THROUGH THE EYES OF TITANS:
Finding Courage to Redeem the Soul of a Nation

THROUGH THE EYES OF TITANS:
Finding Courage to Redeem the Soul of a Nation

Images of Pastoral Care and Leadership, Self-Care, and Radical Love in Public Spaces

Danjuma G. Gibson

CASCADE *Books* • Eugene, Oregon

THROUGH THE EYES OF TITANS: FINDING COURAGE TO REDEEM THE SOUL OF A NATION
Images of Pastoral Care and Leadership, Self-Care, and Radical Love in Public Spaces

Copyright © 2024 Danjuma G. Gibson. All rights reserved. Except for brief quotations in critical publications or reviews, no part of this book may be reproduced in any manner without prior written permission from the publisher. Write: Permissions, Wipf and Stock Publishers, 199 W. 8th Ave., Suite 3, Eugene, OR 97401.

Cascade Books
An Imprint of Wipf and Stock Publishers
199 W. 8th Ave., Suite 3
Eugene, OR 97401

www.wipfandstock.com

PAPERBACK ISBN: 978-1-7252-8421-0
HARDCOVER ISBN: 978-1-7252-8422-7
EBOOK ISBN: 978-1-7252-8423-4

Cataloguing-in-Publication data:

Names: Gibson, Danjuma G. [author].

Title: Through the eyes of titans: finding courage to redeem the soul of a nation: images of pastoral care and leadership, self-care, and radical love in public spaces / Danjuma G. Gibson.

Description: Eugene, OR: Cascade Books, 2024. | Includes bibliographical references and index.

Identifiers: ISBN 978-1-7252-8421-0 (paperback). | ISBN 978-1-7252-8422-7 (hardcover). | ISBN 978-1-7252-8423-4 (ebook).

Subjects: LCSH: Pastoral care. | Pastoral counseling. | Christian leadership.

Classification: BV4011.3 G53 2024 (print). | BV4011.3 (epub).

VERSION NUMBER 010524

Scripture quotations marked (NIV) are taken from the Holy Bible, New International Version®, NIV®. Copyright © 2011 by Biblica, Inc.™ Used by permission of Zondervan. All rights reserved worldwide. www.zondervan.com. The "NIV" and "New International Version" are trademarks registered in the United States Patent and Trademark Office by Biblica, Inc.™

Scripture quotations marked (ESV) are taken from The ESV® Bible (The Holy Bible, English Standard Version®), copyright © 2001 by Crossway, a publishing ministry of Good News Publishers. Used by permission. All rights reserved.

CONTENTS

Introduction: Humanizing the Lives of the Titans | 1

1. The Politics of Silence and Indifference:
   A Brief Practical Theology | 12

2. The Racial Imagination:
   A Brief Pastoral Theology | 23

3. The Psychology of Idealizing Historical Personalities | 58

4. The Audacity of a King:
   On Finding Courage | 70

5. Benjamin E. Mays:
   Your Life-project as Beauty and Resistance | 83

6. Ida B. Wells on Working Through Existential Disappointment:
   The Power of Finding Your Voice | 110

7. Fannie Lou Hamer and the Case for Love:
   What Does Love Look Like? | 141

8. Playing with James Baldwin's Fire:
   Vestiges of Backlash, Redemption, and Hope | 176

9. Pentecostal Worship:
   A Religious Revolution | 200

Bibliography | 209
Index | 217

INTRODUCTION

Humanizing the Lives of the Titans

THE TITANS WERE HUMAN BEINGS, NOT ACTION HEROES

Romanticizing history undermines our capacity to be moral agents in the present time. Idealizing historical personalities distorts their humanity and instead creates myths. This book demythologizes the work and personalities of Fannie Lou Hamer, Ida B. Wells, Martin Luther King Jr., and Benjamin Elijah Mays (herein collectively referred to as *the titans*). Each of them was a public theologian, leader, and spiritual caregiver in their own right. At first glance it would seem that to refer to Hamer, King, Mays, and Wells as titans threatens the very premise of this project. I do not invoke the terminology of titan to suggest that they were superhuman or that emulating their work is beyond the average person's reach. Instead, titan refers to their willingness to engage in the self-work, self-reflexivity, and interior reflection that were required in order for them to accomplish the body of work they are so well known for.

In our collective psychological need for heroes and martyrs, that is to say, people who happily embrace suffering and even death without reservation or hesitation, the titans have been idealized to the point where we have undermined our capacity to learn from them. Instead, their lives remain etched on the pages of books. The practice of engaging with books and other resources about the civil rights movement, anti-racism, or other historical figures who fought for equality and justice has become more fashionable in the first decades of the twenty-first century. In many institutions, the occasional act of learning about history, while commendable, can function as a psychological red badge of courage that takes the place of actually doing the real work of dismantling systemic inequity and oppression. As a result, *reading* about racism and other forms of inequity becomes psychologically soothing, but never translates to actual praxis. Indeed, idealizing historical personalities, and more specifically in this case the titans, has the potential to severely undermine the materialization of a more just society. The insurrection at the US Capitol building on January 6, 2021—which was intended to overturn the results of a national presidential election via the use of violence and deadly force—compels religious and political leaders, and scholars, to reckon with the precarious condition of the democracy and seek to learn from history rather than idealizing it.

The intent of this project is to demythologize the titans and the romanticization of the historical context in which they existed. Once accomplished, the hope is that in our current times, we can see more clearly to emulate the work and practices of freedom they undertook. To demythologize the titans, I perform a psychospiritual examination of key psychological and spiritual themes in each of their lives in a way that expands our imagination about leadership, courage, purpose, resilience, and love, an expanded imagination we desperately need in the current *backlash era* following the first black family to inhabit the White House for eight years. And to be sure, the concept of backlash is nothing new. In his final monograph completed shortly before his assassination, Martin Luther King Jr. brilliantly captures the idea of backlash, undoubtedly the reaction to the passing of the civil rights and voting rights bills within a single decade. Because of its relevance for today, I quote him at length:

> Ever since the birth of our nation, white America has had a schizophrenic personality on the question of race. She has been torn between selves—a self in which she proudly professed the great principles of democracy and a self in which she sadly practiced the antithesis of democracy. This tragic duality has produced a strange indecisiveness and ambivalence toward the Negro, causing America to take a step backward simultaneously with every step forward on the question of racial justice, to be at once attracted to the Negro and repelled by him, to love and to hate him. There has never been a solid, unified and determined thrust to make justice a reality for Afro-Americans.
>
> The step backward has a new name today. *It is called the "white backlash." But the white backlash is nothing new. It is the surfacing of old prejudices, hostilities, and ambivalences that have always been there.* It was caused neither by the cry of Black Power nor by the unfortunate recent wave of riots in our cities. The white backlash of today is rooted in the same problem that has characterized America ever since the black man landed in chains on the shores of this nation. The white backlash is an

expression of the same vacillations, the same search for rationalizations, the same lack of commitment that have always characterized white America on the question of race.[1]

The backlash and social unrest witnessed in 2020 took many by surprise—progressives, moderates, and conservatives alike, especially those privileged to exist at the center of the society (because of their race and class) and away from those forced to exist at the margin (because of their race and class). The idea of progress has been a key mantra in the master narrative of the democratic experiment since the founding of the nation. Moreover, the idea of group progress has been element in American identity formation, for both individuals and as a collective. But the notion of progress is a precarious concept when one considers the extreme violence upon which America was built and that the point of departure in which progress is measured is the genocide of a Native American population, the enslavement and brutalization of black and brown persons and bodies, the subjugation of women, and the exploitation of working class and poor people. The progress narrative runs the risk of leading to a self-aggrandizement and arrogance that covers over the true moral condition of the collective society. How much should a society celebrate when it no longer systematically enslaves, murders, or brutalizes a large segment of its population? Who gets the credit for this alleged progress?

Since the civil rights era, the illusion of so-called American progress has blinded us, inflicting a tonic immobility on our moral imaginations and our wills to act. For decades, we have continued to function as bystanders, overlooking injustice, inequality, structures of racism and oppression, and atrocities against humanity in the form of a burgeoning prison industrial complex and war machine inspired by capitalism. While the very public and brazen murder of George Floyd (which many believed was akin to a public lynching as he was strangled to death in front of a crowd), and the scandalous murders of Ahmaud Arbery, Botham Jean, Breonna Taylor, Tyre Nichols, and the host of unnamed others over the last decade was shocking to many, for a lot of black people, or for those "born with a veil, and gifted with second-sight in this American world,"[2] these murders were no surprise. And while certain constituents in the justice system had the audacity to declare that the death of Breonna Taylor was merely unfortunate and that no one in law enforcement would be held accountable, for those of us who live behind the veil, we knew better. As W. E. B. Du Bois observed, we live with this

1. King, *Where Do We Go*, 72.
2. Du Bois, *Souls of Black Folk*, 3.

> peculiar sensation, this double-consciousness, this sense of always looking at one's self through the eyes of others, of measuring one's soul by the tape of a world that looks on in amused contempt and pity . . . [always feeling his or her] twoness,—an American, a Negro; two souls, two thoughts, two unreconciled strivings; two warring ideals in one dark body, whose dogged strength alone keeps it from being torn asunder.[3]

For many black and brown people, while the aforementioned murders may have been disappointing, for sure, they were not surprising.

The backlash that follows America's first black presidency is characterized by brazen proclamations of racist ideology in social media and the public space, a resurgence of nationalism that is propped up by certain elements of Christian tradition, an increase in wanton political violence, and lastly, a deadly insurrection in the nation's capital aimed at overturning the results of a national presidential election. This current era of backlash embodies the social and political traits of the Redemption period that followed the Reconstruction era in the late nineteenth and early twentieth centuries.[4] To be sure, we have been here before. This is not new. We romanticize history and idealize historical freedom fighters at our own peril.

Even adopting the word *titan* risks undermining the very premise of this book, a premise that suggests we must demythologize these personalities. Our propensity to idealize the lives and humanity of these historical figures undermines our *will to act* and the psychospiritual awareness of a moral obligation to "do good, seek justice, correct oppression; bring justice to the fatherless, [and] plead the widow's cause" (Isa 1:17 ESV). Nevertheless, I use the word *titans* not to suggest that these individuals were super-human, special, or elite, but to *emphasize their audacity to engage in the beautiful but arduous work of becoming and self-actualizing*. I use the word *audacious* when referring to the titans because yielding to the roles and stereotypes preconstructed by the social imagination feuling their racist environments would have been far easier—psychologically, spiritually, and practically—than to engage in the work to become what is herein referred to as a titan.

---

3. Du Bois, *Souls of Black Folk*, 3.
4. Gates, *Stony the Road*.

THE POWER OF SELF-WORK AND THE BEAUTY OF BECOMING

The beauty of becoming is a work of courage in every stage of the human life cycle. For the titans, the alternative was to surrender to the practice of appeasement and assimilating into a racial psychosocial caste system that continues to define America, as well as internalizing racialized typecast roles of human subjugation and subordination that were designed for them by a colonial logic that privileges white life over black life. For it is conceivable that by being docile and compliant to the racial hierarchy that sought to dominate them, they would have lived less stressful lives. Indeed, there is a great temptation to internalize the belief that appeasing and cooperating with structures and cultures of oppression will protect you from harm. But instead, the titans chose the *beauty of becoming*. The difficulty of this self-work cannot be overstated. I engage the wisdom of former Atlanta mayor and US ambassador Andrew Young and feminist scholar bell hooks to delineate what is at stake when envisioning the *psychological and spiritual task of becoming* in a racially antagonistic environment. The evolution of the titans was not a foregone conclusion. In the face of cultural, social, and even religious symbols and innuendos that prop up what Eddie Glaude refers to as the value gap, the risk that the titans could have devolved into self-flagellation and nihilism was great, and in some respects, even understandable had it occurred. In describing the racial imagination in terms of the value gap, Glaude suggests that:

> If what I have called the "value gap" is the idea that in America white lives have always mattered more than the lives of others, then the lie is a broad and powerful architecture of false assumptions by which the value gap is maintained. These are the narrative assumptions that support the everyday order of American life, which means we breathe them like air. We count them as truths. We absorb them into our character.[5]

Similarly, in an earlier work, I describe the *intersubjective milieu* as the shared unconscious space of narratives and stories that exists between individuals and groups. In this shared psychic space, narratives and stories that privilege and normalize the superiority of white life, history, culture, and heritage—at the same time—subordinate, invalidate, or problematize the same categories in black and brown life. Moreover, in the intersubjective milieu, I suggest these shared narratives and stories contribute to individual and group identity formation:

---

5. Glaude, *Begin Again*, 7.

> It is an intersubjective ecology that has been determined by individuals, cultural groups, religion, politics, economics, deep structures of a society, social contracts, historical and contemporary narratives, and unconscious interpretations of nation-state history. The convergence of these discourses can create an intersubjective milieu that props up the psychic structure of the majority [white people] . . . and undermines the psychic space of a minority [black people].[6]

Taken together then, death-dealing intersubjective milieus and value gaps have the potential to undermine black and brown psychospiritual development. They are structured to stamp out black love and black life. Consequently, the role of self-work and self-care in the growth and development of the titans was intentional and purposeful so as to minimize the risk of an enfeebled psychological and spiritual self-structure that was codependent on affirmation from an intersubjective milieu ill equipped to recognize their humanity. For example, while a psychological understanding of human growth and development may not have been front and center on his mind, Andrew Young emphasizes the importance of psychospiritual self-work when he comments on children participating in the civil rights movement in Birmingham, Alabama, in a Jim Crow South. The role of parents and caregivers could not be overstated:

> The idea of it being a children's crusade [the Birmingham civil rights protests in 1963] is a dramatic way to look at it, but in the south you're not a child at 15. You can go to jail, you can get beaten up, you know that you'll get arrested. So, on one side you had segregation training you to accept oppression and be humble and allow yourself to be pushed around. On the other side you had parents who were teaching you how to stand up and be free without doing anything illegal and without getting killed.[7]

In her reflections on teaching and education that are liberative, bell hooks does not ground her work and scholarship in the thinking of prominent scholars or famous models of education. Instead, *her basis of analysis is the memories and experiences of the teachers who taught not only her, but her entire family of origin, while she was in elementary school.*[8] The importance of this cannot be overstated. While scholars such as Paulo Freire may have been instrumental in the formation of bell hooks's thought, the etiology for

6. D. G. Gibson, *Frederick Douglass*, 72.
7. Andrew Young, in S. Nelson, *Rise Up*, 18:04.
8. hooks, *Teaching to Transgress*.

how she conceptualizes education, formation, and *the beauty of becoming*, is lodged squarely in how she was treated by her childhood teachers.[9] That treatment included being taught and embraced by (1) people who loved and understood her (and her family), (2) teachers who did not question whether the manner in which she expressed herself was fully human, (3) teachers who believed in her inherent genius, and (4) teachers who believed that education, at its core, should always be conducive to human freedom. Bondage and the beauty of becoming are always mutually exclusive and will never stand together in terms of healthy self-care and psychospiritual growth. Interestingly enough, bell hooks contrasts her learning experiences at her childhood all-black segregated school, where "attending school then was sheer joy [and that she] . . . loved being a student [and that] . . . school was the place of ecstasy—pleasure and danger [and that] . . . to be changed by ideas was pure pleasure," with what she experienced in an integrated, predominantly white school.[10] Because of its probative value, I quote hooks at length here in her description of how racial integration impacted her educational experience:

> School changed utterly with racial integration. Gone was the messianic zeal to transform our minds and beings that had characterized teachers and their pedagogical practices in our all-black schools. Knowledge was suddenly about information only. It had no relation to how one lived, behaved. It was no longer connected to antiracist struggle. Bussed to white schools, we soon learned that obedience, and not a zealous will to learn, was what was expected of us. Too much eagerness to learn could easily be seen as a threat to white authority . . . Now, we were mainly taught by white teachers whose lessons reinforced racist stereotypes. For black children, education was no longer about the practice of freedom. Realizing this, I lost my love of school. The classroom was no longer a place of pleasure or ecstasy . . . That shift from beloved, all-black schools to white schools where black students were always seen as interlopers, as not really belonging, taught me the difference between education

---

9. In his seminal work *Pedagogy of the Oppressed*, Paulo Freire postulates on the colonizing structure of Western education models, asserting that the basic framework "is an act of depositing, in which the students are the depositories and the teacher is the depositor [and that] . . . instead of communicating, the teacher issues communiques and makes deposits which the students patiently receive, memorize, and repeat [, which can be referred to as] the 'banking' concept of education, in which the scope of action allowed to the students extends only as far as receiving, filing, and storing the deposits" (72).

10. hooks, *Teaching to Transgress*, 3.

as the practice of freedom and education that merely strives to reinforce domination.[11]

It is because the titans engaged in this psychospiritual *self-work of becoming* that they were able to perform the public works of scholarship, leadership, theology, and social justice that they are celebrated for, and that we idealize them for. As such, this book is not an examination of their body of work. Such an examination has already been attended to by other authors and scholars. *Instead, this book is an exploration of the self-work that enabled the titans to produce their body of work.* In understanding their self-work, we can emulate them and conjure a similar courage to imagine a kind of beloved community where we seek to "do good, seek justice, correct oppression; bring justice to the fatherless, [and] plead the widow's cause" (Isa 1:17 ESV). The psychological defenses of romanticizing the experiences of the titans, and idealizing their personhood, both undermine the possibility for their body of work to influence contemporary Christian praxis and expand how we understand leadership and spiritual care.

ANXIETY-PROVOKING WORK

The beauty of becoming is anxiety-provoking work. It is a journey, not a destination. The same applied to the titans, as they labored to find their *courage to become*. They were not born with it. It didn't come naturally as legend would have us believe. They didn't enjoy persecution or fearlessly embrace death in the way that sports entertainment and media outlets would lead us to believe during Black History month in February. The titans were human. The romanticization of historical periods such as Reconstruction or the civil rights era can cause us to lose sight of the fact that the titans were human beings who existed in times not dissimilar to the present, and that we exist in times not dissimilar to the past because of our common humanity. Courage enables us to sacrifice in a fashion similar to the titans. The struggle to find self-courage is constitutional to human experience and perhaps the most significant spiritual exercise that we either embrace or neglect. It is easy to forfeit the pursuit of courage and surrender to the illusion that the love of neighbor and the realization of the beloved community will automatically occur with the mere passage of time. This illusion has cost religious and political leaders dearly, as we are ill prepared to engage the racial animosity and nationalism we face in the twenty-first century. A close parallel to the fallacious belief that the passage of time engenders progress

---

11. hooks, *Teaching to Transgress*, 3–4.

is the belief that silence about the racial imagination and the ongoing legacy of the slavocracy will somehow make it go away and heal our national soul. But such thinking is for the privileged, the naïve, and the bystander.

The titans resisted the temptation to acquiesce to the status quo of accepting a subordinated existence in a racist society. It was because of spiritual, psychological, and emotional self-work that they refused to internalize the common delusion that *time heals all wounds* or that by patiently enduring inequality, then justice, equality, and freedom would automatically materialize because of American innocence, righteousness, and exceptionalism. All of these unconscious or implicit beliefs represent secondary psychological defense processes designed to protect fragile ego structures or communities with weak ego strength. The events of 2020 and 2021 demonstrate the fragility of the democratic experiment. The late congressman John Lewis was brilliant in his observation that "democracy is not a state [but] . . . an act, and each generation must do its part to help build what we called the Beloved Community, a nation and world society at peace with itself."[12]

In finding their courage, the titans experienced a kind of new birth whereby they were no longer *controlled* by the real possibilities of social marginalization, physical harm, or death. This does not suggest that they didn't fear such possibilities, but only that the titans engaged in the requisite psychospiritual self-work that translated into the beauty of becoming and enabled them to be public scholars, theologians, community leaders, and activists, and to engage in the work of pursuing justice and equity. They demonstrated the *will to act*. Today, as much as we tend to romanticize the nature of their work, America stands on the shoulders of the titans. We have benefited from their examples of courage and labor of love. In a post-Obama era of brazen racial backlash, political and social unrest, and what is arguably the most acute racial reckoning since the mid-twentieth century, simply reading or watching documentaries about the titans, in and of itself, does not constitute progress and fulfill our obligation as moral agents. Again, the fundamental task for people of faith and those of good will is to "do good, seek justice, correct oppression; bring justice to the fatherless, [and] plead the widow's cause" (Isa 1:17 ESV). This mandate is foundational to the psychological well-being and *soul health* of every person, group, and institution existing within the American republic. It will be achieved only through a religious and spiritual revolution.

In this book, by examining autobiographical accounts of Martin Luther King Jr., Benjamin Mays, Ida B. Wells, and Fannie Lou Hamer, I

---

12. Quote from an essay authored by John Lewis, "Together, You Can Redeem," which was published in the *New York Times* shortly before his death.

identify psychospiritual practices that contributed to their formation—practices that facilitated the beauty of their becoming. These practices include: (1) finding courage, (2) embracing your life-project and doing your work, (3) working through existential dissapointment and, (4) practicing transgressive love. Through these practices, I suggest that ordinary people like Fannie Lou Hamer, Ida B. Wells, Benjamin Mays, and Martin Luther King Jr., among many others, were able to become the people we know and celebrate them for. Studying their lives can help us redefine how we understand spiritual care and leadership and provide us with an example of how we can respond to racial hatred and resistance to a multiracial democracy in the twenty-first century. In their examples, they demonstrated personal and communal courage to redeem the soul of a nation infected with the legacy of the slavocracy and the colonial imagination. This *soul-infection* remains with us today, as a violent insurrection in the nation's capital and even the attempted kidnapping of a sitting governor are both symptoms of a much deeper corruption of the human spirit—a corruption that has been constantly downplayed or ignored in the name of progress.

The titans were not unique people with a special call to civil rights activism. That sort of thinking provides a ready-made excuse for the church and people of good will to be lazy and act irresponsibly in abandoning their cardinal mandate to love and justice. Instead, the titans were regular people who were informed by their faith to respond to the command to love God as evidenced in loving and caring for their neighbor. They were regular people who responded to the collective call to engage in works of justice. This is a fundamental call that remains for all of us today.

I engage an interdisciplinary approach in this project, analyzing the work of the titans at the intersection of pastoral theology, practical theology, psychohistory, and psychobiography. I approach this work through the lens of *practical theology* as I examine the life and practices of the church in relation to its ongoing complicity in underwriting structures of racial oppression as well as its characteristic silence in this current era of backlash. The canons of practical theology often address how communities and people of faith are adversely impacted by a broken and traumatizing world. But the church is not only affected by a broken and traumatizing world, but in many instances, contributes to the brokenness and traumatization of the world. The contribution to breaking and traumatizing the world is the dark side of the church that often goes unspoken. We are not only image bearers of God (*imago dei*), but image distorters as well. Understood as such, a significant point of departure for practical theology, while not exclusive, stems from a thick observation of problematic practices and experiences of the church that are antithetical to both human flourishing, and the gospel mandate to love God as evidenced in the love of our neighbor. I employ *pastoral theology* in reflecting on how the racial imagination has corrupted the soul of the nation. This text explores how psychospiritual interventions can work—over the long run—to restore the individual and collective moral consciousness that has been ossified by decades of tolerating racial animosity and oppression.

Lastly, this text intersects with psychobiography and psychohistory, as they represent effective interventions for maladaptive forms of idealization. In this work, I seek to develop a spiritual and clinical picture of the titans. Snapshots of a psychobiographical profile have the potential to demythologize the titans. Psychohistory can deromanticize historical eras, as we can better relate to the feelings and emotions of individual and group behavior. Both practices work to demonstrate the repetition of collective patterns of behavior, which is diagnostic in contemplating life-giving social praxis and our overall future. The psychoanalytic examination of autobiographies and history can help us better examine the ongoing sociopolitical cycle of progress by black and brown peoples, which is inevitably met with a violent social and political backlash, followed by a period of social, political, and economic austerity. Psychobiography and psychohistory can both represent mirrors into our own souls. The disciplines give voice to who we can be at our best, and what we are capable of at our worst. They work to orient us to harmful group behavior such as dissociation, denial, and tribalism. Moreover, psychohistory and psychobiography tend to reveal an unsettling truth about our individual and collective nature: with any so-called human progress, you can always count on some form or season of regression. Coretta Scott King, the late widow of Dr. Martin Luther King Jr., brilliantly captures the paradox and mystery between progress and regress in her message to posterity:

> I am counting on the next generation to pick up the still-broken pieces of society on humanity's Jericho Roads and continue the struggle against poverty, greed, and militarism that Martin and I gave our lives to correct, *for struggle is a never-ending process and freedom is never really won. You earn it and win it in every generation.* I believe future generations will have the courage, the love, and the faith to get this done. This is my hope, and this is my prayer.[13]

Given the current season of what I believe is a reactionary backlash to a black presidency, I fear we have not heeded the warning of Coretta Scott King and have instead rested in the *illusion of permanent progress*.

13. Scott King, *My Life, My Love*, 330; emphasis added.

1

THE POLITICS OF SILENCE AND INDIFFERENCE

A Brief Practical Theology

MORE SPECIFIC TO THIS text then, I ask questions about the active role of the church—often in the form of silence and indifference—in perpetuating the religious sanctioning of racial ideology and nationalism. The refusal to talk about the ongoing reality and prevalence of racial animosity is not a mark of individual or group virtue. Silence about the reality of racial hatred is not a milestone to be sought after or valorized. Such silence instead reflects regressed individual and group psychology and psychospiritual immaturity. For example, denying the malevolent and nefarious nature of the Capitol insurrection on January 6, 2021, only blinds us to the ailing soul-condition of the democracy. Perhaps more troubling is that the practices of gaslighting, engaging in selective amnesia, or offering up red herring arguments about the sinister nature of what occurred on January 6 are practices not only enacted in sociopolitical spaces but replicated in many sections of the church in America. The denial that America was on the verge of a violent political coup to overturn a national presidential election reflects a group practice of psychological splitting and disavowal that is reproducing itself in the Christian conscience. This active practice of silence, denial, and gaslighting by the church—in part—reflects a group coping mechanism that protects it against annihilation anxiety. The annihilation in question is the self-perception and group-image of innocence, moral progress, and triumphalism, as there are some truths that are too painful to bear. Hence, the silence is effective in protecting the psychic space of the Western church. Its practice spans generations and is a major contributor to the insurrection of January 6. The makings of what we witnessed on that fateful day didn't occur overnight or even the past year. The insurrection on January 6 reflects the death-dealing wages of the sins of silence and indifference about the ongoing legacy of racial hatred. Silence reflects the politics of indifference and apathy. Ethically, it gives birth to complicity, as the church abandons its call to moral agency and being a seeker of justice.

The politics of indifference and apathy within religious institutions is nothing new. It was observed by William James at the turn of the twentieth century in his psychological reflections on the life of religious communities. James observed that religious symbols and resources were used to justify a life where the self-absorbed pursuit and experience of personal happiness was moralized and then used as a psychic defense to ignore the reality of evil and human suffering. How happiness takes shape, and how it is concurrently experienced, is internally governed by each individual, and in many cases is a communal exercise. For James, "how to gain, how to keep, how to recover happiness, is in fact for most men at all times the secret motive of all they do, and all they are willing to endure."[1] As such, truth about the realities of evil, and in our case the ongoing legacy of racial hostility, can be disruptive to the pursuit and experience of happiness. The realities of white supremacy and nationalism are disruptive to the ideology of exceptionalism and innocence. James recognized that for many groups within Christianity, religious practice (and the corresponding God talk) is constructed to create *proofs and support* of the psychological, moral, or ethical maneuvers required to achieve and maintain happiness. James goes on to observe that "in some individuals optimism may become quasi-pathological . . . the capacity for even a transient sadness or a momentary humility seems cut off from them as by a kind of congenital anesthesia."[2] Silence in the church about racism is an intergenerational practice that spans centuries. But like undiagnosed cancer, the practice of quietness is not benign. Remaining silent about nationalism, the racial imagination, and the events of January 6 is conducive for maintaining communal happiness and comfort in many parts of the Western religious sphere. The observations of William James, in part, offer a degree of explanatory power as they relate to the long-standing practice of the church (and its individual and institutional stakeholders) in America to remain conspicuously silent and painfully inept on matters of racial animosity and inequality.

1. James, *Varieties of Religious Experience*, 78.
2. James, *Varieties of Religious Experience*, 83.

In an earlier work I refer to the muteness that begets apathy and indifference within groups and institutions as the *cult of silence*.[3] In the paradigm of the cult of silence, the idea of a safe space (often understood as being entitled to comfortable dialogue that maintains the status quo) can become a moralized concept that is used to disenfranchise the histories and realities of those who have been forced to exist on the underside of history. Silence and the expectation of happiness are weaponized against those at the margin. It is within the contours of silence that we gain a clear understanding of who and what matters in any given institution, culture, or society. It is within the dialogues of material human experience that disembodied theology becomes enfleshed and dwells among humanity. *Attempts to devalue the importance of dialogue and conversation or to cast them as an exercise in futility ignores how history has shown that silence and indifference about acts of evil and violence, the abuse of power, or any other form of systemic oppression, leads only to a greater loss of life and human dignity.* The human experiences that are included in any group, institutional, or social dialogue give a clear picture as to who matters and who does not matter. In the academy, church, or any institution, and especially in an environment that is experiencing sociopolitical backlash in the wake of the first black family occupying the White House, I conclude that:

> Naming who and what matters (or does not matter) is of vital importance, especially in the current sociopolitical environment. The in-between spaces of not mattering are incredibly dangerous places to exist. It is easy to dismiss experiences that don't matter and to destroy bodies that don't matter. Ambivalence toward bodies and experiences that don't matter is a formidable obstacle to overcome in theological education. That is to say, if you want to know what matters in an academic context, listen for the material conversations that are most often engaged with.[4]

Silence and indifference work as an organic anesthetic towards any story, history, or human experience that disrupts the internal construction of happiness. While silence—and by extension denial—may reflect a group coping mechanism, the near pathological need for happiness is psychologically compensatory in nature. That is to say, happiness and comfort, or whatever sustains the status quo, become the unconscious telos for religious reflection and theological ethics. Happiness and comfort become synonymous with truth. Whatever narrative makes for happiness is equated with

---

3. D. Gibson, "Mentalizing the Classroom."
4. D. Gibson, "Mentalizing the Classroom," 135.

objective truth, with what is deemed right; and whatever conversation or observation that precipitates anxiety is equated with wrong. The veracity of theological reflection and biblical interpretation becomes predicated, in part, on whatever is generative of being comfortable and happy and maintaining the status quo. According to James, "In many persons, happiness is congenital and irreclaimable . . . I mean those who, when unhappiness is offered or proposed to them, positively refuse to feel it, *as if it were something mean and wrong.*"[5] Here, James is emphasizing the psychological experience of unhappy information (i.e., [people] *positively refuse to feel it . . . as if it were something mean*) as opposed to the actual reality or objectivity of the information. This is an important psychodynamic distinction to make. Unless you allow yourself to feel the story, it is unlikely that you can fully understand and comprehend the story. If an individual or group experiences cognitive or moral anxiety because their actions, or the actions that they are observing, are contrary to their stated belief system (or their deliberative theology), there are only three options for relieving the anxiety: alter the stated belief or deliberative theology, engage the cult of silence in the hopes of achieving a degree of happiness or comfort, or engage in an act of moral agency and intervene. The titans chose the last option.

Obviously, the last option of engaging in moral agency in order to intervene on behalf of another is not a common path to be taken up. Over time, this can become spiritually corrosive in systems of religious power where comfort and happiness are emotionally synonymous with truth and right. The pursuit of comfort and happiness becomes the compensatory reaction for relieving cognitive and moral dissonance, or more specifically for our purposes here, racial anxiety. Moreover, it blinds the church to the present realities of evil and a clear vision of our Christian and civic responsibility. This is clearly elucidated in the parable of the Samaritan where Jesus contrasts the stranger's actions towards the wounded person to the actions of the religious leaders. In a stroke of sheer genius, Jesus uses the actions of a non-Jewish personality (and by extension a non-Christian personality) as an example of what it means to be Jesus-like. The ongoing inability of the church, and by extension its stakeholders, to see and better comprehend the reality of racial hegemony and nationalism, as well as its complicity in the matter, is an example of the indifference that William James associates with religious organizations. I quote James at length here because it is imperative to see that the psychological behavior he is observing in the late 1800s and early 1900s is not a function of bygone history, but a cogent observation

---

5. James, *Varieties of Religious Experience*, 79; emphasis added.

of the human project. The happiness of so-called progress undermines our capacity to see evil and react accordingly. He observes that:

> Happiness, like every other emotional state, has blindness and insensibility to opposing facts given . . . [it is an] instinctive weapon for self-protection against disturbance. When happiness is actually in possession, the thought of evil can no more acquire the feeling of reality than the thought of good can gain reality when melancholy rules. To the man actively happy, from whatever cause, evil simply cannot then and there be believed in. He must ignore it; and to the bystander he may then seem perversely to shut his eyes to it and hush it up . . . the hushing of it up may, in a perfectly candid and honest mind, grow into a deliberate religious policy . . . [as] much of what we call evil is due entirely to the way men take the phenomenon.[6]

The religious practice that James recognized over a century ago remains fully functional in the modern-day church. That is, instead of becoming moral agents who address evil, a community can simply change how they talk about what is evil: "Since you make them evil or good by your own thoughts about them, it is the ruling of your thoughts which proves to be your principal concern."[7] Controlling the narrative on how to talk about—or if you even talk about—justice, becomes more important than the call to "do good, seek justice, correct oppression; bring justice to the fatherless, [and] plead the widow's cause" (Isa 1:17 ESV). *Cults of silence* become the by-product of indifference. In the final analysis, while some may question the rationale or efficacy of talking about history (individual or collective), or are dissuaded of the redemptive power of story and narrative because of superficial catch phrases that suggest discussion is cheap and of little value, James is clear that silence and indifference are costly. In assigning the term *healthy-mindedness* to the person or group that is unable to tolerate psychological or emotional dissonance, James warns that we all are susceptible to this frailty of ego and concludes of a majority of American Christian traditions at the turn of the twentieth century that:

> The systematic cultivation of healthy-mindedness as a religious attitude is therefore consonant with important currents in human nature, and is anything but absurd. In fact, *we all do cultivate it more or less, even when our professed theology should in consistency forbid it.* We divert our attention from disease and death as much as we can; and the slaughter-houses

---

6. James, *Varieties of Religious Experience*, 88.
7. James, *Varieties of Religious Experience*, 89.

and indecencies without end on which our life is founded are huddled out of sight and never mentioned, so that the world we recognize officially in literature and in society is a poetic fiction far handsomer and cleaner and better than the world that really is.[8]

The potential maladaptive psychospiritual fallout of what James is postulating cannot be understated. The practice of silence is commonly valorized, being held up as a sign of religious piety. Nevertheless, it is self-deceiving. This quaint educative move, while having an appearance of spiritual asceticism in some quarters and even religious commendation in others, does not come without a cost. Over the long run, moral agency is compromised and the visions of justice, loving God and our neighbor, and what it means to be human are all equally distorted. And similarly to how we assess neurotic psychological behavior in the stages of human development, likewise, we must consider the individual and communal toll that arrested spiritual development takes on the life of a community when silence and indifference cause people to become desensitized to the evils of racial hatred and oppression, incivility, violence, and inhumanity towards our neighbor. It is important to point out here that the veracity of the state of happiness is not what is being challenged. An important part of self-care and flourishing in life is to engage in activities that are generative of happiness. The challenge presented here is when the pursuit and maintenance of happiness, comfort, and convenience are moralized as individual and group defensive mechanisms—effectively becoming psychological and spiritual enablers of denial, indifference, and apathy. *Using religion to comfort self and others is a commendable goal worthy of pursuit and refinement in a variety of forms. The danger however is when religion is used to make us comfortable with our neighbor's suffering and oppression.*

In his practical theology on moral indifference, Ford effectively equates silence, apathy, and passivity to the sin of sloth.[9] While the common understanding of sloth is generally perceived with images of physical idleness, gluttony, or indolence, Ford looks beyond this to connect sloth with moral laziness and intellectual inertia. It is not that a person or community is unable to think. Sloth means that they refuse to think for fear of the cognitive dissonance such thinking will produce (i.e., if it makes me unhappy, don't think about it). The contemporary cultural phenomenon that best captures moral indifference and spiritual laziness is the accusation of being so-called *woke*. When institutions and organizational power

---

8. James, *Varieties of Religious Experience*, 90; emphasis added.
9. D. Ford, *Sins of Omission: A Primer on Moral Indifference*.

structures accuse a person or group of being woke, in my experience it often represents the practice of intellectual laziness and apathy on behalf of the accuser. It is akin to the ad hominem logical fallacy where the person (or group) who accuses another of being woke is really attempting to gloss over, or outright ignore, the underlying argument, question, or concern at hand, and instead attacks the character of the person or group that raised the original question or concern—solely on the basis of the subject matter.[10] The person or group that invokes *woke* nomenclature to their advantage (generally the in-group) is using their institutional or cultural power and privilege to *assume* their presuppositions and worldviews, as opposed to *arguing* them within the community. The claims of the person or group that raised the original concern (generally the out-group) are outright rejected as opposed to being faithfully refuted within the community. Ultimately, any thinking that results in unhappiness is avoided. But over the long run (especially intergenerationally) sloth stunts the moral imagination and arrests intellectual development. It is the condition precedent to tribalism and is a psychospiritual ailment anyone can be at risk for. Because it is a choice not to think, sloth undermines our capacity to correctly appropriate context, history, social location, and place, all of which are critical components for a healthy moral agency. Sloth distorts our understanding of the present, of lived reality, and for our purposes here, the ongoing evils of racial hatred and inequality. Questions about the ongoing legacy of the slavocracy or the reality of systems of racism are less about knowledge deficits of the subject matter and more about intellectual and spiritual sloth. Sloth conforms us to the hegemonic systems of this world and compromises our capacity to be "transformed by the renewal of [our minds] . . . that by testing [we] may discern what is the will of God, what is good and acceptable and perfect" (Rom 12:2 NIV).

---

10. Even more damaging from a psychospiritual perspective is when the woke logical fallacy is invoked by structures of power in Christian organizations and institutions. In such places, claims and concerns classified as woke are generally cast as conversations that real Christians don't involve themselves with. The presuppositions and worldviews of those in power are assumed, as opposed to being argued. Because the woke logical fallacy has the capacity to undermine self-examination, interpersonal accountability, and self-reflexivity in those who use it to suppress painful conversations, over the long run, it results in laziness of intellect and moral agency. In institutional cultures overrun with intellectual and moral sloth, even Jesus's claim in Luke 4:18–19 that "the Spirit of the Lord is upon me, because he has anointed me to proclaim good news to the poor. He has sent me to proclaim liberty to the captives and recovering of sight to the blind, to set at liberty those who are oppressed, to proclaim the year of the Lord's favor" can be perceived as being woke when it is used to challenge systemic sin and injustice.

Ford goes on to compare the sloth *of intellection and moral agency* to sensuality and warns of the danger of delimiting our understanding of the sensuous to lust, sex, and physical gratification. He asserts that sensuality also entails "a willing submission to ideologies, persons, and institutions . . . [and includes] social as well as individual manifestations."[11] According to Ford, Reinhold Niebuhr advocates for two fundamental manifestations of sensuality: idolatry and nothingness. In its idolatrous form, sensuality reflects an abdication of our God-given personal freedom to think and choose, and for the sake of group acceptance, group inclusion, and personal contentment and happiness, a person or group willingly subjugates itself "to some 'other,' whether that other be an ideology, a person, a political movement, or an institution. The victim of idolatry escapes his or her anxiety by accepting the wishes and dictates of someone or something that is conceived to be more powerful, wiser, or more real than oneself."[12] In its nothingness form, sensuality reflects a malignant complacency that blindly accepts the terms and conditions of hegemony, radically resisting any move against the status quo. Ford refers to it as an "arrogant form of indifference" adopted by power structures, which ultimately reflects an abuse of power. Referring to Reinhold Niebuhr's concerns of indifference and complacency around the rising threat of Nazism in the decades prior to the Second World War, Ford asserts that such complacency is relevant today, and that it

> occurs whenever a group becomes comfortable and secure to the point of losing contact with actuality. The powerful can afford to stay comfortably submerged in the routines of life precisely because they can do so with impunity. Without daily reminders of a wide discrepancy between expectation and reality, the powerful lack an inherent context for moral reflection and are thus vulnerable to the complacent sloth of nothingness.[13]

The ongoing practices of silence, the valorization of happiness, and moral sloth, all conspired in a way such that the insurrection of January 6 caught the church off guard—conservatives, progressives, and liberals alike. The point here is not that the future can be predicted, but that silence and passivity are always costly. Over the long run, and especially in the context of human existence at the margin, silence is a component of tribalism and privilege. Affiliation with the ideology of Western/white superiority, coupled with the fear of being expelled from its entrenched status quo, eclipses the

---

11. D. Ford, *Sins of Omission*, 26.
12. D. Ford, *Sins of Omission*, 26.
13. D. Ford, *Sins of Omission*, 29.

necessity of an ethical response. Pastorally speaking, left unchecked, silence results in the searing of the conscience.

Broadly speaking then, moral agency is not a once-in-a lifetime destination. It represents a spiritual journey that must be intentionally engaged over the entire lifespan. To surrender to the comforts of happiness that apathy and indifference produce yields a spiritual sloth that becomes increasingly difficult to rectify over the long run. The actual practice of moral agency begets moral agency. The practice of moral sloth begets moral sloth. Moral agency is a spiritual pedagogy that must be practiced. Moral agency and empathy are both spiritual muscles that are constitutional to what it means to be human. Moral agency is akin to a spiritual muscle that must be continuously exercised. By way of analogy, I am reminded of studying concert piano during my undergraduate years at Morehouse College. Daily practice was essential for success. There were no shortcuts to achieving virtuosity. The professors in the music department could discern which musical selections you practiced, how much you practiced, and if you practiced correctly. Performance doesn't lie. The muscles and dexterity in your hands perfectly matched the effort of your preparation and practice. As you improved, the music was integrated into your very sense of being. It became a part of you such that what you practiced became a part of your very expression. So it is with moral agency and the will to act. Each missed opportunity represents a missed opportunity for becoming more like Jesus, and more human. The observation made by William James over a century ago about the propensity for religious institutions (namely Christian institutions) to hide their head in the sand for the sake of comfort was again lamented by Martin Luther King Jr. as he sat in a jail cell in Birmingham, Alabama. I quote this at length, as this lament still rings true in the twenty-first century. Recollecting on his travels through Mississippi, Alabama, and the southern United States in general, King writes:

> I have looked at her beautiful churches with their lofty spires pointing heavenward. I have beheld the impressive outlay of her massive religious education buildings. Over and over again I have found myself asking: "What kind of people worship here? Who is their God? *Where were their voices* when the lips of Governor Barnett dripped with words of interposition and nullification? Where were they when Governor Wallace gave the clarion call for defiance and hatred? *Where were their voices* of support when tired, bruised and weary Negro men and women decided

to *rise from the dark dungeons of complacency* to the bright hills of creative protest?"[14]

When superficial talk of racial reconciliation covers over or supplants the more critical work of metanoia and justice, such reconciliation-talk is akin to having an *appearance of godliness but denies its transformative power.*[15] Moreover, silence and indifference collude to undermine the interpersonal and communal relationships that racial conciliatory efforts seek to promote. Especially for those who are in positions of authority and have a material influence on the lives of others, or those who serve as mentors, teachers, or spiritual guides—the people we serve are watching us intently. Our silence on matters related to the evils of racism, nationalism, or any form of bigotry and oppression towards another person or group is only a self-delusional fantasy of peace that is violently displaced with events like the January 6 insurrection. Moreover, the people and communities we serve are not deceived. The refusal to talk about racism and injustice does not blind people to the reality of its existence. To the contrary, it speaks more to the quality and authenticity of the communal relationships. Howard Thurman is clear on this point when reflecting on the teacher and mentor who arguably influenced him the most, Rufus Jones. Thurman had great respect for Jones, and Jones was fond of Thurman. Thurman even decided against pursuing a PhD so that he could study instead under the tutelage of Jones as a fellow with the National Council on Religion in Higher Education. Nevertheless, while Thurman held Jones in high regard, the silence of Jones on the racial terror and inequity that oppressed his young student had a lasting impact on Thurman:

> During the entire time with Rufus, issues of racial conflict never arose, for the fact of racial difference was never dealt with at the conscious level. The ethical emphasis in his interpretations of mystical religion dealt primarily with war and peace, the poverty and hunger of whole populations, and the issues arising from the conflict between nations. Paradoxically, in his presence, the specific issues of race with which I had been confronted all my life as a black man in America seemed strangely irrelevant. *I felt that somehow he transcended race; I did so, too, temporarily, and, in retrospect, this aspect of my time with him remains an enigma.*[16]

---

14. King, *Testament of Hope*, 299; emphasis added.
15. Adapted from 2 Tim 3:5 ESV.
16. Thurman, *With Head and Heart*, 76; emphasis added.

Thurman's observation should serve as a warning to all who choose to embrace the sacred role of a mentor, teacher, or guide to others (especially when the student is from a socially marginalized group) but remain silent on weighty matters of equity and justice that require their wisdom and leadership. Moral indifference undermines the mentor/mentee relationship. The moral apathy modeled by Rufus Jones is a common practice today, especially in advisor/advisee relationships in the church and institutions of higher learning. While the power to control the conversation may provide a sense of personal comfort, it is also self-delusional, as it cannot control the hearts and minds of the others in the group. It only contributes to the moral ineptitude of a community and undermines its capacity to satisfy the divine requirement to "do justice, and to love kindness, and to walk humbly with your God" (Mic 6:8 ESV).

2

THE RACIAL IMAGINATION
A Brief Pastoral Theology

TERMS LIKE RACIST OR *racism* are too limiting in their explanatory power of how the legacy of the slavocracy has degraded the human condition. These discrete terms lend to an implicit misconception that interpersonal (or intergroup) dehumanization in the form of *racing another human being* is: (1) largely confined to a historical period, (2) happens only occasionally today, (3) requires conscious intentionality, (4) reflects malice of forethought, and (5) can be (or has been) decisively eradicated from the human psyche for all time (I will engage more on this point shortly). As such, most people disassociate these terms from themselves. That is to say, anything to do with *racist* or *racism* is always *out there and away from the self,* consequently having no relevancy to a person's interior world. In the United States, the approach to understanding the ills of racism (and its resulting violence, injustice, and inequity) reflects a malignant form of individual and collective psychological splitting where the view of the world is clearly divided between two people: a racist and a non-racist. And obviously, most people don't want to be associated with the former. But this imaginary line of demarcation undermines pastoral theological efficacy in its capacity to examine how human animus, contempt, resentment, and oppression emanate from the toxicity of the legacy of race.

Instead of using concrete terms like *racist* or phraseology like "an act of racism," a psychodynamic approach to examine the concept of race is more instructive. Here, I employ the terminology of the racial imagination. While not necessarily novel, as a trained psychotherapist, I am persuaded that the illusion and toxicity of race infect the unconscious more that the conscious, effectively incapacitating the interior world and imagination of the individual, an interior world and imagination that necessarily informs the person's engagement with their exterior world. Predominantly white institutions that serve a diversified public sector are not predominantly white because they cannot find qualified black and brown people. They are predominantly white because they lack the interior capacity to imagine diversity. More than any particular act of racism, the racial imagination corrupts the individual and collective soul. Here I suggest:

> The racial imagination represents an intergenerational socialization of the individual and collective psyche—sometimes consciously, but more often unconsciously—whereby non-white skin tone is the instantaneous visual marker for *experiencing* another person as *not normal, as an aberration of humanity*, or *as a deviation from the center of what it means to be human*. The psychospiritual result is to affectively experience and perceive raced persons—along with their history, heritage, culture, spirituality, and life experiences—as inherently flawed and consequently, subordinated to non-raced persons. That is to say, all things pertaining to black and brown life are rendered secondary, at best, in determining what it means to be human (i.e., normal). In the racial imagination, the *raced* becomes an object of the *racer's* imagination—that is—an object to be acted upon, as opposed to being a critical subject to be taken seriously and engaged with.

This proposed psychospiritual definition of the racial imagination is a corrective to the aforementioned misconceptions of how we understand the nature of race due to concrete terms like *racist* or *racism*, terms that most people distance themselves from and project on others. But what I suggest here about the racial imagination is not entirely novel. There are many black and brown scholars in the psychoanalytic world who have spoken to various aspects of the unconscious or preconscious nature of racism and white supremacy.[1] My use of the term *racial imagination* emphasizes the interior world, which is always the point of departure that eventually manifests itself in the externalization of numerous forms of racial oppression and injustice, violence, inequity. The psychological experiencing of *the other* (or the raced) as subordinate or inferior (to the racer) is the primary emotion that precipitates secondary emotional experiences of *the other* that

---

1. For example, Leary, "Racial Insult and Repair," and "Racial Enactments"; Dalal, *Race, Colour and Processes*, and "Racism: Processes of Detachment"; Gump, "Reality Matters"; Schachter and Butts, "Transference and Countertransference"; Butts, "Psychoanalysis, the Black Community."

can include racial animus, jealousy, envy, or bitterness; paternalism; fear and suspicion; a sense of mystery, bewilderment, or gazing at manifestations of black and brown life judged as being either exotic or deviations from what is considered to be normal when compared to white life; resentment towards the assertion of black and brown agency and subjectivity; resentment towards black and brown protest and resistance; resentment over the affirmation of black and brown creativity and beauty; animus and resentment directed at black and brown intellectualism, or an emotional need to discipline and/or colonize black intellectualism (as opposed to critically engage with it); implicitly perceiving or experiencing black life as criminalized, unscrupulous, incompetent, irreligious, unqualified, and sexually deviant; an emotional need to discipline and/or colonize black religious experience; exhilaration and excitement at the public disciplining of black or brown life, suffering, or experience or excessive rage and aggression when interacting with black- and brown-bodied persons. These are but just a few examples of the *affective states* that take up residence in the racial imagination.

In the final analysis, the combination of the primary psychological need to *experience oneself as better (or better off) than raced persons* with any one of the aforementioned secondary emotional experiences eventually results in outward manifestations of the racial imagination: actions that objectify, brutalize, and subjugate black-bodied people. To speak of systemic or institutional racism then is to describe a communal structure whereby those beholden to racial ideology can interact with black and brown peoples only through perceptions or social terms and conditions controlled by the racial imagination. The alternative to the racial imagination, that is, to experience and affirm another as *equally human* and *just as normal* on terms and conditions authored by them, is a psychic practice foreign to communities entrenched in a communal imagination overrun by the illusion of race. For to interact with all things related to black life as *if* it was just as normative as all things pertaining to white life *feels wrong*. The racial imagination represents spiritual sickness. Individually, it requires a psychospiritual intervention. Collectively, it demands a religious revolution.

The racial imagination can be understood then as an *affective caste system*, where the identity formation of those who inhabit the upper echelons of the emotional caste, in part, have a socialized psychic need for black and brown existence to inhabit the lower rungs of the psychological caste for the sole purpose of propping up the identity and ego of non-raced existence. This represents the psychological core of white supremacy. It bears repeating here that in the proposed understanding of the racial imagination, the destructiveness of race does not begin in the outer world—that is to say, in our daily interactions. The racial imagination suggests that it is the interior world of the individual and the collective that is socialized—intergenerationally—into imagining white superiority (or normality) and black inferiority (or abnormality). The concept of *experienced as* or *self-experience* emphasizes that it is not necessarily objective facts or lived realities that fuel the racial imagination. Instead, it is the racial illusions and delusions of the interior world, imaginations that have been socialized into the interior world of an individual or group across generations, that must be attended to through pastoral intervention.

When the emotional caste system is compromised or inverted (most commonly in the form of black self-determination, flourishing, progress, or success), or if blackness is *experienced as* being equal with or excelling beyond whiteness, what is understood in psychology as narcissistic injury is incurred in the ego(s) of those given to the practice of racing non-white bodies. Left unattended from a psychospiritual perspective, as is commonly the case, the only alternative to soothing the interior anxiety precipitated by racial narcissistic injury is to *restore the long-standing disequilibrium of the affective caste system (i.e., white superiority)* by resorting to maladaptive and death-dealing practices of racial oppression and hegemony. These practices can range from microaggressions and institutional racism, systemic racism, to outright violence.

In several of his autobiographies, Frederick Douglass brilliantly depicts the progression from the racial imagination to outward manifestations of racial brutality and oppression in his explanation of *impudence*, and how it functioned in the slavocracy.[2] Impudence is simply defined as "not showing due respect for another person."[3] Within the slavocracy, the failure of showing due respect to captors, primarily in the form of enslaved individuals not remaining in their subordinated status within the affective caste system, precipitated narcissistic injury to the power structure on the plantation, which ultimately led to physical brutality. Inhabiting the appropriate space within the affective caste system—be it a superior space or and subordinated space—is at the heart of the racial imagination. In his first autobiography written before the Civil War and while Douglass was a fugitive fleeing the Southern enslavement regime, he describes the crime of impudence and how it functions in the imagination of the slavocracy. For the benefit of psychohistory, it is worth quoting Douglass in detail here. Psychohistory illustrates that while we may advance in terms of technology, science, and human innovation, the structures of demonic human imagination don't automatically change over time or fade away without intervention.

---

2. See Douglass, *Narrative of the Life*; or Douglass, *My Bondage*.
3. *New Oxford American Dictionary* (2021).

Psychohistory emphasizes the emotion behind the historical action, thereby compelling us in the present to ponder how similar contemporary emotions could lead to history repeating itself, for better or for worse. Consider how Douglass reflects on the presumptuous attitude of superiority in the racial imagination through the concept of *impudence*:

> A mere look, word, or motion,—a mistake, accident, or want of power,—are all matters for which a slave may be whipped at any time. Does a slave look dissatisfied? It is said, he has the devil in him, and it must be whipped out. Does he speak loudly when spoken to by his master? Then he is getting high-minded, and should be taken down a button-hole lower. Does he forget to pull off his hat at the approach of a white person? Then he is wanting in reverence, and should be whipped for it. Does he ever venture to vindicate his conduct, when censured for it? Then he is guilty of impudence,—one of the greatest crimes of which a slave can be guilty. Does he ever venture to suggest a different mode of doing things from that pointed out by his master? He is indeed presumptuous, and getting above himself; and nothing less than a flogging will do for him. Does he, while ploughing, break a plough,—or, while hoeing, break a hoe? It is owing to his carelessness, and for it a slave must always be whipped.[4]

In another incident where Douglass has been physically brutalized and bloodied by the vicious slave-overseer—*and new Christian convert*—Edward Covey, Douglass attempts to plead his case of brutalization (at the hands of Covey) to the plantation master Thomas Auld. But his claims of innocence, even with a severely beaten body and blood streaming down his face, are summarily dismissed by the functioning of Auld's racial imagination: the need to maintain the illusion of Edward Covey's Christian character and integrity in the affective caste system outweighed the physical evidence of his evil disposition and brutality evidenced by Douglass's broken body. In this example of the racial imagination, it is Thomas Auld's unconscious need to dominate within the affective caste system that drives his conscious decision to repudiate Douglass, reject his claims of abuse, and disavow the brutality that his human sensibilities attested to. Moreover, within the racial imagination, Douglass knew that to quarrel with Auld—that is, to contest the racial logic of the slavocracy—would be viewed and emotionally experienced by Auld as offensive, in furtherance to the crime of impudence:

> I must not affirm my innocence of the allegations which he had piled up against me; for that would be impudence, and would

---

4. Douglass, *Narrative of the Life*, 79.

> probably call down fresh violence as well as wrath upon me. The guilt of a slave is always, and everywhere, presumed; and the innocence of the slaveholder or the slave employer, is always asserted. The word of the slave, against this presumption, is generally treated as impudence, worthy of punishment. "Do you contradict me, you rascal?" is a final silencer of counter statements from the lips of a slave.[5]

In the slavocracy, the enslaved must be silent, docile, and compliant, gladly submitting to the moral reasoning of the slaver. By extension, in the racial imagination of the twentieth and twenty-first centuries, black and brown reasoning, intellectualism, and moral agency are commonly dismissed or ignored, being subjugated to that of white intellectualism.

In Douglass's account of a black woman by the name of Nelly, her offense was her beauty, her aura of self-confidence, and her audacity to be unafraid of a vicious overseer. Taken together, Nelly refused to stay in her subordinated status within a debilitating psychological caste system of the slavocracy. According to Douglass, such violations in the racial imagination led to physical manifestations of racial brutality:

> The offense alleged against Nelly, was one of the commonest and most indefinite in the whole catalogue of offenses usually laid to the charge of slaves, viz: "impudence." This may mean almost anything, or nothing at all, just according to the caprice of the master or overseer, at the moment . . . the party charged with it is sure of a flogging. This offense may be committed in various ways; in the tone of an answer, in answering at all; in not answering; in the expression of countenance; in the motion of the head; in the gait, manner and bearing of the slave.[6]

While Douglass is not using the language of racial imagination, he is clearly referencing the perversion of the interior world of the enablers and custodians of the slavocracy, and by extension, white supremacy. Moreover, Douglass is describing the irreducible connection between the interior imagination of superiority to external acts of brutality and violence designed to substantiate a relationship of power and dominance.

By now, the implications of employing the terminology of *racial imagination* compared to the narrow terminology of *racist* (or any variant thereof) should be clearer. The question is not *necessarily* if a person or action qualifies as racist. Such an inquiry begs the question of when or at what point a person or action crosses the line to being racist, and usually

---

5. Douglass, *My Bondage*, 230.
6. Douglass, *My Bondage*, 92.

results in unconstructive conversation. This is not to say that terms such as *racist* or *racism* are without probative value, but that they are of limited value when attempting to dissect the death-dealing world of systemic and institutional racial animus—the world that the titans confronted in their projects, and the world that remains alive and well with us today. Furthermore, the practice of strictly demarcating who or what action is racist runs the risk of scapegoating those who cross the culturally taboo boundary of what constitutes racism—as if the offender's action(s) are rare and occur only sporadically in the life of the community or contemporary times. As if often the case, when the terminology of racist or racism is invoked, psychological fragility begins to manifest. The community becomes either terrified of or vexed about a conversation on race. No one wants to be considered racist, let alone contemplate the prospect that such a despicable idea is associated with them personally or their community, so all conversation about race is shunned and effectively ignored. Such then are the inner workings of systemic and institutional racism. In both categories, the community gaslights those victimized by its entrenched culture of racial ideology and marginalizes anyone who seeks to undermine the racial status quo. At its core, both systemic and institutional racism thrive in the capacity to appear innocuous and necessary. Systemic and institutional racism gazes upon, critiques, and disciplines black and brown culture, all the while normalizing the institution's own life-limiting practices. All of this occurs against a backdrop of white invisibility. That is to say, in the paradigm of systemic and institutional racism, the concept of culture is delimited to raced individuals, as white is not considered to be a culture, but the global norm upon which all other cultures are judged as to whether they are fully human or not.

The healthier psychospirituality suggested here is to consider the extent that one's reasoning, moral agency, and actions are infected by the racial imagination. For black and brown people, this proposal involves a self-examination of the extent to which there has been an internalization of the racial imagination that precipitates practices of self-hatred and self-flagellation, both as individuals and as a collective community. Pastorally speaking, unless there is a sustained and intentional psychospiritual intervention that addresses the harm that the multilayered legacy of the slavocracy has imposed on identity formation, the racial imagination will remain unscathed and continue to thrive in its ability to socialize people into its demonic web. The mere passage of time does not cure the racial imagination.

There are implications as well for non-raced individuals. The outward subordination and subjugation of black and brown bodies (including Asian and indigenous bodies) that emanates from the racial imagination ranges on a spectrum from brazen violence, conscious and unambiguous bias, and institutional and systemic racism, to microaggressions, unconscious and implicit bias, and the everyday inability for raced people to be experienced by non-raced people as fully human and normal, to outright apathy and indifference to all things that pertain to black and brown life. An intent to harm or ill will are not prerequisites for the racial imagination. The racial imagination is not contained by ideological enclaves of liberal, center, or conservative. The racial imagination does not have to be driven by malevolence. It is fueled by altruism and good intentions as well. Lastly, the racial imagination undermines the misconception that an individual or group must be consciously and intentionally taught racism. To the contrary, *the racial imagination represents complex intergenerational practices of being socialized into a way of experiencing oneself as superior to another human being.* At the core of the racial imagination is the psychic need to experience all things pertaining to oneself *as superior* (or representative to what constitutes normalcy) to all things pertaining to those who have been raced. For individuals privileged enough to be non-raced, the racial imagination represents the intergenerational socialization of internalized superiority. For raced individuals, the racial imagination represents the intergenerational socialization of internalized inferiority and self-flagellation.

THE DANGER OF A PREMATURE BELOVED COMMUNITY

Confining the conversation on racism to conscious, brazen, and egregious actions caused by a person's skin color contributes to the misconception that the practice of *racing others* is a discrete object of human history that can be confined to a specific historical period of time, with only periodic manifestations in the present. Furthermore, this misconception conceivably leads to the thought reverberating in some contemporary anti-racist and racial reconciliation literature that seems to postulate a future where racism does not exist. At face value, such a visionary hope is perhaps admirable, but it is wrought with conceptual problems. Can we imagine a future where there is no human hatred or animosity? Can we imagine a future where human oppression or envy no longer exists? Could we imagine a future where we have eliminated interpersonal resentment or contempt? Would we even contemplate that it is possible to eliminate any of these unhealthy human emotions? To respond to any one of these questions in the affirmative suggests naïve thinking. As such, why do we put such altruistic demands on the issue of racism?

Among the oldest narratives in the Hebrew Scriptures is that of Cain murdering his brother, Abel (Gen 4:1–10). While many interpretations can be gleaned from the story, we clearly see that to subjugate another human being—to the point of death—over the most trivial matters (i.e., envy, jealousy, contempt) is native to the human project. That is to say, to subjugate another human being is constitutional to human history. No one transcends the possibility to subjugate their neighbor for self-serving purposes (i.e., *if you do not do well, sin is crouching at the door. Its desire is contrary to you, but you must rule over it* [Gen 4:7 ESV]). Because Cain failed to *rule over* the insatiable desires that haunted his interior world, it manifested itself outwardly in the murder of this brother, all over what could arguably be conceived as interpersonal competition. Parallels of this construct are evidenced in the Second Testament as well, in Jesus's Sermon on the Mount and in the third chapter of 1 John. In the former, Jesus warns that unchecked animosity in the human imagination leads to the same outer destruction and judgment of a murderer (Matt 5:21–26). In the latter, John postulates unequivocally that the one who harbors animosity and contempt in the heart is the same as a murderer (1 John 3:11–15). The animus and contempt that invades the human imagination and lead to the outward attempt to subjugate *the other* are an indigenous function of the story of humanity that cannot be engineered away, no matter how well meaning the intentions. The animus, or what I refer to later as anti-love, which is elemental to being human, can be managed and mitigated only through an intentional praxis of love in perpetuity.

The matter of racial animus and white supremacy is simply another form of a perversion of the imagination that leads to the interpersonal subjugation of one's neighbor. While the *means of race* is a production of modern history, *the end of its underlying motive* is consistent with any other form of contempt: the subjugation of another human being. Perhaps the genius of Orlando Patterson's work *Slavery and Social Death* was in its recognition that the framework of enslaving another person is endemic to the human project and not predominantly a creation of Western expansionism. For the West, and especially in the Americas, the ideology of racial superiority was created, developed, and refined to be used as a social, moral, and religious justification for the hegemony of slavery. Patterson is clear that:

> There is nothing notably peculiar about the institution of slavery. It has existed from before the dawn of human history right down to the twentieth century, in the most primitive of human societies and in the most civilized. There is no region on earth that has not at some time harbored the institution. Probably there is no group of people whose ancestors were not at one time slaves or slaveholders . . . It was firmly established in all the great centers of human civilization and, far from declining, actually

increased in significance with the growth of all the epochs and cultures that modern Western peoples consider watersheds in their historical development.[7]

Assuming the burden of fashioning a future where racism does not exist has only an appearance of goodness. To do so would also require that the racism-free future be devoid of all human contempt and hatred. Such an idea seems naïve and unnecessarily burdensome. But perhaps more importantly, the notion of a racism-free future risks circumventing the courage needed to cultivate a social praxis of love that challenges racial hatred, and alternatively trying to artificially achieve the post-racial society by creating a façade. This façade is easily constructed by simply controlling the conversation about the ills of race within a community or institution. That is to say, if you don't talk about racism, or minimize the realities of its existence, then you create a synthetic space where racial hatred doesn't exist. Such an environment is nothing more than the wish fulfillment of the privileged. But more importantly, when this vision of a future where racism is totally eliminated is postulated in the church, it runs the risk of politicizing hope.

The politicization of hope is the practice of trivializing a people's fight for freedom and equity. Politicizing a people's hope is the implied suggestion that their aspirations for freedom and equity are an illegitimate form of spirituality that should be replaced by the *more appropriate aspirations* of the majority—aspirations that primarily deny the reality of oppression and maintain the status quo. The politicization of hope is counterproductive to the goal of human flourishing.[8] The politicization of hope ultimately gives way to a form of religion that does not require change, a theology so beholden to culture and tradition that it is unable to inspire moral agency or social ethics, and a spirituality that never leads to the love of one's neighbor. Especially in settings where there is more than one culture or ethnicity, it is dangerous to attempt an all-encompassing definition or vision of hope. When this happens, the resulting vision usually reflects the desires of those in power. The work of theologian James Evans is useful in its analysis of hope in the Christian faith, describing the multidimensional essence of hope and how it is necessarily connected to history and heritage.

Evans details three theological dimensions of hope that include the personal, the communal, and the efficacious (or cosmic). The personal dimension of hope emphasizes that death does not have the final word, that there is life and continuity after death. Instead of romanticizing the reality of the tragedy, evil, horrors, and trauma of all that Good Friday symbolizes

---

7. Patterson, *Slavery and Social Death*, xxvii.
8. D. Gibson, "Black Religion, Mental Health."

in human experience, the personal dimension of hope does not force us to deny or repress the reality of evil. A critical part of the road to psychospiritual healing is the capacity to name and embrace the reality of evil; to be truthful when one is in pain, suffering, or traumatized; and to do so without guilt or shame. The telos of the personal dimension of hope assures us that while suffering, pain, trauma, and even death may prevail on this side of the eschaton, they do not have the final word. There is an Easter event—a resurrection Sunday—to look forward to. The communal aspect of hope, according to Evans, emphasizes that we will be in community again with the friends and loved ones we have been separated from in life, whether it be from death or any other tragedy. Lastly, what Evans calls the cosmic dimension of hope, or what I refer to as the efficacy of hope, emphasizes that there is no person beyond the power of redemption. Despite the vigorous efforts of the institutional church to build taller barriers to entry, or to squander its time determining who belongs and who does not belong in its social enclave, the efficacy of hope constantly ponders the critical question, "If salvation is not possible for the worst of us, can it be a certainty for any of us?"[9]

More important to the argument here (i.e., how the idea of a race-free society runs the risk of undermining the work of shalom) is how Evans borrows from the work of Max Weber to establish the relationship between history and social location, and the mechanics of hope.[10] Hope cannot be reduced to abstract proclamations and religious platitudes about the future. An articulated narrative of hope that represses the past, engages in revisionist historicizing, looks above the suffering of the one's neighbor, and trivializes the necessity of justice and metanoia as it relates racism and inequality, represents a bankrupt theology that does little in the way of healing, redemption, and the construction of a beloved community. History, heritage, and social location will necessarily impact how a community constructs hope. *Hope is politicized when the ambitions of the powerful and privileged are uncritically imposed upon the disinherited and then purported as representing the most appropriate yearnings for all of humanity.* According to Weber, hope, more often than not, is unconsciously conceptualized in conjunction with social location and class. There is no such thing as a disinterested hope or doctrinal purity in terms of what constitutes hope. Because of this common and gross misunderstanding of how the ethic of hope is construed in Western Christianity, Weber is worth quoting at length. I suggest hope is one of many subcategories in what Weber suggests about religion and how

---

9. Evans, *We Have Been Believers*, 180.
10. See Weber, *Sociology of Religion*.

people use it to justify and provide meaning to their existence and ambitions. According to Weber, in the case of the upper social classes, and for our purposes those who enjoy the privilege of being non-raced:

> *Their sense of self-esteem rests on their awareness that the perfection of their life pattern is an expression of their underived, ultimate, and qualitatively distinctive being*; indeed, it is in the very nature of the case that this should be the basis of the elite's feeling of worth. On the other hand, *the sense of honor of disprivileged classes rests on some concealed promise for the future which implies the assignment of some function, mission, or vocation to them*. What they cannot claim to be, they replace by the worth of that which they will one day become, to which they will be called in some future life here or thereafter.[11]

Weber suggests that a combination of history, culture, and social location feeds into the functionality of religion for any community. The implication is significant as it relates to any racial conciliatory praxis sponsored by the church: the religious space must always be a co-created space between the advantaged and the disadvantaged, or the inherited and the disinherited, if such a space is to maintain even the faintest modicum of salvific value. The telos of hope for what Weber refers to as the nobility class is different than the telos of what he calls the disprivileged class. Weber goes on to observe that:

> Other things being equal, classes with high social and economic privilege will scarcely be prone to evolve the idea of salvation. Rather, they assign to religion the primary function of legitimizing their own life pattern and situation in the world . . . When a man who is happy compares his position with that of one who is unhappy, he is not content with the fact of his happiness, but desires something more, namely the right to this happiness, the consciousness that he has earned his good fortune, in contrast to the unfortunate one who must equally have earned his misfortune. Our everyday experience proves that there exists just such a psychological need for reassurance as to the legitimacy or deservedness of one's happiness, whether this involves political success, superior economic status, bodily health, success in the game of love, or anything else. What the privileged classes require of religion, if anything at all, is this psychological reassurance of legitimacy.[12]

---

11. Weber, *Sociology of Religion*, 106; emphasis added.
12. Weber, *Sociology of Religion*, 107; emphasis added.

Understood in this light, the narrative of hope for Weber's *nobility class* can tolerate abstract propositions that are discursive in nature and void of any concrete ethical mandate for repentance or disruption of the racial status quo; the existing way of life is to their benefit. Alternatively, for Weber's disprivileged class, the narrative of hope tends to include elements of the temporal and the eternal, an ethical mandate for metanoia, a disruption of the racial status quo, and an irreducible requirement for justice and equity. To be clear, in the narrative of hope for the disinherited, freedom and equity are never incidental to eschatological hope. They are foundational.

Among the most compelling historical examples of the politicizing of hope is found in the correspondence between Martin Luther King and eight white Birmingham clergymen. While most are familiar with King's letter from a Birmingham jail, now considered among the most prestigious literary works of the twentieth century, fewer are familiar with the context and the open letter authored by seven Protestant ministers and a Jewish rabbi that occasioned the now famous letter from a jail cell. Earlier that year in January of 1963, prior to King being arrested because of the Birmingham civil rights protests that would occur in April, the same eight white ministers, with three others, penned an open letter in the local newspaper entitled "An Appeal for Law and Order and Common Sense."[13] In that open letter, they warn Birmingham residents that because of a series of court decisions, schools in Alabama would eventually be desegregated and all citizens should abide by the decision of the courts. In that same letter, the ministers condemn both defiance of the court's decision, and violence because of the decision. Clearly, the ministers had *good intentions, but good intentions do not meet the standard of becoming moral agents and responding to the divine ethical mandate for justice.*

By April of 1963 after King was arrested because of the nonviolent protests, the same core group of white clergymen issued another open letter in the local newspaper denouncing the protests and characterizing the work of King and his associates as inciting hatred and violence.[14] Moreover, the group of clergymen urged the black community in Birmingham to withdraw their support from the civil rights demonstrations and delimit their redress on civil rights to local constituents and resources. Perhaps the most commonly quoted line from this second open letter is "we are convinced that these demonstrations are unwise and untimely." Notable highlights from King's letter include responses such as "We know through painful experience that freedom is never voluntarily given by the oppressor; it must

---

13. See Harmon et al., "Appeal for Law."
14. See Harmon et al., "Call for Unity." See further Bass, *Blessed Are the Peacemakers*.

be demanded by the oppressed ... [and] I have never yet engaged in a direct action movement that was 'well-timed,' according to the timetable of those who have not suffered unduly from the disease of segregation"[15] and "You deplore the demonstrations that are presently taking place in Birmingham. But I am sorry that your statement did not express a similar concern for the conditions that brought the demonstrations into being."[16] But perhaps the following excerpt captures the essence of the letter and is worth quoting at length:

> I must make two honest confessions to you, my Christian and Jewish brothers. First, I must confess that over the last few years I have been gravely disappointed with the white moderate. I have almost reached the regrettable conclusion that the Negro's great stumbling block in the stride toward freedom is not the white citizens' "Councilor" or the Ku Klux Klanner, but the white moderate who is more devoted to "order" than to justice; who prefers a negative peace which is the absence of tension to a positive peace which is the presence of justice; who constantly says "I agree with you in the goal you seek, but I can't agree with your methods of direst action"; who paternalistically feels that he can set the timetable for another man's freedom; who lives by the myth of time and who constantly advises the Negro to wait until a "more convenient season." Shallow understanding from people of good will is more frustrating than absolute misunderstanding from people of ill will. Lukewarm acceptance is much more bewildering than outright rejection.[17]

This exchange between King and the eight white ministers in Birmingham has tremendous instructional value in terms of how we envision racial reconciliation and Christian praxis. This exchange is a mirror into our individual and collective souls. When we examine the emotional and psychological dynamics of the situation, we see, perhaps to the chagrin of many, that we are not that far removed from an era of American history that many would like to forget, or even deny. It is suggested here that we witness the politicization of hope when the eight ministers presumptuously assumed that they could unilaterally construct a narrative of hope for all of Birmingham. This comes across most vividly when they assert in their open letter, "We are now confronted by a series of demonstrations by some of our Negro citizens, directed and led in part by outsiders. We recognize

---

15. King, *Testament of Hope*, 292.
16. King, *Testament of Hope*, 290.
17. King, *Testament of Hope*, 295.

the natural impatience of people who feel that their hopes are slow in being realized. But we are convinced that these demonstrations are unwise and untimely."[18] Furthermore, I suggest we see the racial imagination in play when they paternalistically claim to know what is in the best interest of an oppressed black community and declare, "We further strongly urge our own Negro community to withdraw support from these demonstrations, and to unite locally in working peacefully for a better Birmingham."[19] The object of hope for the white ministers and their constituents was peace and tranquility. The object of hope for their black neighbors was freedom from a racial oppression that had terrorized their people for centuries. James Evans's conceptualization of the Christian hope captures the gap in the narratives of hope between the white ministers and the black community when Evans asserts that "a hope that does not come to terms with history can become unbridled optimism and idealism, or the cover for unchecked expansionism. History anchors hope. Because history and hope always belong to a specific community, they can mean different things to different people . . . hope takes on the connotations that reflect the social location of the community in question."[20]

In many respects this dynamic remains in the church today when we talk about racial reconciliation: those in a white power structure set the terms and conditions for constructing the narrative of Christian hope. I will also observe here that in both of the open letters authored by the eight ministers, the authors never argue for desegregation on a biblical or theological basis, like Martin Luther King, who richly argued his position for the nonviolent demonstrations from a biblical and theological perspective. Instead, the eight ministers argue their position of tenuously accepting desegregation only on the basis of abiding by the decision of the courts. From a theo-ethical perspective, their position reflects the religious tyranny of half-truths. By remaining silent on racial hatred and the evil system of segregation from a biblical and theological perspective, and arguing only that citizens should comply with the court's decision to desegregate, the religious leaders engage in the sin of sloth by averting the formidable challenge of having to become moral agents and denounce an evil apartheid system—regardless of any court decision. In effect, they are saving face and hiding behind the court's decision in their open letter. The religious leaders imply that freedom from oppression is only a social matter, and as such, is not worthy of theological reflection. And if it is not worthy of theological reflection, the

---

18. As quoted in Bass, *Blessed Are the Peacemakers*, 376.
19. As quoted in Bass, *Blessed Are the Peacemakers*, 377.
20. Evans, *We Have Been Believers*, 165–66.

natural progression is that people of faith—namely the Christian church—are not ethically obliged to repent for generations of racist contempt and the racial imagination. This approach adopted by the eight ministers represents an effective mental strategy for dealing with cognitive and moral dissonance associated with trying to *be a Christian* (as opposed to *acting like a Christian*) and at the same time affirming—implicitly or explicitly—the tenets of white supremacy that have defined the US for generations.

The same emotional patterns and psychological framework that undergird this historical episode are still at work today, especially in religious institutions. Many who watch images or documentaries of water hoses and police dogs being unleashed on children participating in the nonviolent demonstrations are appalled, and rightfully so. Such images are atrocities. Likewise, it is easy to idealize Martin Luther King and his writing of the famous letter from prison—and then, simultaneously with the idealization, to mentally and emotionally associate yourself with the principles and values outlined in the letter, and imagine that you would have *easily* thought, felt, and engaged in the acts of protest and civil disobedience displayed by King, his associates, and the protestors. However, *we should not fail to see ourselves in the eight local ministers as well*, who publicly denounced the nonviolent civil rights demonstrations because of the tension and discomfort the demonstrations caused, and instead advocated for the path of least resistance that prioritized peace and tranquility—an alternative that involved maintaining a death-dealing system of racial segregation.

But the eight local ministers were not alone in their resistance to the demonstrations. In the work of undoing the harmful effects of idealization, we must also see ourselves in certain portions of the black middle class that strongly opposed the nonviolent protest and instead preferred to find a way to cooperate with the status quo for the sake of peace and tranquility. King makes specific mention of this dynamic in his letter from prison, noting that "because of a degree of academic and economic security, and because at points they profit by segregation, [some middle-class black people in Birmingham] have unconsciously become insensitive to the problems of the masses."[21] And according to Julian Bond, "More work was needed to secure the support of Black Birmingham. Despite the careful work SCLC had done in preparing for the community, they were taken aback by the opposition the first days' protests raised among Birmingham's Black middle class, who were fearful that King's movement would upset the transition from a racist wild man Connor to the more sophisticated segregationist Boutwell."[22] At

---

21. King, *Testament of Hope*, 296.
22. Horowitz and Theoharis, *Julian Bond's Time*, 216.

least through the eyes of Bond and King, there is a misguided attempt by some to address the evil of segregation by appeasing it. That is to say, in order to keep the peace, the implicit thinking is to find a more palatable way to maintain an oppressive system, to find a right way to do wrong. Appeasing structures of racial terror oppression only emboldens it. On September 15 of that same year, after the nonviolent demonstrations, a bomb detonated during the morning worship service at Sixteenth Street Baptist Church, killing four girls: Carol Denise McNair, Carole Robertson, Cynthia Wesley, and Addie Mae Collins. *The peace that comes with appeasement is little more than a façade of progress.*

Idealization is useful in the development of transcendent ideas. Every human being engages in idealization in our personal identity formation. However, if it is maintained in an unhealthy way because of our own repressed anxieties and unmet needs, idealization undermines our developmental formation as moral agents. It can delude us into believing that we are already doing the work that we idealize. Furthermore, it can undermine our ability to engage in the necessary self-introspection that will enable us to do works of justice.

RACISM AND THE IMAGINATION: A PSYCHOSPIRITUAL SICKNESS

The racial imagination is a sickness of the interior world. It infects the psychic space of a community, a polis, and a nation. Manifestations of racism reflect a sickness of the soul that requires a psychospiritual intervention. A significant amount of scholarship on the topic of racism has attended to its impact in groups, organizations, institutions, and society at large. Other scholarship has put forth prospective remedies to address its ill effects, including caring for (mainly reactively) individuals and communities harmed by its demonic effects. *But not nearly enough attention or literature has focused on how the individual and collective soul of the racial oppressor has been corrupted by the ongoing legacy of the slavocracy.* More attention in the literature, and perhaps rightfully so, seems to have been given to examining the destructive effects of racial ideology. The unintended consequence of this approach, in part, is an implicit belief that racial justice equates to doing favors for, providing charity or concessions to, or giving handouts to those who have been raced or who have suffered under the crushing burden of a system of racial apartheid; hence, the often-heard messaging of "haven't we done enough for them." *Rarely is it understood as psychospiritual sickness that deteriorates the humanity and soul of those immersed in the racial imagination. And in terms of remedy, even more seldom is the race problem understood in terms of devising a psychospiritual intervention to reverse the harmful effects of the individual and collective soul infected by the ideology of inherent superiority based on skin tone and heritage.*

This oversight, perhaps in every sector of the republic, has been shortsighted, causing scholars and political and religious leaders to underestimate at best, or outright overlook at worst, the corrosive nature of the racial imagination—over the long run. Like an undiagnosed disease, the racial imagination ossifies the moral compass of the body politic until only a horrific event can quicken the inert conscience: hence a violent insurrection to harm and murder elected officials in order to overthrow a national election. Predominantly white organizations and institutions err greatly when it is assumed that because there are little to no ethnic minorities in their midst, that racial ideology is irrelevant to their context. It is an organizational misconception to believe that matters of race are merely topics for black and brown people. Such thinking undermines the health of any community. Moreover, in the halls of the academy and ivory tower, merely asserting that racism (and by extension nationalism) has already been discussed in academic scholarship and mainstream literature is a deceptive *check-the-box approach* that reflects a long-standing gaslighting strategy and misses a deeper point: how (and why) the ongoing legacy of the slavocracy and the racial imagination continues to corrupt the psychic space and soul of the academy, and the larger republic.

Perhaps one of the most overlooked personalities that captures the essence of how racism is a soul-sickness is that of Lillian Smith. Smith was the owner and director of the Laurel Falls Camp for Girls in Clayton, Georgia. She was also a best-selling author and magazine editor. But even with no formal role in a national civil rights organization, Smith found a way to use her platform and body of work to challenge segregation and white supremacy. As a white woman living in the South in the mid-twentieth century, it is easy to see how she existed before her time given her revolutionary stances against segregation.[23] But she understood that she didn't need a national platform, significant financial resources, or notoriety to do her part in the work of justice. She is a prime example of how psychohistory can be used to demythologize how we think of the civil rights era. In her public writings and speeches, she challenged the alleged wisdom of moving slowly when it came to ending segregation, and more importantly, about how racism inflicted the souls of those beholden to racial ideology.

---

23. See Gladney and Hodgens, *Lillian Smith Reader*.

At the beginning of one of her speeches to a group of student protestors in Atlanta, Smith laments, "I regret that there are so few white students, as yet, working side by side with you; I am sorry they have not yet realized that segregation is their enemy also; that it harms their minds and souls as much as it does yours; that it blocks their freedom and their future as severely as it does yours. When they do see they will not be afraid to do their share; they too have courage; it is vision they do not, as yet, possess."[24] Here, Smith models a pedagogical principle that can still be emulated in predominantly white institutions of higher learning today: in the formation of our students, engaging matters of oppression and injustice as they relate to our neighbor cannot be merely reduced to a matter of personal prerogative or thought of as a personal preference for social justice, but must be understood as an ethical obligation that the professor must unequivocally profess—lest the student fail to grasp *love of neighbor as both a moral imperative and a matter of personal and communal integrity and morality.*

In another well-known speech entitled "The Right Way Is Not a Moderate Way," Smith challenges the common wisdom that desegregation should be slow, moderate, and at a pace deemed acceptable by the local population. According to Smith, the call for moderation when it comes to destroying a system of racial apartheid is nothing more than code for the real sentiment that says, "We want to freeze things; we want to be neutral; we don't want to move a step either way. Things suit us as they are: why should we change them? Change is painful; so let's don't change." Smith's observation about the psyche of the system of segregation is still relevant today and is consistent with the heart of institutional racism. But in an even more genius way, Smith associates the workings of racial segregation to her own personal bout with cancer, arguing that both cancer and racial segregation will not end well with any person or community plagued by the disease. Similarly to how people are inclined to ignore a cancer diagnosis out of fear, she asserts the call for moderation (or ignoring the problem of race relations) is done out of fear. Smith articulates the racial imagination as a spiritual sickness that is worth quoting at length here. In discussing the racial crises in the mid-twentieth century, Smith says:

> People behave this way in other crises, too; not simply in this one of race relations. There are people who react in a similar way when they are told they have cancer. They decide to be moderate and do nothing; to rock along and postpone thinking about it. Why? Because they are scared. And, because of their fright, they

---

24. Smith, "Are We Still Buying," 480.

convince themselves that if they do nothing, if they take a few vitamins, maybe, the cancer will go away.

The tragic fact is, neither cancer nor segregation will go away while we close our eyes. Both are dangerous diseases that have to be handled quickly and skillfully because they spread, they metastasize throughout the organism. We have seen this happen, too often, to people who have delayed doing anything about cancer. We have also seen sick race relations metastasize throughout our country—and indeed, throughout the whole earth.

Because of the nature of both diseases—one physical, one social—because you cannot wall these problems in, you do not have time to lose with cancer; nor today, do we have time to lose in facing up to segregation . . . the critical moment is on us. Now is the time to deal with it.[25]

Idolatry is the theo-ethical interpretation of the racial imagination. It is a perversion of faith whereby the ideology of the superiority and greater worth of non-raced people over that of raced people is stacked against the revelation of God and the knowledge that all the peoples of the earth are created in the image and likeness of God. The mechanics of idolatry are fueled by fear, self-loathing, and pride. The truth of human finiteness, depravity, and the inherent sameness of all the peoples of the earth is feared. The reality of this essential human condition then fosters self-loathing compelled in part by the psychic need to be fundamentally better than *the other*; as opposed to a healthier identity formed on *who a person is*, rather than an identity that is co-dependent on *not being like one of them*. Finally, through the practice of pride, this handcrafted imago of superiority, exceptionalism, and purity is granted primacy over the revelation, wisdom, and knowledge of God. At the heart of idolatry is the creation of a god-image that can be manipulated and controlled to provide religious sanctioning of the racial imagination.

In his classic text *Racism and the Christian Understanding of Man*, George Kelsey, perhaps better than any religious scholar in the twentieth century, interprets the structures of racism—at its core—as a perversion of religiosity, as a spiritual sickness, and a metastasizing form of moral decay. The importance of this work cannot be overstated, as the church and Western Christian tradition are indicted for their role in the construction and maintenance of racism in the American story, and what I am referring to as the racial imagination. When it is argued in the church, and by extension theological education, that Christian approaches to anti-racism must be

---

25. L. Smith, "Right Way Is Not," 336–37.

adopted, such thinking reflects an unending, if not troubling, irony, as the argument fails (if not refuses) to recognize the ongoing role of the church in perpetuating the racial imagination. Kelsey masterfully articulates the conspiracy between the church, Western Christian tradition, and the legacy of race. According to him:

> Racism is a faith. It is a form of idolatry. It is an abortive search for meaning . . . It did not emerge as a faith . . . But gradually the idea of the superior race was heightened and deepened in meaning and value so that it pointed beyond the historical structures of relation, in which it emerged, to human existence itself. The alleged superior race became and now persists as a center of value and an object of devotion. Multitudes of men gain their sense of the "power of being" from their membership in the superior race.
>
> By and large, Christians have failed to recognize racism as an idolatrous faith, even though it poses the problem of idolatry among Christians in a way that no other tendency does. Racism is especially problematical not only because of the peculiar nature of the racist faith, but because it is a "Trojan horse" within organized Christianity and Christian civic communities.[26]

The implications of this Trojan horse in organized Christianity in the West cannot be overstated. The term *syncretism* is often employed in the church and theological education (pejoratively, if we are honest) to describe how non-Western cultures that practice the Christian faith do so in a compromised way when they integrate Christian ideas and practice with other indigenous religious practices or concepts. The very usage of the word *syncretism* reflects the ideology and illusion of purity itself—as if any person or culture can embody the faith without it being fused with the social dynamics of the culture in which it is embedded. In my own classroom, I discourage students from using the word *syncretism* unless they are willing to acknowledge how Christianity in the West is enmeshed with Western values and ideologies (i.e., capitalism, neo-liberalism, consumerism, etc.). More specifically, the church in America fails to comprehend, let alone acknowledge, how its embodiment of the faith is infused with racial ideology. On this point, Kelsey argues:

> The fact that racism exists alongside other faiths does not make it any less a faith. Rather, this fact is *testimony to the reality of polytheism in the modern age*. In its maturity, racism is not a mere ideology that a political demagogue may be expected to

---

26. Kelsey, *Racism and Christian Understanding*, 9.

> affirm or deny, depending upon the political situation in which he finds himself. *Racism is a search for meaning.* The devotee of the racist faith is as certainly seeking self-identity in his acts of self-exaltation and his self-deifying pronouncements as he is seeking to nullify the selfhood of members of out-races by acts of deprivation and words of vilification.[27]

This unacknowledged practice of syncretism and polytheism in the church lends itself to the uninterrogated assumption that the US is inherently a Christian nation. It blinds the church to the fact that it has been a major progenitor in racial ideology and terror. In some respects, because of the idolatry of the racial imagination and the practices of polytheism and syncretism, it becomes nearly impossible to engage in an honest conversation about Christian faith in the US without talking about racism, and vice versa. Faith has been syncretized with the ideologies of race, capitalism, consumerism, and class, such that to excel or be successful in any of these categories is to be automatically conferred with salvific virtue. Bearing the fruit of love, joy, peace, patience, kindness, goodness, faithfulness, gentleness, and self-control—all of which reflect the work of the Spirit—becomes irrelevant in the paradigm of racial idolatry.

Understood as idolatry, the sin-sick soul is fixated on the illusion of individual and group purity, endeavoring to achieve this through an obsession with the methodologies of exclusion. The politics of exclusion is achieved through the intrapsychic process of projection, where unwanted elements of the human condition (i.e., sin, frailty, finiteness, suffering, brokenness, depravity, etc.) are projected onto *the raced other*. When a community is consumed with the methodologies of exclusion, *who belongs* and *who does not belong*, or *who is one of us* and *who is not one of us*, are the pervasive preoccupations and fears that fuel a deep sense of annihilation anxiety. Consequently, instead of a self-identity that is formed through an awareness of *what I am* as a human being created in the image and likeness of God, individual and group identity is cultivated by a preoccupation of *what I am not*. This resulting self-image of *what I am not*, driven by the fear of finiteness and human frailty, and created through the methodology of exclusion, is given priority status over and against the knowledge of God, and then against all others created in the image and likeness of God. Scripture compels a Christian identity informed by the apostle Paul's assertion:

> In Christ Jesus you are all sons of God, through faith. For as many of you as were baptized into Christ have put on Christ. There is neither Jew nor Greek, there is neither slave nor free,

---

27. Kelsey, *Racism and Christian Understanding*, 23; emphasis added.

there is no male and female, for you are all one in Christ Jesus. And if you are Christ's, then you are Abraham's offspring, heirs according to promise. (Gal 3:26–29 ESV)

By contrast, the idolatry underwritten by the racial imagination seeks to reestablish the human-value caste system eviscerated by Jesus in the passion and Easter events. Instead of human beings who—in Christ—also happen to be (unashamedly and unapologetically) Jewish, Greek, female, male, slave, or free, the idolatry of the racial imagination (similarly to how it seeks *to race* human beings) insists on the material reality of a Jewish Christian, Greek Christian, male Christian, female Christian—or for our purposes here, a white Christian (along with its religious histories and heritage) and the assertion of its religious, theological, and spiritual superiority (or value) over that of a black or brown Christian (along with its religious histories and heritage). On this point, I quote Kelsey at length as he crystalizes, in great detail, how racial idolatry undermines the Christian witness:

> *Therefore racism as a faith is a form of idolatry, for it elevates a human factor to the level of the ultimate. The god of racism is the race, the ultimate center of value.* "What does it mean to have a god, or what is God?" Martin Luther inquires. Proceeding to answer his own question, Luther says, "trust and faith of the heart alone make both God and idol . . . For the two, faith and God, hold close together. Whatever then thy heart clings to . . . and relies upon, this is properly God." *For the racist, race is the final point of reference for decision and action, the foundation upon which he organizes his private life, public institutions and public policy, and even his religious institutions.* When men elevate any human or historical factor to so great a height that it has the power to give substance and direction to all cultural institutions, no matter what the *raison d'être*, that human or historical factor has become a god.[28]

My assertion that the racial imagination represents the sin of idolatry, in part, explains the perpetual silence of the church in relation to generations and centuries of systemic racism and terror: the church has been, and continues to be, neck-deep in the practice of an idolatry that has taken root in the ecclesial imagination. Paul Tillich is useful in understanding how idolatry infects the human imagination. Borrowing from John Calvin to make the connection between idolatry and anxiety, Tillich asserts, "The human mind is not only, as Calvin has said, a permanent factory of idols, it is also a permanent factory of fears—the first in order to escape God, the

---

28. Kelsey, *Racism and Christian Understanding*, 27; emphasis added.

second in order to escape anxiety; and there is a relation between the two . . . The basic anxiety, the anxiety of a finite being about the threat of nonbeing, cannot be eliminated. It belongs to existence itself."[29] At the heart of idolatry then is the attempt to address our internal fears of annihilation anxiety, and the fear of having to be true, transparent, and authentic in the presence of the Divine.

The idolatry of the racial imagination is far reaching, with devastating effects in the church: it undermines moral agency and efficacious Christian praxis. The apostle Paul is clear about how idolatry (or racial idolatry for our purposes here) corrupts the Christian heart and mind. Moreover, left unattended to, this corruption metastasizes in the collective soul of the polis, when pride (i.e., confiding more in the logic of racism as opposed to the law of God), the arrogance of the racial imagination, and the *faith of racism* all collude to challenge the revelation of the true God. Racial idolatry left unchecked is bound to manifest itself not only in repetitious acts of violence, but greater, and more destructive and sinister, forms of evil and violence. Over the long run, racial idolatry gives way to a process whereby the violence that we are more accustomed to inevitably evolves into insatiable self-interest, human carnage, and destruction for which there is no logic—or what could be understood as radical evil (consider the horrors of the American slavocracy, or the Holocaust, or Jim Crow and the prevalence of lynching). Martin Beck Matuštík describes radical evil as:

> gratuitous destruction and invidious violence . . . [whereas a] thief might commit murder to avoid being caught in the act of robbery, betrayed lovers might kill in the heat of passion or out of anger and jealousy, and wars might be waged for political and economic gain . . . [radical evil in the form of] mass murders have no such reasonable telos . . . With aimless evil, it is difficult to negotiate reasons or pursue normative goals. Shaming radical evil's logical self-contradiction or rational and moral incoherence does us existentially no good. Radical moral evil lies in humans [sic] willing destruction even at the cost of their own downfall.[30]

This description of radical evil appropriately captures the much of the racial terror and violence witnessed in the western hemisphere in the nineteenth and twentieth centuries. Moreover, when it is tolerated through indifference, it spiritually and emotionally immunizes individuals, institutions, nations, and even the church. Whereas guilt, compassion, and even shame

---

29. Tillich, *Courage to Be*, 39–40.
30. Matuštík, *Radical Evil*, 8.

would normally prompt people to protest and resistance, apathy becomes the governing reaction to human atrocity. It is my assertion that the apostle Paul captures this psychospiritual dilemma in the first chapter of Romans:

> Furthermore, *just as they did not think it worthwhile to retain the knowledge of God, so God gave them over to a depraved mind, so that they do what ought not to be done.* They have become filled with every kind of wickedness, evil, greed and depravity. They are full of envy, murder, strife, deceit and malice. They are gossips, slanderers, God-haters, insolent, arrogant and boastful; they invent ways of doing evil; they disobey their parents; they have no understanding, no fidelity, no love, no mercy. *Although they know God's righteous decree that those who do such things deserve death, they not only continue to do these very things but also approve of those who practice them.* (Rom 1:28–32 NIV; emphasis added)

Paul articulates the ramifications of the collective decision to place greater confidence in human dogma (i.e., racial ideology) than in the knowledge of God: a society overrun with mayhem and human atrocity. In order to satisfy the insatiable concupiscence and passions of the human heart—and for our purposes here, the racial imagination—there is no amount of violence and hatred that would be considered off limits in order to secure the desires of the idolatrous heart. Consider the growing apathy towards mass shootings, or the black and brown victims of hate crimes and massacres at the hands of those beholden to ideologies of racial purity or white supremacy. A massacre can occur on one day, and the attention of the country can turn to sports entertainment within hours of the killing. The collective soul of the nation is becoming numb to radical evil, with the result being that it takes even greater acts of human atrocity to grab our attention for even a brief moment.[31] While some theologians use the first chapter of Romans as one of their go-to passages regarding matters of sexuality, I suggest the passage speaks more directly to the sociopolitical lawlessness and mayhem produced by idolatry over the long run—the idolatry spoken to by John Calvin, George Kelsey, Paul Tillich, and the apostle Paul. The Rom 1 passage is describing the Western democratic experiment. Paul is speaking to us!

> The wrath of God is being revealed from heaven against all the godlessness and wickedness of people, *who suppress the truth by their wickedness, since what may be known about God is plain to them, because God has made it plain to them.* For since the creation of the world God's invisible qualities—his eternal power

---

31. See Means, *Trauma & Evil*.

and divine nature—have been clearly seen, being understood from what has been made, so that people are without excuse. *For although they knew God, they neither glorified him as God nor gave thanks to him, but their thinking became futile and their foolish hearts were darkened. Although they claimed to be wise, they became fools* and exchanged the glory of the immortal God for images made to look like a mortal human being and birds and animals and reptiles. (Rom 1:18–23 NIV; emphasis added)

The racial animosity and strife that we are witnessing in the twenty-first century, a racial contempt and nationalism that precipitated the violent insurrection in January 2021, in part, is due to decades of appeasing racial idolatry coupled with the long-standing notion *of moderation*. The practice of moderation prioritized a superficial racial harmony and a façade of the beloved community. It privileged the *religion of happiness* and moral apathy but failed in the much more difficult work of curing the individual and collective soul infected by the racial imagination. In her work, Smith does not view the dismantling of racial apartheid as providing concessions and charity to black and brown people. Instead, she is clear that the freedom of white people is at stake and includes "the freedom to do right . . . the freedom to obey the law . . . the freedom to speak out, to write, to teach what one believes is true and just [and]. . . the freedom from fear."[32] According to Smith, the freedom to "teach what one believes is true" was related to teachers having to sign documents prohibiting them from teaching on desegregation and white supremacy, at the risk of incurring penalties or even losing their jobs. While Smith remarked on this in 1956, such prohibitions on teaching about the ills of racial ideology and white supremacy have resurfaced in the twenty-first century in the form of local governments and school boards across the country banning the teaching of any theory about race that highlights its systemic and endemic natures. The resurfacing of such prohibitions in education reflects, in part, what happens when only the symptoms of racism are addressed as opposed to dealing with it as a spiritual disease.

In his psychological description of racism, Neil Altman describes racism as a disease of the psyche whereby the ailments and vulnerabilities of the human condition are externalized and then projected on a *racially constructed other*. Among the most compelling examples of this in American history is the way in which the nation viewed and experienced the crack cocaine epidemic that ravaged black and brown communities in the latter half of the twentieth century, and the opioid epidemic that ravaged white

---

32. Smith, "Right Way Is Not," 339; emphasis added.

middle-class communities in the first part of the twenty-first century. In the former example, black and brown communities became the face of drug addiction, with the primary sociopolitical response being that of draconian prison sentences, as the addictions were deemed to reflect deficits in personal character where all that was necessary was to "say no to drugs." In the latter twenty-first century example, the prevailing sociopolitical response has been that of empathy in the opioid epidemic that has ravaged primarily white middle-class communities, a response that has yielded multibillion-dollar payouts from pharmaceutical companies accused of aiding and abetting in the chemical dependency of thousands of people. How do we account for the vast difference in public response to drug abuse, where black and brown communities were demonized and white communities were humanized? In part, it reflects how Altman describes the disease of racism where human frailty and vulnerability are externalized and projected on raced communities. That is to say, to be black or brown becomes the metaphor for criminal, weak, faulty, substandard, inadequate, sinful, or profane, so that white becomes the counter-metaphor for the mastery and goodness of the human project. For Altman, "racism is a symptom, a manifestation, of *an underlying disease* that might be defined as an organization of experience around power, or a dominant-submissive structure that affects all of us."[33]

BUT HAVEN'T WE TALKED ABOUT RACE ENOUGH?

If understood as a psychospiritual sickness, it seems that instead of asking whether or not we have discussed racism enough—a question that is often asked in the ivory tower as well as in mainstream society—a more helpful analysis is to understand the cultural and sociopolitical backdrop upon which that very question is being considered. Especially in the halls of academia and in religious institutions, given the racial tensions being witnessed in a post-Obama age, the notion that we have already written and talked enough about racial ideology is turned on its head. This sort of thinking is especially prevalent in the ivory tower that tends to have an overdeveloped view of its efficacy in society by merely noting that a topic—in this case, racism—has been addressed in the literature. What is often missing in the thinking of ivory tower culture is whether or not what has already been written has been effective in dismantling the structures of racial oppression. The obvious answer is no! Moreover, the mandate to avoid addressing an academic topic that has allegedly been previously addressed discourages future generations of scholars, especially from black and brown communities,

---

33. Altman, *Analyst in Inner City*, 103.

from engaging phenomena that are relevant to their own communities (under the guise that it has already been discussed somewhere in the academy). That is, current and future scholars of color are disincentivized (at the risk of not receiving tenure or simply not being employed) to do research, innovate, and engage topics that existentially matter in their own culture and heritage, especially if that area of focus is not of interest in the culture of the ivory tower. bell hooks speaks cogently to the matter of navigating the academe, knowing and loving her audience and, as a result of that, engaging in scholarship that matters to that audience when she constructs feminist discourse. hooks asserts, "I have written elsewhere, and shared in numerous public talks and conversations, that my decisions about writing style, about not using conventional academic formats, are political decisions motivated by the desire to be inclusive, to reach as many readers as possible in as many different locations."[34] In many respects, this reflects the current state of affairs as it relates to the body of literature on racial oppression. Its efficacy is being measured against and judged by the volume of similar literature in the ivory tower, instead of being measured by its usefulness towards fostering change the broader society. It seems to me that using violence to overthrow a national election suggests that we need to revisit, *in a significant way*, how we have understood and discussed racial ideology in the academe—both in theological education and secular education.

To suggest that race has already been discussed in the church and the academy is woefully inadequate to the cause of liberty and justice. Instead of thinking of racial oppression as one of many topics inscribed within the story of America, perhaps we are better served by understanding racial oppression as being embedded in the very pages upon which the American story is inscribed. The conventional point of view that suggests racial oppression has yielded a limited, and even benign, influence on the American story, and, as such, can be disregarded in the construction of historical narratives is a misguided perspective that is taken up and deconstructed quite compellingly by Toni Morrison in her analysis of the American literary imagination. Morrison seeks to critique a conventional wisdom among literary historians and critics who seem to believe the traditional American literary body of work is unaffected by the violence upon which the American democratic experiment is founded. According to Morrison:

> This knowledge holds that tradition, canonical American literature is free of, uninformed, and unshaped by the four-hundred-year-old presence of, first, Africans and then African-Americans in the United States. It assumes that this presence—which

---

34. hooks, *Teaching to Transgress*, 71.

shaped the body politic, the Constitution, and the entire history of the culture—has had no significant place or consequence in the origin and development of that culture's literature. Moreover, such knowledge assumes that the characteristics of our national literature emanate from a particular "Americanness" that is separate from and unaccountable to this presence.[35]

Morrison's observation of how Western literary tradition attempts to disavow the story of black and brown people, including centuries of racial oppression in America, can also be made in other traditions and discourses. The impact of the racial imagination is considered incidental at best, or outright denied at worst. The choice of whether or not to entertain the effects of racial ideology reflects the invisible nature of non-raced culture. In describing the philosophical differences that informed the strategies of Black Power activists and civil rights activists during the 1960, historian Matthew Countryman describes the backdrop of white invisibility compellingly when he observes that the activism of civil rights proponents "had been based on the liberal presumption that racism was an unfortunate distortion of American values and institutions and that it could be remedied through specific legal and political reforms."[36] Countryman contrasts this understanding of America with Black Power activists who "viewed racism as constitutive to the American social structure."[37] Understood in this way, engaging the business of racial oppression is no longer understood as white people offering charity or concessions to black and brown people. This long-standing view reflects the narcissistic grandiosity of white supremacy. Instead, it means that the liberation of the oppressed—at the same time—represents the healing and redemption of the soul of the oppressor.

For the most part, racial discourse, both in theological education and the North American church, has tended to adopt the former paradigm described by Countryman. This can have an unintended consequence of configuring the pastoral imagination to understand racial ideology as being an occasional problem that has been greatly mitigated through progress and goodwill since the mid-twentieth century. In this paradigm, being colorblind, turning a blind eye to the workings of white supremacy, and looking above the suffering of *the raced other*, is valorized, and in some communities (especially Christian communities) deemed a mark of maturity. Herein is the fallout of the notion of progress when it infiltrates pastoral imagination and praxis. When it comes to race relations, the concept of

---

35. Morrison, *Playing in the Dark*, 4–5.
36. As quoted in Horowitz and Theoharis, *Julian Bond's Time*, 300.
37. As quoted in Horowitz and Theoharis, *Julian Bond's Time*, 300.

progress—understood as one-off achievements by ethnic minorities—whether it be individuals, groups, or communities, can represent a misleading marker of so-called progress. Generally, these one-off achievements are seen as reflecting a community or institution becoming more inclusive, rather than it being seen as reflecting the hard work and resiliancy of the individual or group.

Moreover, it is suggested here that progress is less about any particular one-off gain or achievement, and more about what gain or achievement is sustainable, and recognizing the individual and communal practices that make the gain or achievement *more likely* to remain sustainable. The long-standing practice of attributing the one-off achievements of black and brown persons to white racial progress reflects the paradigm outlined Matthew Countryman that portrays the violent racial ideology at the foundation of the American story as "an unfortunate distortion of American values and institutions." Here again, James Evans warns against conflating the notion of Western exceptionalism and progress with Christian hope. Western idealism and Christian hope are mutually exclusive and incompatible with the biblical witness. According to Evans, eschatological hope in the discourse of black theology does not overstate any one-off achievement and ascribe it to permanent progress. Permanent progress is an illusion. Because of the ubiquitous nature of racial ideology, any progressive achievement must be intentionally sustained. This is most clearly seen in history with one-off achievements like the Reconstruction period after the Civil War, or the election of the first black president. According to Evans, eschatological hope in black theology:

> makes *every historical gain only penultimate*. In the struggle for a new social order, there is a *great temptation to forget the tragic and ironic dimensions of historical efforts*. In the exhilaration of revolutionary zeal, the eschatological vision will not let the Christian settle for anything less than the perfect reign of God. One might say that the difference between the Christian revolutionary and the secular revolutionary is that the Christian asks each day, *"How can we make it better?" Eschatology provides the historical model of perfection that prevents us from sacralizing any human social order.*[38]

---

38. Evans, *We Have Been Believers*, 179; emphasis added.

TOWARDS A PEDAGOGY OF RACIAL JUSTICE AND EQUITY

This project challenges the conventional wisdom about racial reconciliation, per se, which has become in many ways a red herring topic that diverts from the reality of how the racial imagination and the legacy of the slavocracy has corrupted the human soul. As a condition precedent to racial reconciliation, the psychospiritual sickness of the racial imagination must be attended to. The pastoral assumption being made here is that once the individual and collective soul begins the work of repentance and recovery from debilitating effects that the racial fantasy has imposed on a person's subjectivity, moral compass, and spirituality, the goals of reconciliation will occur more effectively through an organic—rather than acquisitive—epistemology.[39] That is to say, *racial reconciliation, when preceded by metanoia and justice, will represent a social and religious praxis that is more caught than taught.*

More specifically, a community cannot simply read about racial equity to achieve racial equity. The community must ready itself (cognitively, emotionally, and spiritually) to *do and practice equity* if it is to learn and understand equity. Institutions must be willing to accept the messiness, tension, and growing pains that accompany cultural paradigm shifts. Reading about cross-culturalism doesn't automatically engender a healthy culture of multiplicity. No matter its level of emotional readiness, no matter how risky and uncomfortable it may feel, a community must *do and practice diversity*

---

39. In using the terminology of *organic* vs. *acquisitive* epistemology, I am challenging the common belief (which is an extension of Cartesianism) that *if a person knows better, they will necessarily do better.* This approach to pedagogy, and human growth and development, presupposes that the cognitive acquisition of knowledge necessarily leads to maturity and character development. While anti-racism and other resources and literature related to cultural diversity have grown significantly in the first part of the twenty-first century, what is often overlooked is that very little in this literature reflects new knowledge about racism and equity that has not been addressed by previous generations of scholars, writers, artists, community activists, and leaders. This is not to say that such literature is useless, but it must be understood as only a tool that prepares individuals and communities for the work of justice. In many institutions that unconsciously adhere to an acquisitive epistemology, the acquisition of anti-racism literature become an idolatrous end—as opposed to representing only a means to an end. In such cases, institutions and communities are deluded into believing they have made progress or are racism-free or have achieved racial reconciliation because they read a book, watched a documentary, or engaged with any number of resources that deal with the legacy of racism, all the while leaving racist practices, ideologies, and structures in place. There is no right way to do wrong. There is no liberative way to patronize oppressive structures. An organic epistemology assumes that growth and development towards racial reconciliation are painstaking, slow, but inevitably occur through processes of repentance, recovery, and justice.

and justice if it is to learn about and understand other cultures. As a southern white woman advocating for radical change in her own community, Lillian Smith knew this all too well. Smith understood the mechanics of what a transformative pedagogy of racial justice entailed: *doing the change, no matter the risk to status quo, was the only way to unlearn centuries of racial oppression.* She claims, "The time has now come when it is dangerous not to risk . . . we must do something big and imaginative and keep doing it until we master our ordeal . . . [and] in dramatizing that the extreme way can be the good way, the creative way, and that in times of ordeal it is the only way, you are helping the white South find its way, too. You are giving young white Southerners hope. You are persuading some of them that there is something worth believing in and risking for. You are stirring their imaginations and hearts."[40]

Perhaps another way to make this observation is this: there is no correct way to maintain white supremacy, no right way to remain wrong, or no healthy and commendable way to maintain oppressive systems. An acquisitive epistemology of equity and justice, taken by itself, risks commoditizing diversity, equity, and inclusion resources, using them only to save face and cover the backside of an institution hell bent on maintaining and justifying a culture and tradition of resistance to racial diversity. But with an *experiential pedagogy* of diversity, equity, and inclusion, the probability of its efficacy and longevity will increase. *This is at the heart of an organic epistemology—learning, growth, and development are more caught than taught.* Moreover, if there is no understanding, contrition, and repentance from the sin of white superiority, any efforts at racial reconciliation are premature, short lived, and reflect a façade of so-called progress. In an earlier work I outline the pastoral and psychospiritual implications of the legacy of the slavocracy:

> The unmourned legacy of the slavocracy precipitates a spiritual and clinical picture of neurosis and pathology in white subjectivity just as it does in black subjectivity. It does not follow that because an individual or group is in a position of power that their spiritual or clinical picture is normative and should be used as a baseline upon which to judge the psycho-spiritual health of all other people. To speak of a culturally traumatized black subjectivity in the intersubjective milieu necessarily means to speak of the pathology of whiteness and its related subjectivity in the same intersubjective space. Pastoral theology often overlooks this important dynamic.[41]

---

40. L. Smith, "Right Way Is Not," 340–41.
41. D. G. Gibson, *Frederick Douglass*, 178.

To avoid the downside of idealization and engage the process of demythologizing the titans, I embrace the intersection of the aforementioned disciplines as a methodology to help us better understand the emotional dynamics of historical figures like the titans (as opposed to simply romanticizing their lives), and then like them, how we can accomplish the task of *finding our courage* and then engaging in *the will to act*. No matter how modernity valorizes cognition, as a practical matter, affect trumps cognition every time. Consequently, while I engage historical contexts in this book, my purpose is not an objective recounting of historical fact. Historiography is not my focus. I am less concerned with *what occurred* historically, and *more intrigued with the psychological and soul dynamics that underwrote how and why it occurred (psychologically speaking), and the collective psychic space* that functioned as the emotional container in which the titans existed, as well as the ensuing actions for which they are celebrated.

IDEALIZATION: THE DANGER OF DISTORTING TRUTH

When viewed through a conventional historical lens, categories such as *Reconstruction* or the *civil rights era* have an unintended consequence of romanticizing those time periods, leading us in the present to believe that bigotry and racial hatred, and human oppression and degradation, were evils confined to the past. Romanticizing history leads us to believe that the work of confronting such evil was particularly suited for those historical periods, and that American society has naturally evolved beyond such human limitations through intellectual genius, Christian identity and virtue, and the inevitability of Western progress. Concurrently, many of the individuals previously identified, who were on the front lines of resisting racial violence and inequity in these historical periods, are commonly idealized as unique and special individuals—that is, people having a special calling, personal desire, and unique gifts that especially suited them to do the work for which they are now celebrated. Moreover, it is now common practice to culturally appropriate the lives and work of these individuals without giving due recognition to the values and principles for which they fought and suffered.

Unfortunately, the combined effect of romanticizing history and idealizing its actors results in the undermining of contemporary Christian praxis—where the telos centers primarily on the Sunday morning event and the privatization of faith—at the expense of doing the work of faith, religion, justice, and mercy in the public space. This failure of leadership and undermining of Christian ethics and moral accountability is often rationalized and dismissed as residing beyond the purview of Christian accountability and ministry. The prophetic dimension of calling to account the immorality of powers and principalities, the priestly dimension of equipping the church for works of mercy and justice, and the pastoral dimension of caring for the least of these among us—is all but forgotten. This project serves as a corrective to the work of romanticizing and idealizing—inviting us to consider a transformative praxis in our pastoral care and leadership.

Case in point is the deaths of John Lewis and C. T. Vivian. Both occurred on the same day (July 17, 2020) and were met with a rightly deserved outpouring of sympathy and gratitude across the nation. Both men were towering figures in their own right who fought against white supremacy and racial injustice on behalf of many forced to exist at the margin in the richest country in the world. In watching the news coverage of their passing, especially coverage in relation to John Lewis, I took notice of how their lives and what they stood for were extolled by politicians, scholars, theologians, and laypersons alike, on television and across social media. Even those who were diametrically opposed to (and that is to put it mildly) the perspectives and values of these two titans seemed to take hold of their legacies and personalize them—as if they had somehow embraced Lewis and Vivian (and the communities they represented) all along.

In making this observation, I am less interested in differences among policymakers (although that is only an extension of one's core values). For it could easily be said that while people may have differed with Lewis at the policy level, they respected him as a person and the values that he stood for. But this does not seem to square with the historical record (to say the least). The way that Lewis and Vivian were treated in their lifetime suggests that for many individuals, these men were anything but beloved figures. In fact, they were a thorn in the flesh of American idealism and status quo. I recall mentioning to several colleagues that as the death of John Lewis was mourned, we must resist the temptation to romanticize his life and legacy. American society has the neurotic habit of celebrating and idealizing freedom lovers and freedom fighters in their deaths. Yet, it is so quickly forgotten how those same freedom fighters (and the values they stood for) were despised, disregarded, and rejected while they were alive. Moreover, it seems to me that those of us who inhabit spaces of influence in the church, theological education, and society at large, have a responsibility not to let John Lewis's legacy be limited to the memory of one or two historical acts of activism. It would suggest that his life's work was a sidebar to what it means to be a Christian and plays into the practice of privatizing the faith. John Lewis's life was not simply incidental to what it means to be a person of faith but is foundational to religious expression. He showed us how to be lovers. John Lewis's legacy and his entire body of work represent a rich source for biblical and theological reflection and imagination. So, it is ill advised to allow his project to become fodder for idealism and fairy tales. Lewis has exemplified for us what it is to be inspired and compelled by God's love for us, and then as a result of that divine love, to pursue justice for the least of these among us, and to exemplify and pursue a radical love for neighbor.

3

THE PSYCHOLOGY OF IDEALIZING HISTORICAL PERSONALITIES

For the purposes of this text, I use the terms *idealization* and *romanticization* somewhat interchangeably, with idealization used to describe how we idealistically (albeit unrealistically) imagine—and then psychically affiliate ourselves—with people, groups, or institutions. Romanticization is used more with how we idealistically reflect upon and interpret historical and contemporary events or contexts. Critical to understanding idealization and romanticization is this: individuals and groups use both idealization and romanticization to stave off debilitating anxiety and to feel good about themselves. When we idealize individuals, groups, or institutions, we project on them our internal images and needs for omnipotence, great ideas, innocence, virtue, perfection, strength, and security. These emotional needs reflect internal deficits in our own ability to construct ideas, philosophies, or conceptions that are self-sustaining. As such, we look to others and imagine them to possess the ideas, values, or character traits that we believe we lack as individuals. As such, idealization is a normal part of human development.[1] Our need to connect with what we personally perceive as a great idea or value system reflects a fundamental psychological task of meaning making. Over the course of the human life cycle, this need never dissipates. At various points in the life cycle, the need to psychically merge with greatness or idealized people, goals, or institutions, will be triggered. Without idealized figures, pursuits, or goals in our lives, "the healthy capacity for enthusiasm will be lost—the enthusiasm for goals and ideals which people

---

1. H. Kohut, *How Does Analysis Cure.*

with a firm self can experience vis-à-vis the admired great who are their guide and example or with regard to the idealized goals that they pursue."[2] When we project these psychological or spiritual needs onto others, we set out to merge—psychically or emotionally—with our mentally idealized figures. Normally, these idealized figures begin with our parents or some other caregiver.

Neither idealization nor romanticization are inherently good or bad. Both are value neutral. A critical point to keep in mind is that when we idealize people, places, institutions, or great and noble ideas, the inherent psychological need is to merge with and/or stay close to the object of the idealization. Consequently, as it relates to how images of well-known personalities during the civil rights era such as Rosa Parks or Martin Luther King Jr. are invoked by organizations or groups that eschew the very ideas and principles they stood for, from a psychological perspective, what we are witnessing is the *need to merge with great ideas*, even if the same person or institution does not practice the ideas that were espoused by a Rosa Parks or Martin Luther King Jr. This reflects a regressed manifestation of idealization, where truth and reality are compromised (to put it mildly) at the expense of maintaining the idealized object—whether it be a person, goal, organization, or noble idea. The omnipotence of the idealization must be maintained at all costs, as the individual or group identity is co-dependent on the object of the idealization. I believe Martin Luther King Jr. observes this regressed form of idealization in the collective American psyche when he asserts in his final sermon before his assassination, "'Be true to what you said on paper.' If I lived in . . . any totalitarian country, maybe I could understand the denial of certain basic First Amendment privileges, because they hadn't committed themselves to that over there. But somewhere I read of the freedom of assembly . . . the freedom of speech . . . the freedom of the press. Somewhere I read that the greatness of America is the right to protest for right."[3]

What King is postulating here, psychologically, is an example of regressed idealization: the *emotional need to merge*, followed by the actual psychic merger with a noble idea or an omnipotent figure (be it a group, organization, or institution), becomes so integrated into the ego that it blinds the idealizer from the reality of their actions. Practically speaking then, agreeing with an idea, or having good intentions about a noble idea, is mistaken for being the idea, doing the idea, or living out the idea. Good intentions are mistaken for Christian praxis. Across the American landscape,

2. H. Kohut and Wolf, "Disorders of the Self," 419.
3. King, "I See the Promised Land," in *Testament of Hope*, 282.

the idealization and infatuation with civil rights icons and freedom fighters, which has led to the commercialization of their stories, likenesses, and even deaths, has blinded the country to its *actual soul condition* or blinded it to the fact that its structures and policies contradict its noble ideas. The proliferation of anti-racism literature, while laudable, has in part become a product for public consumption in the service of feeding the idealization of iconic freedom fighters, instead of serving the purpose of being a tool that helps in the disruption of the racial imagination and redeeming the collective soul of America.

The refusal by nearly half of the US Congress to certify the results of a national election that survived state audits and the courts does not reflect the sentiments of just a few elected officials. It was reflective of the collective racial imagination in a malignant form of groupthink.[4] It was the *tip-of-the-iceberg* representation of the sentiments of nearly half the electorate. Beneath the iceberg was a desperate attempt to counter a perceived threat to a *raced view* of both the (1) American landscape and (2) individual and group identity, hence the initiative to *make America great again*. This is perhaps the most brazen form of groupthink in the twenty-first century, whereby "group members attempt to maintain a shared positive view of the functioning of the group in the face of a threat [and they] . . . experience a collective threat [that involves] . . . an attack on the positive image of the group [and they] . . . use a variety of tactics to protect the group image."[5] Even with the lack of material and coherent evidence to justify misconduct and corruption in the presidential election, the implicit and often erratic messaging was that "if we say the election was rigged, then it must have been rigged." This is the force of unchecked groupthink when people of faith and goodwill appease actions that they know to be unethical and sinful. It is the posture of the bystander. History has clearly demonstrated that appeasing violence and injustice only sets the stage for greater human atrocities.

Those who participated in the January 6 raid of the Capitol building did not represent the desires of just a few. Participants in the raid only possessed the necessary personality valence that enabled them to act out the racialized acrimony that lay dormant in the psychic space of a much larger mass. This attempt to overturn the certification of a presidential election evidences an ailing psychospiritual condition of the soul of America: (1) the democratic experiment remains infected with the violence of colonialism, racial ideology, and white supremacy; (2) consequently, what cannot be had by a fair and legal election (which reflects the will of the electorate)

---

4. See Janis, *Groupthink*; *Victims of Groupthink*; and *Crucial Decisions*.
5. Turner et al., "Threat, Cohesion," 789.

will then be taken by force, deadly if necessary; and (3) all such actions will be morally justified and granted religious sanctioning—often in the form of conspicuous silence by the church. This, despite the talk of a post-racial America after the election of the first black president, and the proliferation of anti-racist and racial reconciliation literature over the past two decades. It is hard to overstate this point, as it has grave theological, spiritual, and psychological implications. This reflects the same psychospiritual condition of the collective soul that was foundational to the creation of an American imperial democracy. Moreover, it reflects psychological splitting at a group level, in part, caused by the illusion that idealization creates—that being emotionally close to the idealized object, which in our case represents the work of the titans, is confused with actually doing the work of freedom and justice. In an earlier work, I address group-level splitting and the contradictions of character and morality it creates and sustains:

> Splitting provides the requisite emotional repertoire for an individual or group to unconsciously enact racial ideology, embody injurious behaviors and attitudes, and exact violence while at the same time extolling values of human decency and liberty, democracy, and good will. Although not comprehensive in its explanatory power, the concept of splitting—applied to group-level functioning—provides compelling historical insight into how some of the most heinous atrocities committed against humanity (the trans-Atlantic slave trade, America slavery, the Holocaust, Native American genocide, etc.) were carried out by group and nations that espoused moral virtue and democracy.[6]

Idealization works best in the process of human development as we develop the psychic and spiritual maturity to be less dependent on the idealized figures. The psychospiritual benefits of idealization are maximized as we learn to tolerate or survive the inevitable disappointment caused by our idealized goals, figures, or objects or ideas of greatness and omnipotence. Learning to tolerate these disappointments leads to psychospiritual maturity, as we become less dependent on idealizing others, and slowly realize and experience ourselves as individuals and people who can also develop great ideas and goals that are life-sustaining. Healthy idealization enables us to humanize the people we idealize. Kohut and Wolf argue that:

> However great our disappointment as we discover the weakness and limitations of the idealized selfobjects in our early life, their self-confidence as they carried us when we were babies, their security when they allowed us to merge our anxious selves with

---

6. D. G. Gibson, "When Empathy," 619.

their tranquillity—via their calm voices or via our closeness with their relaxed bodies as they held us—will be retained by us as the nucleus of the strength of our leading ideas and of the calmness we experience as we live our lives under the guidance of our inner goals.[7]

Developed properly then, idealization makes us less co-dependent on others, enhances our capacity for self-agency, and contributes to our ability to live confidently and interdependently with other. The alternative is developmental arrest, where insecurity and a poor sense of self-worth become the primary governors that inform our actions and decisions. Ultimately, human frailty and the challenges of life will challenge and even destroy our idealizations. Nevertheless, even amid painful reality checks, our exposure to the disruption of our ideas should not be debilitating.

As such, for our purposes here, I am interested in how an idealized historical record, especially as it relates to America's long-standing history of racial discord and animosity, is recounted and remembered by individuals and communities. This book takes a look at how the romanticization of history has influenced the body politic and undermined our collective ability to learn from history and to avoid repeating the same mistakes. Lastly, this book shows, in part, how the idealization of history influences the social contracts that govern how we see and experience other people and groups, especially black- and brown-bodied persons by whom we have learned and practiced otherizing for centuries.

THE PATHOLOGY OF IDEALIZING HISTORY

The idealization of historical personalities engaged in the work of fighting for human rights and freedom in the nineteenth and twentieth centuries has done significant damage to the Christian imagination and our capacity to imagine liberative praxis in the twenty-first century. A psychospiritual intervention is necessary to undo that damage. By engaging the genre of spiritual autobiography and using the tool of psychobiography, I hope to expand how we imagine pastoral leadership and care in the twenty-first century context. I attempt to demythologize how we view and understand the work of the titans, as well as the historical contexts in which they existed. Instead of romanticizing their lives, their work, and confining them to ideological categories (such as civil rights era, black history, liberation theology, etc.), this book will use elements of autobiographic accounts in a way that

---

7. H. Kohut and Wolf, "Disorders of the Self," 417.

demythologizes how we understand their work and the times in which they lived, and augment how we understand Christian praxis today. Even in the wake of the January 2021 insurrection and attempted coup in Washington, DC, that so evidently revealed the ongoing legacy of white supremacy in America, it is important to recognize that as a nation, we have been here before. Lovers of freedom and justice have a template for perseverance and resilience. Especially in the academe and predominantly white institutions (religious and secular), there is a tendency to create myths of the titans, and then confine the interpretation of their lives, as well as the implications of their work, to black life and heritage. The implied belief is that the work of the titans is tertiary at best, or irrelevant at worst, to white life and heritage. The point here is not that historical categories (such as the civil rights era) are wrong, it is just that they tend to underwrite a maladaptive idealization of history and restrict our understanding of the contribution of the titans and their articulation of what it means to be human, and what it means to be image bearers of God. Using a psychospiritual lens to analyze salient themes in the lives of the titans, I hope to contribute to the lineage of other black and brown scholars that showcases an Africana *interpretation* of Christian faith and praxis.

Idealizing the work of historical figures undermines our capacity to fully appreciate their context and their work. It compromises our ability to act morally and responsibly today in the face of rabid xenophobic and racist violence. The titans were not special people living during a unique time period that made the fight against racial hatred and oppression more conducive for success. Instead, they were regular people with fears, insecurities, hopes, and dreams. They lived in perilous contexts with no automatic promise of a bright future. Survival of the community was not a forgone conclusion. Instead, the titans mustered the self-determination to fight for the future of posterity. The titans did not assume that progress in justice, equity, and human rights just naturally occurs in the American story. They knew the only future that was *manifest* in the *destiny* of black and brown people was the continued status quo of subordination to white supremacy. For them, faith was manifested in courage and the will to act, as they knew that the mere passage of time would not automatically generate progress. For the titans, there was no distinction between their Christian faith and the work of freedom, no distinction between a personal Savior and a public Savior. Indeed, the romanticization of the work of the titans in the mid-twentieth century has undermined the Christian imagination in a way that causes a large segment of the contemporary church to be mesmerized by evil, thereby abdicating moral agency and responsibility in the face of the brazen violence and racial hatred that has revealed itself in response to a black president. Indeed, the fight against racial domination that the titans engaged in was not a story confined to twentieth-century American history. As we have seen in the wake of the first black family leaving the White House, the fight against racial hatred—sometimes more benign, sometimes more malignant—remains with us.

At stake here is an understanding of how the errors and horrors of history will repeat itself without intentional and preventative actions. The common axiom that history repeats itself comes from philosopher George Santayana. Retentiveness, that is, a recollection of history, is a condition precedent to human progress. Change in and of itself does not constitute progress. Yet, this is the common mistake that derails the democratic experiment. Change, uninformed by the teachings of history, parades itself as a façade of progress, but devoid of developmental growth, maturity, and wisdom, and as a consequent, deceives the individual and collective ego that prides itself in superficial modifications. For Santayana:

> Progress, far from consisting in change, depends on retentiveness. When change is absolute there remains no being to improve and no direction is set for possible improvement: and when experience is not retained . . . infancy is perpetual. *Those who cannot remember the past are condemned to repeat it.*[8]

Remembering history is not merely an academic exercise to be engaged in one's spare time. It is a condition of one's very being and humanity. Santayana goes on to warn:

> When retentiveness is exhausted and all that happens is at once forgotten; a vain, because unpractical, repetition of the past takes the place of plasticity and fertile readaptation. In a moving world readaptation is the price of longevity . . . [and] a succession of generations or languages or religions constitutes no progress unless some ideal present at the beginning is transmitted to the end and reaches a better expression there; without this stability at the core no common standard exists and all comparison of value with value must be external and arbitrary. *Retentiveness, we must repeat, is the condition of progress.*[9]

The practice of forgetting is a hallmark of Western society. Sometimes being equated with forgiveness, it is valorized, even moralized, and often mistaken for a sign of spiritual or emotional maturity. In a capitalistic society where human worth is evaluated by professional accomplishment, productivity,

---

8. Santayana, *Life of Reason*, 172; emphasis added.
9. Santayana, *Life of Reason*, 172; emphasis added.

and the accumulation of wealth, the messaging that is often levied towards ethnic minorities is that personal character is measured by the extent to which they can function *as if* the past didn't exist, is irrelevant, or has no influence on the present or on our capacity to imagine the future.

The practice of remembering is conducive to psychological and spiritual well-being. What is remembered, and how it is remembered, are equally important. Unpacking the collective psychic space in which the titans and their antagonists existed is crucial to understanding the current psychosocial unrest after eight years of the first black family in the White House. It is the psychic space of any group or community, the emotional and psychological atmosphere, and the collective psychosocial environment, that informs and instigates the thoughts, motivations, and actions that transpire within any time period, and ultimately creates what we like to deny or repress: disturbing and painful history. Just as important as it is to know history, it is also important to understand the psychological and emotional container—the psychic space—that constructs the historical record.

Psychohistory helps us to accomplish this task of demythologizing. Psychobiographic reflections help us to better illuminate and interpret the lives and actions of those under analysis.[10] It can help us understand how the titans lived into their authentic selves in a world hell bent on subjugating the true selves of black-bodied people, how racists and an oppressive context may have given rise to individual and collective maladaptive behaviors, and help crystallize how the titans maintained their sense of identity, calling, and dignity in an environment meant to deny the value of their existence and subjugate their heritage, culture, and ultimately, humanity.[11] History and culture inform psychology, and psychology provides us better insight into understanding both historical and contemporary human phenomena and events.[12] Understood in this way, psychohistory helps to demythologize the titans and return the human element to their body of work. As long as we perceive historical personalities as heroes, we can never use history as a mirror to reflect into our own souls to see what we are capable of doing or achieving—for better or worse. The work of the titans forced them to exist in a way whereby they were constantly subjected to being misunderstood, maligned, alienated, socially marginalized (outside of their communities and sometimes within), and character assassinated by the media and the American status quo. Moreover, they existed under the constant threat of bodily harm and the fog of death. While many of the titans may be

10. Runyan, "Progress in Psychobiography," 319–21.
11. Anderson, "Recent Psychoanalytic Theorists."
12. T. A. Kohut, "Psychoanalysis as Psychohistory."

celebrated across the country today, we can be certain that they did not feel like they were celebrated or appreciated in their lifetime (at least in the way they are idealized today).

Surveys compiled from Cornell University's Roper Center for Public Opinion Research show the extent to which idealization has distorted our understanding of history, making us believe that somehow the civil rights era was destined to occur because of the goodness of America. Nothing, however, could be further from the truth. A survey conducted by Gallup between May 28 and June 2 of 1962 showed that 61 percent of respondents disapproved of what the Freedom Riders were doing, compared to 22 percent of respondents approving. Another 18 percent were ambivalent on the matter. When asked about whether sit-ins at lunch counters and other demonstrations would help black people be integrated in the South, 57 percent of respondents felt it would hurt, with only 28 percent believing it would help and another 16 percent being ambivalent on the matter. Just days before the March on Washington in August of 1963, another Gallup survey found that 60 percent of adults surveyed were against the march, compared to only 23 percent being in favor of the march and another 17 percent being undecided. In another national survey conducted by Louis Harris & Associates in October of 1966, 85 percent of white respondents felt that civil rights demonstrations have done more to hurt the advancement of rights for black people.[13]

Simply put, opposition and criticism to contemporary movements like Black Lives Matter is nothing new. Resistance (by a majority of the population) to movements that promote human equality is core to the American democratic experiment. The idealization of the various protests we now venerate from the civil rights era in the mid-twentieth century (a veneration with a peak season in February where multibillion-dollar media outlets selfishly co-opt images of protest and resistance against racial oppression to enhance their own corporate or institutional image as if they always, if ever, supported racial equality) reflects the ongoing emotional need in the American psychic space for a revisionist history. The requirements of this revisionist history include omitting or suppressing any historical data that clearly points to the fact that violence, and racial animosity and oppression, have been and continue to be core tenets of the American story. The void is filled with a kind of religious-oriented narrative that props up a sanctimonious image of America. This religious revisionist history confiscates the stories of suffering by the very few (relatively speaking) who fought and died for racial and human equality and appropriates their stories into a master

---

13. Izadi, "Black Lives Matter."

narrative that suggests America, in its divine manifest destiny, has always stood for the rights and equality of all its citizens. It is a divine revisionist history that in part underwrites Christian nationalism.

Using the outgrowth of the gun lobby as an example in her description of how Christian doctrine and Scripture were used to fashion an ideology that suggested American history was representative of a Calvinist-inspired covenantal relationship with God, Roxanne Dunbar-Ortiz suggests that not only documents written by the Founding Fathers are sacralized to endorse violence, but even symbolism from the civil rights era:

> In other modern constitutional states, constitutions come and go, and they are never considered sacred in the manner patriotic US citizens venerate theirs . . . From the Pilgrims to the founders of the United States and continuing to the present, the cultural persistence of the [Calvinist] covenant idea, and thus the bedrock of US patriotism, represents a deviation from the main course in the development of national identities . . . *Patriotic US politicians and citizens take pride in "exceptionalism."* Historians and legal theorists characterize US statecraft and empire as those of a "nation of laws," rather than [in actuality] one dominated by a particular class or group of interests, *suggesting a kind of holiness.*
>
> The US Constitution, the Mayflower Compact, the Declaration of Independence, the writings of the "Founding Fathers," Lincoln's Gettysburg Address, the Pledge of Allegiance, and *even Martin Luther King Jr.'s "I Have a Dream" speech are all bundled into the covenant as sacred documents that express the US State religion.*[14]

Dunbar-Ortiz concludes her thought by highlighting how contemporary gun lobbyist view themselves as "descendants of the old settlers" and as such stand for "the people."[15] This morbid romanticizing of history and historical documents leads to a sanctification of the Second Amendment that is akin to a religious confessional that justifies the kind of violence we saw in 2020 when protesters with guns actually entered the Michigan state capitol building just to protest COVID-19 restrictions. Indeed, idealization in its pathological form can lead to religious violence and terrorism. It is hard to imagine that the public would have had the same calm reaction had the armed protestors been black or brown people. Ultimately, when we view the titans through the lens of a romanticized history, it is all too easy to

---

14. Dunbar-Ortiz, *Indigenous Peoples' History*, 50; emphasis added.
15. Dunbar-Ortiz, *Indigenous Peoples' History*, 50.

engage in psychological idealization, which leads to the assumption that the values and actions of the titans were self evident, easy to understand, and something that we all would immediately subscribe to. We idealize them, romanticize the context and times in which they lived, uncritically (and even unethically) appropriate their actions and values as our own, only to become complacent about matters of injustice, inequity, and oppression.

Perhaps Julian Bond, one of the founding members of the Student Nonviolent Coordinating Committee and among the chief architects and interpreters of civil rights era, most brilliantly captures the romanticized version of the work of the titans in what he refers to as the master narrative of the civil rights movement. It seems that the master narrative outlined by Bond lies dormant in the preconscious of the collective American psyche and is among the sacred stories that make up what Dunbar-Ortiz refers to as the US State religion. According to Bond:

> Traditionally, relationships between the races in the South were oppressive. Many Southerners were very prejudiced against Blacks. In 1954, the Supreme Court decided this was wrong. Inspired by the court, courageous Americans, Black and white, took protest to the street, in the form of sit-ins, bus boycotts, and the Freedom Rides. The nonviolent protest movement, led by the brilliant and eloquent Reverend Martin Luther King, aided by a sympathetic federal government, most notably the Kennedy brothers and a born-again Lyndon Johnson, was able to make America understand racial discrimination as a moral issue. Once Americans understood that discrimination was wrong, they quickly moved to remove racial prejudice and discrimination from American life, as evidenced by the Civil Rights Act of 1964 and 1965. Dr. King was tragically slain in 1968. Fortunately, by that time the country had been changed, changed for the better in some fundamental ways. The movement was a remarkable victory for all Americans. By the 1970s, Southern states where Blacks could not have voted ten years earlier were sending African Americans to Congress. Inexplicably, just as the civil rights victories were piling up, many Black Americans, under the banner of Black Power, turned their backs on American society.[16]

As a former student of Julian Bond, Jeanne Theoharis asserts, "In this master narrative, as Professor Bond made clear, injustice is obvious, decent people took action, and the good guys triumphed—and then Black Power came

---

16. Julian Bond, as quoted in Payne, *I've Got the Light*, xiii–xiv.

along and ruined everything."[17] Lastly, I suggest that the internalization of this master narrative of the era of the titans has made us sleepwalkers in both the church and the academy, blind to the realities of what the ongoing toleration of racial injustice and oppression will yield in the months and years to come. In the decades since the civil rights era, romanticizing history made us ill prepared for the likes of an insurrection on January 6, 2021. While the presidential election of 2020 was probably the most contentious in modern US history, who could have imagined in the fourth quarter of 2020 what would occur in January 2021?

What future terror are we not imagining now?

17. Horowitz and Theoharis, *Julian Bond's Time*, xv.

4

THE AUDACITY OF A KING

On Finding Courage

ON SEVERAL OCCASIONS I'VE had the opportunity to visit the Dexter Parsonage Museum, the home for Martin, Coretta, and their first child, Yolanda, while Martin served as the senior pastor of Dexter Avenue Baptist Church in Montgomery, Alabama. On one occasion when I visited the museum, I was especially aware of the curator commenting on the interior design of the house and a door in the home that was designed to withstand (as best it could) the explosive impact of a bomb. Prior to the parsonage actually being bombed on the evening of January 30, 1956, the King family had been under the increasing threat of violence. Adjacent to this spot in the house was the kitchen. It was in this kitchen where King makes mention of what I believe is perhaps one of the most overlooked, but crucial moments of the civil rights movement. Because of his decision to take up a leading role to challenge segregation laws in Montgomery, Alabama—a place that symbolized and embodied the heart of the former Confederate South—King had to reckon with the prospect of the inevitability of self-harm, and ultimately, the violent ending of his life. That is to say, in this moment, *King had to engage in the work of finding his courage.*

Much scholarship has been produced in relation to Martin Luther King's body of work in terms of his writings, his speeches, lectures, and sermons, and his larger social and political accomplishments. But it is suggested here that this entire body of work rested upon this foundational psychospiritual practice: the difficult and anxiety-provoking work of finding one's courage. While there are general references to the courage of all who may have been active participants doing the work of the movement—both those of national repute as well as the thousands of unknown and unsung heroes of freedom—there has not been significant attention given to *how* King and others engaged in the work of finding their courage.

As such, it seems the vital question is not about the necessity of courage, but *how we find such courage* when providence and life circumstances force us to exist in personal or social adversity and propel us to the edges of meaning. Viewed through the lens of King's personal experiences expressed in his autobiography, *I construct a brief psychospiritual picture of how he engaged in the work of finding his courage.* As a practical theologian, I suggest that it is less about knowing what to do, what is right, what is moral, and what our ethical mandate requires as people of faith, and *more about finding the courage* to do what is right, moral, and ethical. Amidst the proliferation of the literature on race since the mid-twentieth century, there tends to be a misguided notion that we are in need of the one magic resource that will resolve and heal the terror of racial hegemony inflicted over the past four hundred-plus years. The BIPOC members in many communities, organizations, and institutions are often tasked to shoulder the burden of addressing inequity, injustice, and racial tensions, being encumbered with questions like "what do you want us to do" or "how should we solve this" or "what do you expect from us." Questions like this cleverly shift the responsibility of thinking and responding from the majority to the minority, suggesting that if there is a problem, it is because people of color have not thought creatively enough about the situation. There is no magic bullet or antidote when it comes to engaging the racial imagination in its legion of demonic manifestations (i.e., we are many). Instead, it is more about finding the courage to do right and act responsibly, with an alternative of cowering into a space of silence and compliance to an oppressive status quo of the racial imagination that represents a core part of the American story.

Fundamentally, courage is the externalization of the *fear-conquering reflections* within a person's interior world, where the end result is to take action in spite of the fear associated to the action. Courage is not the abatement of fear or the nonattendance of terror. Courage is taking action in defiance of the fear and terror. Without action, there can be no assurance that what you have is true courage, as the fear-conquering reflections remain imprisoned within interiority. Understood in this light, courage can manifest itself in people overcoming their fears in a variety of ways: public speaking, heights, medical procedures, pain, death, suffering, or anything that imposes fear upon the heart. While important, this is not necessarily the courage that redeems the soul from the racial imagination. Taken in isolation, the courage here is delimited to being a countermeasure related to individual phobias. In his analysis on the psychology of courage, Warren Poland makes an important distinction between machismo and courage, noting that "a courageous act satisfied enduringly by protecting cherished values, while a counterphobic act provides only temporary relief from a private dread . . . [and that] the modesty seen with courage driven by ideals stands in strong contrast to the spiritual pride of the self-righteous person . . . [whose] posture of moral superiority . . . comes through as smugness."[1] In a somewhat similar fashion, Salmon Akhtar distinguishes between physical courage, intellectual courage, and moral courage, and then details pathological manifestations of courage—namely an overreaction to a persona phobia and, most notoriously, cowardice. For him, "the phenomenon of courage has two psychopathological counterparts. One is marked by a peculiarly exaggerated absence of fear. The other is characterized by a weak-kneed response to life's challenges. The former leads to behaviors that are at best called 'foolhardy' while the latter results in gutless avoidance of risks. The two syndromes are those of counterphobia and cowardice."[2]

While the courage to overcome personal phobias is commendable, on balance, this is not the courage that moved the titans. I suggest that the courage that motivated Martin Luther King was more akin to what I refer to as *noble courage*. Noble courage is what we see in the life of Jesus, and is a manifestation of courage that is constantly fueled by this question: *Who is my neighbor?* Responding to this vital question with the one, definitive answer for all time (a practice that is commonplace in religious education) does not yield the greatest psychospiritual fruit. Instead, it is the capacity and the willingness to engage with the question of neighbor, as a matter of Christian ethics, over the entire lifespan, that yields the greatest benefit in terms of being more Jesus-like and emulating the work of the titans. With the question of *who is my neighbor*, we are reminded that none of us lives and dies to ourselves, but that our actions, our words, our scholarship (particularly that of a religious and theological nature), and the work that we do will always impact the life of another person or group—especially if the person or group is forced to exist on the lower tiers of our sociopolitical and racial caste system.

In this well-known parable of the good Samaritan, Jesus is responding to the question of a lawyer who is inquiring about the criteria for eternal life (Luke 10:25–37). The passage makes clear that the motivation for the lawyer's question is twofold: to test Jesus and to justify himself. While there can be many interpretations as to the nature of the alleged test, I suggest

---

1. Poland, "Courage and Morals," 257–58.
2. Akhtar, *Good Stuff*, 8.

here that the test was one of social fundamentalism—that is, to see if Jesus's response would be favorable to the worldview of the ruling class and the establishment theology that underwrote their privileged existence. Such a response reflects fundamentalism in that it wouldn't require Jesus to think for himself, but simply reply to the lawyer's question through a set of preestablished doctrines and propositional statements constructed by the social elite. From the lawyer's perspective, *the test was to see if Jesus was one of us*. People of color are constantly subjected to this same sort of suspicion and testing in predominately white institutions to verify that they are not a threat to the institutional status quo, that they are safe, and that they have indeed accepted the invitation to assimilation as evidence of competence and qualifications. Likewise, the lawyer needed to proctor a test to see if Jesus met the standard to sit at the table of the ruling elite—a table that Jesus ultimately turned over when he entered the temple shortly before being executed by the state. In terms of self-justification, the lawyer's question to Jesus (of who is my neighbor) reflects a deep-seated emotional need that every human being is guilty of: using religion and spirituality in a way that affirms our core sense of self.

Jesus's response to the lawyer, in the narrative of the good Samaritan, suggests that the point of departure for determining our neighbor is not identifying people we are most comfortable with, familiar with; or who think, act, and behave like us; or who like and affirm the same people we extol, and hate and repudiate the same people and groups we hold in contempt. This understanding of neighbor is nothing more than tribalism. Alternatively, the response of Jesus suggests that the point of departure for neighbor is responding to those in our sphere of influence, power, and control who represent the class of the downtrodden and outcast, and to those who have fallen victim to the material reality of human suffering—especially when that suffering reflects the evil intent and actions of other human beings. As such, it is based on Jesus's response to this critical question of who is my neighbor that I suggest the following definition of *noble courage*:

> Noble courage reflects the externalization of a person's fear-conquering reflections, as well as their contemplation of the critical question of *"who is my neighbor."* Noble courage is operationalized in responding to relieve or alleviate human suffering within one's sphere of power, influence, and control. It will most likely result in personal inconvenience and discomfort at best, or invite harm and injury to self, or even death and destruction to one's very existence at worst. Noble courage, by definition, is designed to relieve or alleviate human suffering, or to undermine or eliminate the cause of the suffering. Similar to

phobia-based courage that does not require the elimination of fear, but responds in defiance of that fear, noble courage does not require the abatement of the fear of self-harm. Instead, noble courage responds to the needs of neighbor in full defiance of an awareness and likelihood that responding to alleviate or eliminate human suffering compels the holder of such courage to contemplate the *inevitability* of personal demise and destruction, or even death.

Inherent in this understanding of noble courage is that an individual *does not have to respond* to their neighbor, but they instead *choose to respond*. The Samaritan could have walked by, but chose to stop, not knowing how responding to human suffering may compromise personal comfort and convenience. Additionally, phobia-based courage and noble courage are not mutually exclusive, but independent. That is to say, when phobia-based courage works in the service of fostering noble courage (i.e., in the context of the titans, they had to deal with fears of physical suffering and harm like going to jail, lynching, etc.), such phobia-based courage reflects a redemptive pretext to noble courage. Noble courage is what we see in Jesus. Noble courage is what we see in the titans. And it is noble courage that we see manifested in the biographical accounts of Martin Luther King. Now, the critical question is more about *how we find our noble courage*. To address this question, I turn to the well-known kitchen event in the story of King. To understand this account, I quote at length the following passage from his autobiography.

> One night toward the end of January I settled into bed late, after a strenuous day. Coretta had already fallen asleep and just as I was about to doze off the telephone rang. An angry voice said, "Listen, nigger, we've taken all we want from you; before next week you'll be sorry you ever came to Montgomery." I hung up, but I couldn't sleep. It seemed that all of my fears had come down on me at once. I had reached the saturation point.
>
> I got out of bed and began to walk the floor. I had heard these things before, but for some reason that night it got to me. I turned over and I tried to go to sleep, but I couldn't sleep. I was frustrated, bewildered, and then I got up. Finally I went to the kitchen and heated a pot of coffee. I was ready to give up. With my cup of coffee sitting untouched before me I tried to think of a way to move out of the picture without appearing a coward. I sat there and thought about a beautiful little daughter who had just been born. I'd come in night after night and see that little gentle smile. I started thinking about a dedicated and loyal wife,

who was over there asleep. And she could be taken from me, or I could be taken from her. And I got to the point that I couldn't take it any longer. I was weak. Something said to me, "You can't call on Daddy now, you can't even call on Mama. You've got to call on that something in that person that your Daddy used to tell you about, that power that can make a way out of no way." With my head in my hands, I bowed over the kitchen table and prayed aloud. The words I spoke to God that midnight are still vivid in my memory: "Lord, I'm down here trying to do what's right. I think I'm right. I am here taking a stand for what I believe is right. But Lord, I must confess that I'm weak now, I'm faltering. I'm losing my courage. Now, I am afraid. And I can't let the people see me like this because if they see me weak and losing my courage, they will begin to get weak. The people are looking to me for leadership, and if I stand before them without strength and courage, they too will falter. I am at the end of my powers. I have nothing left. I've come to the point where I can't face it alone."

It seemed as though I could hear the quiet assurance of an inner voice saying: "Martin Luther, stand up for righteousness. Stand up for justice. Stand up for truth. And lo, I will be with you. Even until the end of the world."

I tell you I've seen the lightning flash. I've heard the thunder roar. I've felt sin breakers dashing trying to conquer my soul. But I heard the voice of Jesus saying still to fight on. He promised never to leave me alone. At that moment I experienced the presence of the Divine as I had never experienced Him before. Almost at once my fears began to go. My uncertainty disappeared. I was ready to face anything.[3]

To craft a clinical picture of Martin Luther King finding his courage, I borrow from the work of Heinz Kohut and his reflections on courage of three martyrs in Nazi Germany who were executed for refusing to comply with the dictates of Nazi Germany during the Holocaust. But before examining this, it is important to emphasize that in examining how King (and others) may have found their courage, it should not be implied that for millions of others there was no courage. There are many unsung heroes of the civil rights movement, people whose names we will never know on this side of the eschaton, who mustered noble courage to survive hardships in the Jim Crow South. Judging individuals who were forced to exist in a context of unbearable extremity serves little constructive purpose. In his lecture "White Supremacy and the Founding of the NAACP," Julian Bond

3. King, *Autobiography*, 77–78.

succinctly captures the essence of Southern hegemony and the backlash to Reconstruction:

> Reconstruction had collapsed. Blacks were disfranchised across the South, beginning in Mississippi in 1890; by 1910, state constitutions barred Black voters in North Carolina, Alabama, Virginia, Georgia, and Oklahoma. In Louisiana, slightly more than 50 percent of the electorate was Black in 1890; by 1910, less than 0.1 percent was Black. Murder and brutality—including lynching, ritual human sacrifice, state-sponsored and private terror—accompanied the removal of Blacks from every sphere of public life. Between 1880 and 1923, a Black person was lynched every two and one-half days in the United States.

Terror was a factor of everyday life for black and brown people who existed in the South. The full extent of the brutalization of white supremacy still remains unknown to most people who have a general awareness of history, let alone for those who choose to ignore it. Some were more active in their participation in the movement for freedom, while others chose to adopt a more passive role for the sake of survival. The Rev. William J. Barber II brings a pastoral lens to the reality of death-dealing suffering when comparing those who were more involved in the civil rights movement and those who were less involved. Barber says, "I don't do a lot of judging of that, because you would get your church blown up. You would get your head shot off. *But I often wonder what could have been if there was full unity. If there was a complete engagement, a total commitment of every Black denomination, could we have gone much further?*"[4]

Heinz Kohut, a Jewish psychiatrist and psychoanalyst, offered up a psychological study on the presence of courage in three martyrs of the Holocaust: Franz Jaegerstaetter, an Austrian farmer, and Hans and Sophie Scholl, two siblings who were involved in the 1943 Student Conspiracy in Munich.[5] Franz Jaegerstaetter was executed for refusing to serve in the army of Germany, while Sophie and Hans Scholl, both anti-Nazi political activists, were executed for their attempts to undermine support for Nazism. According to Kohut, in addition to their using religious symbols as a way to foster courage, he also observed that the presence of a sense of humor, the presence of a significant level of empathy, and the presence of serenity were all contributing factors to the presence of courage in these individuals. I suggest these four elements—more or less—are present in the autobiographical accounts of Martin Luther King and contributed to his ability to

---

4. Gates, *Black Church*, 145; emphasis added.
5. H. Kohut, *Self Psychology and Humanities*.

find courage in the context of extremity. Much of what King experiences in the highlighted passage, and at other points in his life, parallels what Kohut attributes as elements of courage when describing the three individuals who were martyred in Nazi Germany. In what follows then, I will briefly discuss the importance of these factors in the journey to finding courage, as well as offer up what I believe is a crucial fifth element in finding courage: travailing the existential threat of nonbeing.

I begin this analysis with *travailing the existential threat of nonbeing* as being a necessary component of finding one's courage. The above passage in the kitchen of the Dexter Avenue Baptist Church is a familiar episode to most scholars of King, but customarily, the events of this passage have not been considered as being fundamental to his body of work. I suggest here that what we witness in this passage is the work of King finding his courage, and that without it, we would not have known him in the way that we know him today. More importantly, I suggest that he would not have achieved what he did without the important work of finding his courage. The episode begins with King receiving death threats against himself and his family, which unfortunately had become commonplace. After this particular threat, he is overwhelmed with fear. He is at a breaking point. According to King, after he prayed, he felt the presence of God as he had never experienced, and as a result, he also felt the fear dissipate almost immediately. But here, I suggest that the process of King finding his courage had already been initiated days earlier when he was arrested for a minor traffic violation (i.e., going thirty mph in a twenty-five mph zone). The city of Montgomery had initiated a "get tough" policy in response to the bus boycott. As King was being driven to jail by two police officers, perhaps because he was relatively new to the city, he didn't recognize the way they were going. King began to deduce that he was being taken away to be killed, and his fears were not unfounded. Such actions were commonplace for people considered to be agitators in the Jim Crow South:

> As we drove off, presumably to the city jail, a feeling of panic began to come over me. The jail was in the downtown section of Montgomery. Yet we were going in a different direction. The more we rode, the farther we were from the center of town. In a few minutes we turned into a dark and dingy street that I had never seen and headed under a desolate old bridge. By this time I was convinced that these men were carrying me to some faraway spot to dump me off. "But this couldn't be," I said to myself. "These men are officers of the law." Then I began to wonder whether they were driving me out to some waiting mob, planning to use the excuse later on that they had been overpowered.

> I found myself trembling within and without. Silently, I asked God to give me the strength to endure whatever came.
>
> By this time we were passing under the bridge. I was sure now that I was going to meet my fateful hour on the other side. But as I looked up I noticed a glaring light in the distance, and soon I saw the words "Montgomery City Jail." I was so relieved that it was some time before I realized the irony of my position: going to jail at that moment seemed like going to some safe haven![6]

While this particular event was not planned by King, and while he may have wished to avoid it (like any sensible human being), it was forced upon him. He was forced to travail—from beginning to end—a psychospiritual encounter with the ultimate existential threat of not only being killed . . . but killed in a particularly vicious way. Ultimately, while he was not killed (it appears that he simply didn't recognize the way they were taking him to jail), I suggest there was a psychospiritual benefit from the experience: *he metabolized the existential threat of nonbeing into his core self, as opposed to the experience of the threat remaining unintegrated and outside of his core being, where it could taunt and terrorize him*. But note how he concludes the event: "I was so relieved that it was some time before I realized the irony of my position: going to jail at that moment seemed like going to some safe haven." After successfully travailing the existential threat of nonbeing, the fear of going to jail (a fear that many had in the early days of the movement) was experienced as miniscule to nonexistent. I suggest this event here initiated the process of King finding his courage and was continued during the well-known kitchen episode. Evidence of King finding his courage was manifested only a few nights later after the kitchen event when his home was bombed while he was attending a church meeting. While Coretta and Yolanda were not harmed, upon initially receiving the news, King was not aware of their fate. Yet, he testified in his autobiography, "Strangely enough, I accepted the word of the bombing calmly. My religious experience a few nights before had given me the strength to face it."[7] This suggests a metabolization of the threat into King's self-experience as opposed to the threat functioning as an unintegrated provocateur.

This critical milestone of *travailing the experience of the existential threat of self-harm* in the pursuit of courage suggests to us today that being co-dependent on comfort and convenience as determinants of what constitutes right or wrong when it comes to challenging the structures of racial

---

6. King, *Autobiography*, 74.
7. King, *Autobiography*, 79.

oppression and injustice is woefully inadequate to the task of finding our courage and challenging the hegemony of racism that has defined America. The point here is not that you put yourself in death's way, necessarily, to psychologically and emotionally metabolize a fearful event. That is not what King did. But the effects of what he experienced were beneficial to his self-structure and additive to his pursuit of courage. Many of us today do not have to put ourselves, necessarily, in death's way. But far too many of us do not want to put ourselves on any path that would lead to discomfort, inconvenience, or place us in jeopardy of being rejected by the people, communities, institutions, or power structures we cling to for affirmation and/or unconscious identity formation. Hence, our capacity for moral agency is curtailed by the limits of emotional safety and comfort. Again, it is acceptable to use religion to comfort us. But when our religion or theological ethics make us comfortable, it runs the risk of undermining our ability to find our courage. The point here is that the beginning of the journey to finding our courage requires that we, to some extent, place ourselves within the proximity of that which we are most uncomfortable with or that which we fear the most, in order to facilitate the psychological and emotional process of integrating into our inner world (or our inner self-structure) the perception or narrative of what we fear or are uncomfortable with. What this looks like will differ for each individual or group, but the thrust of what is being suggested remains the same. In some ways, this parallels the process of trauma recovery put forth by Judith Herman where Herman asserts that "acknowledging the trauma and naming its consequences begin the process of meaning making . . . [because] survivors come to understand . . . that their symptoms [including fear and anxiety] make sense in the context of a formative relationship of coercive control. This understanding is a powerful antidote to the feelings of malignant shame and stigma that afflict so many survivors."[8] What I am suggesting here is that travailing the experience of the existential threat of self-harm is akin to a trauma survivor having to recount their traumatic story in order to initiate the meaning-making process. Meaning making has the potential to undermine the debilitating relationship of coercive control that our fears or anxieties have over us. For Martin Luther King, I suggest that the meaning-making process began for him in the car ride to the Montgomery jail, and was further developed in the famous kitchen experience.

In Kohut's reflections on the courage of three martyrs in Nazi Germany, he emphasizes the use of religious icons, a sense of humor, what he

---

8. Judith Herman, "Foreword," in Ford and Courtois, *Treating Complex Traumatic Stress*, xiv.

refers to as a high degree of empathy, and pervasive sense of serenity as key elements in fostering the courage of the martyrs.[9] Kohut would not be the first psychologist to observe the benefits of using religion and spirituality to bolster endurance and courage. Perhaps what is most useful as it relates to the work of Kohut is understanding how religious symbols and resources are used by the subject to: (1) mirror back to the individual and affirm the specialness of their personhood and veracity of their joys, hopes, and concerns; (2) psychically or emotionally merge with a symbol or source of idealized strength, comfort, valor, or nobility; or (3) function as a type of twin or alter-ego whereby a person can see themselves in another as a source of psychic companionship.[10] In the passage from the kitchen event, we see where King used a confluence of Scripture and hymns to mirror back to him and affirm his loneliness and fear, and the legitimacy of his cause. We also see an element of using Scripture to form an alter-ego connection, a suggestion that his plight was not unlike the persecution Jesus experienced when he sought after justice for the oppressed.

In terms of a sense of humor, Kohut observed that the Austrian farmer Franz Jaegerstaetter, even when faced with execution, wrote his wife sarcastic and humorous letters about how her household chores had increased because he was incarcerated. For Kohut, humor was not a sign of immaturity or insecurity, but symbolic of a mature personality that had little use for grandiose narcissism. According to Kohut, "To be humorous is not the same as to be self-belittling or to be lacking in enthusiasm. Humor is fully compatible with a secure sense of self-esteem or with a warm devotion to values and ideal."[11] We see a strategic use of humor in the life of King as well when he jokes about what he would say in the eulogies of the staff members if they were ever assassinated or otherwise killed in the civil rights movement.[12]

In noting the ubiquitous presence of serenity in Sophie Scholl on the day of her execution, Kohut seems to attribute it to Sophie being perfectly consumed by her "idealized values" that were internalized into the core of her being. And perhaps this is correct. But Kohut also mentions that on the day of her execution, Sophie communicated to her cellmate that in her dream from the previous night, she recalls carrying a baby to the top of a mountain to be baptized. When she reached the top of the mountain, she took note of the abyss below her and was able to place the baby safely to

---

9. H. Kohut, *Self Psychology and Humanities*.
10. H. Kohut, *How Does Analysis Cure*.
11. H. Kohut, *Self Psychology and Humanities*, 17.
12. See the commentaries of Clarence Jones, Andrew Young, and C. T. Vivian in the documentary film directed by Peter Kunhardt, *King in the Wilderness*.

the side before falling into the abyss. Sophie reports to her cellmate that her interpretation of the dream was that the anti-Nazi student movement would go on after her death. Based on this dream, I suggest that the serenity Sophie experienced, in part, was not just happenstance or due to the fact of her being aligned with her idealized values. Instead, it was the awareness of posterity and continuity that provided Sophie with the sense of serenity. One of the key steps in finding one's courage is living a life of generativity where your values, resources, and benefits stemming from your body of work don't simply vanish at the time of your demise or death, but instead, are manifested in the continuity of life as you share your life, gifts, and talents with others for their benefit and for the sake of posterity. The concept of psychological generativity suggests a capacity to experience fulfillment and joy at witnessing the flourishing and prosperity of posterity, a future generation that has benefited from you. Here, I suggest that a praxis of posterity yields the ubiquitous phenomenon of serenity that Kohut interpreted in the life of Sophie. Moreover, I suggest that a praxis of posterity is accretive to finding one's courage. This praxis of posterity is evidenced in the final stanzas of King's sermon "The Drum Major Instinct" where King asserts that he doesn't want his many accomplishments mentioned in his eulogy, but only references to those whom he tried to help in life.[13]

Lastly, in what Kohut interprets as a "high degree of empathy" in Hans Scholl (the brother of Sophie), he comments on Hans briefly stepping off a train en route to the Russian front where he and his military company were headed for active duty. Hans deboarded the train to give a flower to a young girl engaged in heavy labor, along with a group of other young girls and women, on the train tracks. The girl initially throws the flower back at him, but Hans makes a second attempt by putting the flower on a food package and placing it at her feet. As the train departs and he looks back, Hans can see where the young girl has placed the flower in her hair. Again, through this event, Kohut interprets the capacity for a "high degree of empathy" as being a component of courage, and perhaps his observation is accurate. Nevertheless, I suggest it does not go far enough. What we are witnessing with Hans is a romantic flirtation with a young girl—even in a context of profound hardship and adversity. This raises a vital proposition to consider. Even for the most noble causes of equity and justice, it is unhealthy to allow a cause or movement to solely define us. In times of extreme adversity, the psychospiritual tendency is to become regressive and transactional in nature, subordinating aesthetic elements of human existence that include beauty, love, integrity, honesty, decency, compassion,

---

13. See King, "The Drum Major Instinct," in *Testament of Hope*, 259–67.

tenderness, and kindness, and instead prioritizing only actions that are necessary for the corporeal survival of the species. As important as resisting racial oppression is to the survival of black and brown people, resisting the evil structures of oppression cannot become the governing principle that defines us. Even in the context of extremity, we must make time for love, creativity, imagination, art, sensuality, intimacy, and empathy—things that may not be absolutely necessary for biological survival but are necessary for the survival of our humanity.

Kohut is clear that most people do not achieve the level of courage he references in Sophie, Hans, and Franz—all martyrs of Nazi Germany. And perhaps the same can be said for the noble courage I have identified in Martin Luther King and the other titans. In observing the difference between those who have courage and those who do not, Kohut observes:

> The remarkable psychological quality that individuals like . . . [Sophie, Hans, and Franz] possess is their capacity not to withdraw from an inner conflict of extraordinary proportions. Their conflict concerns the performance of certain interrelated tasks. They must identify their nuclear self, resist their tendency to disown it, and ultimately resolve to shape their attitudes and actions in accordance with the basic design of the nuclear self, despite inner doubts and external threats and seductions.[14]

The point is not to be judgmental, but to challenge our propensity to romanticize courage, and then imagine that we automatically possess such courage when in actuality we remain in spaces of safety and comfort, appeasing life-limiting practices of the racial imagination and turning a blind eye to injustice (just as long as it doesn't affect us). Noble courage is not bestowed upon us like an honorary degree. It cannot be bought. Noble courage is earned, built, and constructed over time. Like King and the titans, we must labor to find our courage.

---

14. H. Kohut, *Self Psychology and Humanities*, 15.

5

BENJAMIN E. MAYS

Your Life-Project as Beauty and Resistance

I've only just a minute,
Only sixty seconds in it.
Forced upon me, can't refuse it,
Didn't seek it, didn't choose it,
But it's up to me to use it.
I must suffer if I lose it,
Give an account if I abuse it.
Just a tiny little minute,
But eternity is in it.

—Author Unknown

To be able to stand the troubles of life, one must have a sense of mission and the belief that God sent him or her into the world for a purpose, to do something unique and distinctive; and that if he does not do it, life will be worse off because it was not done.

—Benjamin E. Mays

You use up everything you got trying to give everybody what they want.

—Nina Simone

It's important, therefore, to know who the real enemy is, and to know the function, the very serious function of racism . . . is distraction. *It keeps you from doing your work.* It keeps explaining, over and over again, your reason for being . . . *None of that is necessary.*

—Toni Morrison

In this chapter, I briefly reflect on Dr. Benjamin Elijah Mays's capacity to know and implement his life-project in a way that served as a function of self-care and self-flourishing, and as a counter-hegemonic praxis against the racial imagination and racial oppression. In this brief chapter, *knowing and carrying out your life-project is also referred to as doing your work.* The life-project or doing your work does not refer to an occupation. It does not refer to the activities you engage in on a daily basis in the normal course of a job. Your life-project reflects the confluence of activities, commitments, tasks, practices, and endeavors, along with governing philosophies and values informing them, that you engage with over the entire life span, which gives ultimate meaning and definition to the formation of your identity. It is living into your divine calling, which is not to be confused with participating in organized religious activities or ecclesial tasks. Your life-project reflects you doing the work that God has ordained for you, a work that transcends a temporal dualism of sacred vs. secular tasks. While very few people are lucky enough for their life-project and daily occupation to intersect, one of the key differences is that you are driven to do your life-project whether you receive remuneration or not. Metaphorically speaking, your life-project represents your signature on the cosmos. Your life-project is akin to trace evidence that you leave behind in the significant places of your life, evidence that suggests you inhabited a particular space in time and that you brought some degree of value, meaning, or significance to that place. Failure to engage in your life-project results in an existential void in your life, a kind of restlessness and chronic melancholy that can be resolved only by doing your work.

For generations of Morehouse men, Benjamin Elijah Mays compelled them to understand their life-project. He knew that there was a *beauty of becoming* in doing your work, and that it was also the best practice of resistance to the hegemony of racial oppression. The idea of being sustained through the awareness of your life-project—of doing your work as an act of self-care and self-affirmation—is consistent with Viktor Frankl's observation of how personal meaning increased the probability of a person surviving a Nazi concentration camp during WWII. What I am referring to as life-project runs parallel to Frankl's concept of logotherapy, of how helping people discover their personal meaning in life is accretive to psychological well-being and of tremendous value in surviving a context or season of suffering:

> There is nothing in the world, I venture to say, that would so effectively help one to survive even the worst conditions as the knowledge that there is a meaning in one's life. There is much wisdom in the words of Nietzsche: "He who has a *why* to live for can bear almost any *how*." I can see in these words a motto which holds true for any psychotherapy. In the Nazi concentration camps, one could have witnessed that those who knew that there was a task waiting for them to fulfill were most apt to survive. The same conclusion has since been reached by other authors of books on concentration camps, and also by psychiatric investigation into Japanese, North Korean and North Vietnamese prisoner-of-war camps.[1]

In a similar fashion, Benjamin Mays understood that such meaning was essential for black men matriculating through Morehouse College. This philosophy is captured in Mays pervasive allusion to "God's Minute."

Dr. Benjamin Elijah Mays is often credited with authoring the poem "God's Minute." Whether or not that is ultimately the case, his usage of it was frequent, and quite compelling, as he endeavored to motivate and inspire scores of students and other black and brown people to live into their essential life-calling. When I personally attended Morehouse in the early 1990s, this poem was instilled into the student body, especially the freshman cohort. Benjamin Mays regularly cited this poem within the Morehouse community over his twenty-seven-year term as president. The poem begins by calling us to reconsider the value of the one remarkably precious, but depreciating asset on the balance sheet of life: time. That is to say, time is arguably the most valuable commodity. Moreover, our life-project is encapsulated in time. While other assets in our lives, whether it be money or any other material possession, are important, if we suffer a loss, we still have the possibility to recoup those assets. But that is not the case with time,

---

1. Frankl, *Man's Search for Meaning*, 97.

as whatever is wasted, or loss, is done so in perpetuity. As such, for Mays, reorienting our conception of the value of time to the very seconds that constitute a minute has psychospiritual significance as well as theo-ethical implications. For example, Mays had a keen awareness of the poor financial condition Morehouse was in during his tenure as president. And while raising money was a priority, he couldn't allow himself or the institution to accept money from places that were antagonistic to the very existence of black life. Oddly enough, when a white friend of the college, Elizabeth Whitehead, attempted to solicit fundraising from her circle of associates, one of the checks that came to Morehouse was from Samuel Green, head of the Atlanta Ku Klux Klan.[2] Mays sent the check back to Green. While at first glance this may seem like the obvious choice, when it comes to money, we fool ourselves if we think anyone in Mays's position would have done this. Given the financial exigencies, many would rationalize a decision to keep the money by rationalizing that all money spends the same and that the college was in dire straits, financially. When teaching pastoral ethics to my own students, I suggest that it is wholly unethical to probe about the spiritual condition of the poor or needy as a precondition to caring for them, when the same is not done to donors and givers when the church is collecting its tithes and offerings. Mays, contrasting his philosophy to that of another black college president, Booker T. Washington, claims "Booker T. Washington may have been right when he said that the only thing wrong with 'tainted money' is that 'it taint enough,' but money from Mr. Green was too tainted for Morehouse to use. The amount didn't matter—it would have been refused had it been for a million dollars."[3] *To accept the money from Green would been a perversion of the invaluable commodity of time that Mays and the college would spend ingratiating themselves to someone who could not even recognize their full humanity.*

For Mays, understanding your life-project, or doing your work, was inherently accretive to healthy identity formation and human flourishing. Moreover, Mays understood that doing your work was probably the most effective countermeasure—individually and communally—to the onslaught of white supremacy and the instantiation of the racial imagination. It is conceivable that the reason Mays referred to the "God's Minute" poem so much with the student body was that it reflected an orienting life-philosophy that grounded him, spiritually and psychologically. The ideological framework of the poem was conducive to creating boundaries for himself and the Morehouse community, who and what he would involve himself

2. Mays, *Born to Rebel*, 204.
3. Mays, *Born to Rebel*, 204.

with, and how he understood his life-project; that is, the ultimate work he was born for, and what the events in his life prepared him to providentially carry out. *"God's Minute" provides a definitional framework for understanding your life-project, or for doing your work.* In the particularity of Mays's location, time, and space, it is conceivable the focus on the seconds in a minute reflects Mays's poetic call for black and brown folk not to waste time trying to successfully negotiate the futile practice of identity politics or the politics of respectability for the purpose of being liked and accepted into a Southern racial caste apparatus that was never designed to recognize and affirm black life. For Mays then, if the ultimate understanding of success is measured simply by the extent to which a person has curried the favor of gatekeepers and power brokers to inhabit spaces traditionally not given to recognizing the full humanity of black and brown people, and such effort is put forth without due regard to how it impacts the health and vitality of the individual and collective soul of that individual's community, then your efforts are a *perversion of time*—an investment loss that you can never recoup.

The "God's Minute" poem suggests that while geographic location and position in time and space may not be of your choosing or beyond your control, you still have a divine mandate to use time in a manner that is faithful to your personhood, and accretive to the purpose for which you have been called and prepared. The poem warns that there are consequences to desecrating our life-project: (1) there will be suffering in some form or another (be it yourself or others) if we fail to do our work, and (2) we will be held to account for neglecting or abusing our life-project. Both of these considerations emphasize the gravity of the life-project. Doing your work is a sacred task. Mays understood that in the oppressive regime of the Jim Crow South, black and brown people are understandably compelled to prioritize survival, perhaps even at the expense of self-flagellation. In an oppressive institutional environment or in a social context of extremity, human creativity and imagination become secondary at best, or tertiary at worst. The beauty of becoming and living into your life-project is developmentally arrested in the service of trying to survive racial terror and oppression and living to see another day.

The relative eclipse of creativity and imagination is a consequence of internalizing a key narrative in the racial imagination: your life does not matter. Failure to take seriously one's purpose and calling is the end result, as you internalize the practice of cheapening your own life—a practice that is replete within the racial imagination. When Mays rehearses the section of "God's Minute" that reads "I must suffer if I lose it, give an account if I abuse it," he is sending a fundamental message to Morehouse students: *You matter. Your life matters. Your life-project is sacred. Treat it as such. Take your humanity and your work seriously.* Through a traumatic encounter Mays experienced as a teenager with a medical doctor by the name of Wallace Payne, he knew all too well about the death-dealing ethos of the racial imagination—that black life is cheap, irrelevant, and does not matter—and the danger of unconsciously internalizing it, for the sake of surviving the real threat of death. I am intentionally using the term *traumatic* in the clinical sense. While Mays penned his autobiography during his sixties, and his encounter with this wicked medical doctor occurred when he was a teenager, Mays is clear that "this humiliating experience is as vivid in my mind today as if it happened yesterday."[4] As Mays went into the local post office to retrieve mail for his mother, he was slapped—quite arbitrarily—by Dr. Payne and told "get out of my way" for the sole purpose of maintaining racial hierarchy within the post office. In his description of Dr. Payne, Mays articulates the broader social attitude:

> The racial attitude of Wallace Payne and others like him was summed up in that sentence: "Get out of my way, you black rascal; you're trying to look too good anyway." I was black; and a black man had no rights which he, Wallace Payne, was bound to admit, let alone respect. My life meant no more to him than that of a rabbit. I was black and he was white; accordingly, with or without provocation, he could—with impunity—do to me what he wished. A rascal is one who is unprincipled and dishonest, and I supposed that Dr. Payne's conception of all Negroes was that they were unprincipled and dishonest. *My greatest sin, of course, was that I was "trying to look too good."* I was standing erect . . . But *a Negro was not supposed to look neat or intelligent, or to stand erect around Dr. Payne.*[5]

Mays's own life experiences then made him acutely aware of the dangers of internalizing the precepts of the racial imagination and its cancerous pedagogy of self-hate, self-deprecation, and self-flagellation. If internalized and allowed to metastasize, the cancer of racial ideology all but ensures the psychospiritual decay of the human spirit. The individual and community aspire to become nothing more than objects of the racial imagination and its concomitant ideology and caste system. Mays did not want this for his Morehouse students. Moreover, he knew that engaging the life-project and doing your work was the psychospiritual intervention to guard against internalized racism and self-hate. He captures the educative philosophy of Morehouse in the following reflection:

4. Mays, *Born to Rebel*, 45.
5. Mays, *Born to Rebel*, 45; emphasis added.

What did Morehouse teach her students about the injustices that bore down upon them every minute of every hour, every hour in the day and every month in the year? Did *Morehouse teach her students to prepare themselves for active attempts to change society, to accept segregation submissively*, or to protest against it with the hope that someday the situation would change? Morehouse certainly did not teach students to accept, let alone gloss over, the environment as they found it. Though *no one at Morehouse taught submission*, neither did anyone encourage Morehouse students to attempt by force to overthrow or change the system. At least, by precept and example, *the Morehouse student was taught never to accept the system in his own mind as being inescapable or right. Never was his intelligence or his pride insulted by his being asked to believe that the cruelty and injustice of racism were the "will of God."*[6]

The observations and concerns of Mays cannot be overstated. Mays was compelled to prepare the Morehouse man to *know his life-project and with that, to engage in doing his sacred work*. This would be the foundational psychospiritual strategy that would lead to human flourishing and at the same time resistance to the oppression of a racial caste system. The idea that Morehouse did not teach accommodation to segregation and racial ideology—moreover to internalize it as God's will—is a pedagogical philosophy that is not limited to Morehouse but is a governing philosophy of many HBCUs (historically black colleges and universities). The same cannot be said of many predominately white institutions of higher learning, including theological education, where the implied messaging—implicitly communicated through institutional silence and appeasement when it comes to matters of racial animosity and injustice—is to be docile and quietly accommodate the evils of the racial imagination, especially when silence and accommodation are in the best interest of *keeping the peace* in the broader community. Knowing this, Mays laments, "It is discouraging and disturbing to me that there are indications of a subtle move afoot to abolish black colleges . . . black colleges, in the thinking of many, are not academically strong enough to train bright-minded blacks, but a white college—*any* white college—is so qualified. So the money flows one way—to the white college. Automatically, *whatever is white is better*."[7]

The final stanza of the poem alludes to eternity inhabiting each minute of our lives. For Mays, I believe such a philosophy turned on two crucial themes that ultimately define your *life-project and doing your work*: (1) the

6. Mays, *Born to Rebel*, 90; emphasis added.
7. Mays, *Born to Rebel*, 192.

potential for a religious moment, and (2) the eschatological plot. Doing your work is generative of a prospective religious moment. A religious moment is episodic in nature, a transitional space where a person encounters and grapples with the Divine—that is to say, the ultimate concern—while in the process of doing their work.[8] In this episodic sacred space, there is a transition to a deeper, more substantive understanding of calling and the nature of one's work. It is a space where you are compelled to transcend the individuality of your work so as to better understand how your life-project is not only consequential to self-interest, but to the interest and well-being of a larger community. In the religious moment, you gain a deeper awareness that you neither live nor die to yourself, but in relation to others as well. In this space, the telos of your life-project is better crystallized, as well as the implications and cost of doing your work. It is important to emphasize that performing an explicit religious activity or functioning in an official capacity of any organized religious organization is not necessary to experience a religious moment. Instead, it is being involved in your life-project, that is, doing your work, that is precipitous of the religious moment. For example, the kitchen incident referred to by Martin Luther King was a religious moment for him. While King was not involved in a specific ecclesial activity, his leadership of the Montgomery bus boycott reflected a component of his life-project. According to Julian Bond, "On Friday night, sitting in his kitchen, King experienced a religious moment setting him on the path that would consume the rest of his life."[9] In another example, Susannah Heschel, daughter of Abraham Heschel, claims that her father experienced a religious moment when he marched with King for voting rights in March of 1965. Again, while Heschel was not involved in an explicit religious activity, involving himself in the march was consistent with his life-project and precipitated a revelation in his inner world in relation to the parallels of what King was doing and Judaism. According to Susannah Heschel, "For my father the march was a religious moment. He wrote in his memoir: 'I thought of my having walked with Hasidic rabbis on various occasions. I felt a sense of the Holy in what I was doing . . . I felt again what I have been thinking about for years—that Jewish religious institutions have again missed a great opportunity, namely, to interpret the civil-rights movement in terms of Judaism. The vast number of Jews participating actively in it are totally unaware of what the movement means in terms of the prophetic traditions.'"[10]

---

8. See Tillich, *Dynamics of Faith*.
9. Horowitz and Theoharis, *Julian Bond's Time*, 80.
10. Heschel, *Moral Grandeur*, xxiii–xxiv.

The outcome of the religious moment is twofold: you are compelled to move forward in your life-project and do your work even when faced with challenges, adversity, or the threat of harm or demise, and you develop a greater sense of piety. In this definition of piety, I am not referring to the sacralization or valorization of asceticism simply for the sake of asceticism, which is nothing more than self-defeating legalism. Instead, I refer to an idea of piety put forth by Cornell West whereby piety is the awareness that you stand on the shoulders of *others who laid the groundwork for you to carry out your life-project and do your work*. Piety recognizes that many of those in the *great cloud of witnesses died in faith, and even suffered and were killed in pursuit of the ultimate concern*,[11] *not having received the things promised*, but nevertheless proceeded in spite of the real likelihood that they wouldn't live to receive the things promised. Such individuals, *many of whom the world was not worthy of, still persisted in doing their work* for the sake of future generations and for the well-being and potential flourishing of posterity.[12] Using Frederick Douglass as an example, West asserts that "piety is but a way of talking about the reverent attachment that we have to those in family, in social movements, in civic institutions, in various social networks who help us make who we are . . . [and] it becomes a source of good in your life, and it becomes the very launching pad for you in terms of your future, the wind at your back in the present."[13] For West, piety protects against narcissism and yields a sense of gratitude in a person's inner world. He rounds out his idea of piety by suggesting that "if piety is understood as the debts you owe to those who came before tied to the tradition and community and legacy of struggle . . . [then] there is an indescribable joy in serving others . . . [which] is qualitatively different than pleasure in leading others."[14]

---

11. In *Dynamics of Faith*, Paul Tillich describes Christian faith in terms of what a person or community is ultimately concerned about. According to Tillich, "Faith is the state of being ultimately concerned: the dynamics of faith are the dynamics of man's ultimate concern . . . but man, in contrast to other living beings, has spiritual concerns—cognitive, aesthetic, social . . . [and] political" (1). Using ancient Israel as an example, Tillich goes on to suggest that "faith, for the men of the Old Testament, is the state of being ultimately and unconditionally concerned about Jahweh and about what he represents in demand, threat and promise" (3). For our purposes here, I invoke the terminology of ultimate concern to challenge the self-deluding temptation (especially in the West) to believe (and then suggest to other persons or groups) that religious praxis reflects pure altruism and is free from temporal self-interest or selfish ambition. The terminology of ultimate concern has the potential to deconstruct modernity's false divide between sacred and secular.

12. See Heb 11.

13. West, *Black Prophetic Fire*, 18–19.

14. West, *Black Prophetic Fire*, 96.

Lastly, the final line in "God's Minute" that references eternity in each minute reflects the notion of the eschatological plot put forth by Edward Wimberly. In much of black religious tradition, the idea of the eschatological plot blurs the divide between sacred and secular components of individual and communal life—a divide that is commonly witnessed in Western Christian traditions. In the eschatological plot, the entirety of the individual life—whether it entails involvement with organized religion and ecclesial activities, or involvement with secular organizations, pursuits, career ambitions, or vocations—is considered to be subsumed in a providential plot to redeem and restore all things back to God. For many black and brown people, incorporating this narrative into your life story does not require formal participation in organized religion. This takes on special significance for a people forced to exist on the underside of history, where religion, particularly Christian theology and biblical interpretation, has been used to justify their oppression. The eschatological plot reflects a narrative etched in eternity, a narrative that suggests justice and redemption will ultimately prevail. According to Wimberly, what black people took "away from the encounter with God in Scripture is the eschatological plot, understood as redemptive and liberating . . . African Americans interpreted the texts of terror within the context of God's unfolding drama of salvation, and the eschatological plot had to be envisioned in light of the coming of God's rule on earth . . . [As such] in the lives of African Americans, slavery, racism, and oppression are real, but within the eschatological plot of God, they are not the final chapters. There is more to come."[15]

To this end, the manner in which life unfolds is understood in terms of this fundamental question: *What has God called me to do?* In my time as a pastor, I didn't understand this phenomenon in the way that I understand it in hindsight. Even for people who occasionally attended church (at best), or perhaps were not involved in the church at all, but nonetheless knew that I was a pastor, when speaking with me, they would tend to talk about their lives through biblical narratives they may have learned from their parents or grandparents. They would articulate the stories of their life in a manner that suggested they imagined themselves being involved in a larger overarching divine plot that included their flourishing, success, healing, or redemption. Common narratives would center around themes like *all things work together for good*, or *the race is not given to the swift or the strong but to those that endure to the end*.[16] At the time, I didn't appreciate the cultural

---

15. Wimberly, *African American Pastoral Care*, xiii.

16. In the common usage of biblical themes like *all things work together for good*, or *the race is not given to the swift or the strong but to those who endure to the end*, the purpose was not to derive a precise exegetical interpretation, but to use Scripture as a space

wonder that I was witnessing in these testimonies (and in fact, my formal theological training taught me to dismiss it or look negatively upon it): core values and beliefs that sustained the African diaspora. The psychospiritual strength of this cultural and religious phenomenon is captured brilliantly in the work of Cooper-Lewter and Mitchell and the concept of soul theology. For Cooper-Lewter and Mitchell, soul theology represents the implied theological framework derived from generations of black life, love, and suffering; constructed in oral tradition; and distributed through black religious tradition. Core values and beliefs are at the heart of soul theology but can sometimes be misunderstood as being old-fashioned, legalistic, or austere. But for Cooper-Lewter and Mitchell, "rather than being considered rigid, core beliefs are seen as a necessary anchor in life's storm. Without formal or sophisticated rationale, the oppressed people holding core beliefs tend to assume that God takes good care of them. Old prayers thanked God that 'He woke me up this morning, clothed in my right mind.' . . .[So consequently] what looks like rigidity to some people is seen [for an oppressed people] . . . as stability and strength."[17] Perhaps among the most foundational tenets of soul theology is the notion of divine providence and its importance in the meaning-making process for an oppressed people. According to the authors, many black people

> may not have so precise a word for it, and they many even know [or care for that matter] that the idea they cling to so naturally is called a doctrine. But in Africa and Afro-America, the most treasured and trusted word about our life here on earth is that God is in charge. This faith guarantees that everyone's life is worth living. The Bible passage that expresses it best is Paul's famous word to the Romans: "And we know that God works in everything for the good of those who love him and are called according to his plan."[18]

The idea being put forth here, that the life-project is informed by a larger providential scheme that does not bifurcate sacred and secular but views the entire life cycle in an eschatological plot, reflects a view of religion and life with African roots. While some scholars of religion and

---

of redemption and healing, where the person could envision the entirety of their life in the story of the text. For example, the latter theme ("the race is not given") represents the combination of passages taken from the First and Second Testaments. While this may run afoul in the ideology of certain Western exegetical approaches, for black and brown people, the approach represented a wholistic view of interpreting Scripture in a way that reflects the love and justice of God.

17. Cooper-Lewter and Mitchell, *Soul Theology*, 4–5.
18. Cooper-Lewter and Mitchell, *Soul Theology*, 14.

sociology suggest that the transatlantic slave trade severed much of African culture from those in the diaspora forced to exist in the Americas, Peter Paris argues that much remained in terms of the overarching paradigms that defined African spirituality. Among those fundamental paradigms was an understanding of spirituality that transcended organized religion or the institutional church. According to Paris:

> One of the most important marks of continuity between Africans on the continent and those in the diaspora is their common belief in a transcendent divine power primordially related to them as the creator and preserver of all that is . . . There is no evidence that either the slaves or their African forebears ever believed in the modern Western distinction between sacred and profane. Rather, both presupposed a sacred cosmos. That is to say, in traditional African thought all reality (human and natural, animate and inanimate) was thought to be derived from a common, primeval, divine source on which its continuing existence depended. Hence they viewed everything as sacred in some respect and saw nothing as totally profane.[19]

The paradigmatic continuity between spirituality in Africa and the spirituality of black people in America that Paris is describing aligns squarely with the idea of grasping your life-project and doing your work: God's call and plan for your life transcend the confines of organized religion and the institutional church and connect with every facet of your life and being. For generations of black men who would have no choice but to live, thrive, and flourish in a racist society, or who would be compelled to thrive within institutions lacking the capacity to affirm their full humanity, or to inhabit spaces that never had them in mind when those spaces were designed, Benjamin Mays knew that these men would have to be equipped to see eternity in each minute of their life, to construct an eschatological plot, and to maintain a soul theology with sufficient integrity to understand their life in a larger providential story that transcended the racial imagination and caste system.

Currently in North American theological education, the idea of clergypersons being bi-vocational or multi-vocational, as well as literature on faith and work, are all gaining traction, albeit in a reactionary way, as pressure on church finances over the last several decades is pressuring more faith communities to consider the idea of multi-vocational leadership as well as the ensuing theological implications. However, to be clear, there is nothing new about this phenomenon—in terms of scholarship or praxis— as black and brown clergypersons who have matriculated through the ivory

---

19. Paris, *Spirituality of African Peoples*, 33–34.

tower culture have been engaged in multi-vocational praxis for generations. Instead, the multi-vocational human experiences of black religious tradition were dismissed as being a dysfunctional aberration of what it meant to be a clergyperson and never considered to be a suitable exemplar of ecclesial praxis and Christian tradition. Benjamin Mays was a preacher, educator, scholar, and college president, all at the same time. In my own professional career, in some form or another I was some combination of a banker, pastor, scholar, and psychotherapist. During that time, especially as a pastor and banker, it was occasionally suggested to me (in the form of a polite question) that I couldn't do both, I shouldn't do both, and that one vocation diminished my capacity to engage in the other. By the time I began my doctoral studies, a few professors offered *unsolicited observations*—in a somewhat passive aggressive way—along the lines of "it is hard for students who have worked in other professions to accept that they are at the bottom again or that they are at an entry-level phase again."

Strangely enough, I never understood the pursuit of my doctoral degree (after a career in financial services) as starting over, but simply as the ongoing unfolding of my lifework. Nevertheless, as gatekeepers of the ivory tower, some of the professors' intended messaging was clear: in their view of the world, there existed a rather extensive portion of my life that was deemed irrelevant to the space of the theological academe, an elite space that was primarily underwritten by Eurocentric religious experience, privileged the sacred/secular binary paradigm that required vocational allegiance to one or the other, and confined scholarly identity formation to isolated disciplinary silos that undermined interdisciplinary praxis, created life-limiting (and even death-dealing) echo chambers, and impaired much-needed creativity and imagination to address needs and deficits in an emerging scholar's own religious tradition and heritage—the very community that sent them to seminary in the first place. It was only when I graduated with my doctoral degree and was interviewing for academic positions that a former professor in my doctoral program, responding to my question about what experiences I should include on my resume, strongly asserted: "*You should include everything about your past academic and career experiences on your resume. Every aspect of your past life is important and relevant to who you are today. It is left up to you to figure out how it is relevant.*" Her wisdom functioned as a healing balm at the end of my academic journey. Until then, the implicit messaging was that there was only a limited portion of my personhood that stood a chance of being recognized and accepted into the theological academy. Said differently, in the words of James Baldwin, the *price of the ticket* for admittance into this privileged world would require me to contort my personhood, scholarly imagination, and voice into a form deemed acceptable to the gatekeepers of the system.

Benjamin Mays's focus on engaging your life-project suggested a different approach. Again, in many black and brown communities, while economics may have been a part of the reason for being multi-vocational, *it more so reflected the concept of doing your work*, where instead of a parochial understanding of religious work through a bifurcated lens of sacred or secular, they alternatively viewed their participation in organized religion as only one particular manifestation of their life-project—the entirety of which was divinely ordained and pneumatologically inspired. Consequently, in black religious tradition, it was not necessarily uncommon to see a black clergyperson who was also a politician or politically active. It was not because they had a divided mind, but because they understood and were called to a multipronged approach to serving the community. In another place Paris asserts, "Since authentic worship reflects the life of the people and their pressing needs, African peoples have always viewed the political struggle for freedom as mirrored in their worship."[20] When religious experience is understood in this light, it is not entirely clear to me that predominately white churches with multicultural aspirations grasp the full implications of what they are really aspiring to when touting the multicultural vision. It is far more than adding a few songs by black authors to the worship-song list. It requires a shattering of a preexisting paradigm—a shattering that holds the possibility to expand what it means to be human and how we conceptualize a Triune God.

LEGALISM: THE ENEMY OF THE LIFE-PROJECT

In a previous work, I broached the question of why Frederick Douglass would find it necessary to write four autobiographies. I suggested then that it was, in part, a coping mechanism to guard against the psychological and spiritual degradation embedded in the slavocracy, as it invested Douglass with the agency to construct and interpret his own life story, not a story imputed on him by others. His writing represented "an act of resilience to prop up his internal force of being, as he existed in [a context of] extremity . . . [and his] ongoing passion to craft a counter-narrative over and against the overarching narrative of white supremacy and black subjugation is clear in his repeated efforts to write down the story of his existence and selfhood."[21] What I didn't make clear at the time was that the writing of his autobiographies,

---

20. Paris, *Spirituality of African Peoples*, 47.
21. D. G. Gibson, *Frederick Douglass*, 127.

in part, represented his life-project. The amalgamation of Douglass's writings, lectures, and speeches represented his work. It was his signature on the cosmos, upon what Martin Luther King referred to as the arc of the moral universe,[22] trace evidence that Douglass was a contributor to the American democratic experiment. While I believe it is debatable whether the arc of the moral universe actually bends towards justice, it is clear to me that *the weight of our life-project, of doing our work, must contribute to pitching the arc in the direction of justice.*

The opposite of doing your work is to engage in the practice of legalism: the betrayal of yourself and your life's work in lieu of conforming to a status-quo archetype of who and what you should be for the sake of communal and cultural acceptance. The prevalence of the theme of legalism in the Second Testament of Scripture was not because people were so bad or sinful, but because legalism is the far easier alternative to living into the life-project. *Legalism holds out the illusion that we are actually doing our work.* Legalism caters to our need to be accepted, affirmed, or to fit in to a given community, as it is far easier than the hard work of reaching beyond ourselves to a transcendent purpose and calling that eclipses the immediacy of our fears, insecurities, and our need for safety and security. Legalism is living and practicing life in a way that sublimates your voice and subjectivity in the service of conforming to the vision and expectations that a larger social system has for your life—all for the purpose of being accepted by that social system. Legalism doesn't require individual or communal contemplative work or self-reflexivity. Instead, it valorizes the unexamined life. Legalism doesn't require you to ask why you do what you do, or to question the efficacy of existing practices; it privileges action, conformity, and compliance, for the sake of action, conformity, and compliance.

If the writing of four autobiographies was reflective of Frederick Douglass doing his work, then perhaps the most illustrative example of legalism in the life of Douglass would have been if he had betrayed himself in order to be accepted by the Northern abolitionists. That is to say, had Douglass chosen to comply with the vision for his life as imagined by Northern abolitionists (people who were friends of Frederick Douglass and who were adamantly against slavery but were nonetheless infected by the racial imagination) just to remain in their good graces and be accepted into their inner circle, such a move would have epitomized legalism and all but sidetracked the life of Douglass as we know it today. Moreover, the American democratic experiment would have suffered an immeasurable setback, as it would have been deprived of the impact of Douglass's life-project. In his third

---

22. Washington, *Testament of Hope*, 207.

autobiography Douglass laments the embarrassment he experienced when his own friends—associates who were for the cause of abolition—wanted him to talk and behave as they imagined an enslaved person on a plantation should talk and behave:

> "Give us the facts," said Collins, "we will take care of the philosophy." Just here arose some embarrassment . . . "Tell your story, Frederick," would whisper my revered friend, Mr. [Lloyd] Garrison . . . "People won't believe you ever was a slave, Frederick, if you keep on this way," said friend Foster. "Be yourself," said Collins, "and tell your story." *"Better have a little of the plantation speech than not," it was said to me; "it is not best that you seem too learned."*[23]

Influenced by the racial imagination, Douglass's abolitionist friends had a greater interest in appropriating his black body than they had in a relational connection with his mind and subjectivity that were informed by his black experience. The racial imagination rejects black intellectual tradition. *They needed Douglass to be a black man as they imagined a black man*, on terms and conditions that were acceptable to them and suitable to their ego-strength, in order for them to feel as though they were white men whose lives were synonymous with freedom and the ideology of manifest destiny, as well as life, liberty, and the pursuit of happiness. Simply put, *the abolitionists needed Douglass to be black so they could be white*. The racial imagination is more comfortable with subjugated and imprisoned black bodies than it is with black and brown intellect. And especially in the church, the racial imagination is far more comfortable with black and brown bodies it perceives as being in need of salvation than it is with engaging with black and brown theological tradition. In another place Frederick Douglass asserts, "When a black man's language is quoted, in order to belittle and degrade him, his ideas are put into the most grotesque and unreadable English, while the utterances of negro scholars and authors are ignored . . . [and] a hundred white men will attend a concert of white negro minstrels with faces blackened with burnt cork, to one who will attend a lecture by an intelligent negro."[24] Had Frederick Douglass surrendered to the desires of the racial imagination of his abolitionist friends just for the sake of receiving their approval, acceptance, and admiration, he would have subverted his own life-project and perverted the very core of his being. Had Douglass made the decision to be black on the terms and conditions laid out by his abolitionist associates (even while they may have had the best of intentions) just for the

---

23. Douglass, *Life and Times*, 218.
24. Douglass, *Lessons of the Hour*, 19.

sake of being successful, by definition then he would have chosen a spiritual life of legalism and sin.

In her description of the psychodynamics between master and slave, Jessica Benjamin provides insight into the kind of behavior we read about between Frederick Douglass and his abolitionist friends. According to Benjamin, there is no such thing as an independent self-aware subject or human being. In order to be a self-aware subject, we depend on others, in part, to recognize us. But such a dependence of the recognition of others creates potential insecurity and vulnerability. As such, Benjamin asserts, "domination [of another human being] begins with the attempt to deny dependency."[25] If dependency on another person is necessary to be a healthy self-aware human being, it is more comfortable, psychologically speaking, to be able to exercise control over that person or for them to be in a subjugated position, relatively speaking, than to have to depend on a person you have no control over. This is at the heart of the psychodynamics between master and slave, being free versus unfree, and the social construction of what it means to be white versus the social construction of what it means to be black. In each instance, within the racial imagination, there is a need for the latter to exist in a subjugated manner so that the former can experience the fullness of their humanity. This is the psychospiritual cost of being socialized in the racial imagination across generations. It is indeed a high cost that cannot be remediated overnight. Within the racial imagination, non-raced people have internalized a sense of superiority that must be attended to via a pastoral and psychospiritual intervention. According to Benjamin:

> Since the subject cannot accept his dependency on someone he cannot control, *the solution is to subjugate and enslave the other—to make him give that recognition without recognizing him in return.* The primary consequence of the inability to reconcile dependence with independence, then, is the transformation of need for the other into domination of him.[26]

While William Lloyd Garrison and his abolitionist colleagues were staunchly against slavery and sincerely wanted to break the back of the system of evil, the fallenness of their own interior world—a world influenced by the racial imagination—still required Douglass not to be as intelligent, as well spoken, as informed, or as refined as they desired to be. Their friend Douglass had to be in some way subordinate to their personhood.

This is an interpersonal and intracommunal dynamic that can be present in many communities and organizations today, particularly the

---

25. Benjamin, *Bonds of Love*, 52.
26. Benjamin, *Bonds of Love*, 54.

church, when the community has been formed and developed in isolated cultural enclaves characterized by high social barriers to entry and sustained through de facto segregation. The implicit master and slave dynamic becomes unconsciously entrenched in the culture of the community and risks undermining any effort to create a more culturally diverse institution if ignored. Left unchecked (via an institutional praxis that emphasizes the biblical, theological, and spiritual value of cultural multiplicity), the sort of psychospiritual degradation that undermined the abolitionist's capacity to recognize the full humanity of Douglass can upend the racial progress of any community, regardless of whether or not they see themselves as conservatives on the right of the sociopolitical spectrum, or so-called progressive and liberal on the left of the sociopolitical spectrum. In the collective psyche of the community, individuals with *raced bodies* (i.e., black and brown people) are expected to think, feel, talk, act, and function in a way that is consistent with the fantasies of the racial imagination, and that contributes to the psychic well-being, comfort, and narcissistic ambitions of those with *non-raced bodies*.

This manifestation of social oppression is no respecter of persons in terms of where they fall on the political spectrum. When ethnic minorities who inhabit predominantly white institutions are relationally engaged with through prefabricated psychic archetypes or stereotypes of who they should be, it represents a form of psychic violence and emotional brutality that flattens their history, heritage, and life story. Moreover, it robs them of human dignity. The racial imagination is a product of the human condition, not a sociopolitical schematic. If Frederick Douglass had betrayed the core of his selfhood and complied with the desires of his abolitionist friends—just for the sake of fitting in and remaining in their good graces—it would have represented a life-limiting praxis of legalism that over the long run would have resulted in a disintegrative psychospiritual death. Of course, this did not happen with Douglass because instead of complying with the desires of his friends, he engaged his life-project and committed himself to doing his work. And while the Northern abolitionists did many good works, nevertheless, they still were in need of a religious and spiritual intervention that targeted their racial fantasies.

Benjamin Mays understood that Morehouse students would encounter dynamics similar to what Frederick Douglass experienced for the rest of their lives. This is why he stressed the importance of them understanding their life-project and doing their work: it functioned as resistance against the onslaught of racial oppression, as well as the point of departure for psychospiritual flourishing. Perhaps the best example of Mays advocating for students when it came to doing their work was when he advocated for a young Martin Luther King Jr. during his tenure as the pastor of Dexter Avenue Baptist Church. Mays stood in solidarity with Martin Luther King to return to Montgomery, Alabama (from Atlanta, Georgia), to continue leading the bus boycott—a move that was strongly contested by King's father because of the threat to Martin's life and the lives of his wife and daughter, as well as the threat of being imprisoned. While in Atlanta visiting with his parents, Martin Luther King recalls a day when his father, Martin Luther King Sr. (commonly referred to as Daddy King) invited several prominent local leaders over to his house to discuss the matter of his son returning to Montgomery. Daddy King wanted their wisdom and input. Those local leaders included Benjamin Mays (who was the president of Morehouse by that time), Rufus Clement (president of Atlanta University), Bishop Sherman L. Green of the AME church, and several other prominent businessmen. Initially, there was a general agreement with Daddy King that Martin should not return to Montgomery. But then at a pivotal moment, Martin Luther King recalls the following:

> There were murmurs of agreement in the room, and I listened as sympathetically and objectively as I could while two of the men gave their reasons for concurring. These were my elders, leaders among my people. Their words commanded respect. But soon I could not restrain myself any longer. "I must go back to Montgomery," I protested. "My friends and associates are being arrested. It would be the height of cowardice for me to stay away. I would rather be in jail ten years than desert my people now. I have begun the struggle, and I can't turn back. I have reached the point of no return." *In the moment of silence that followed I heard my father break into tears. I looked at Dr. Mays, one of the great influences in my life. Perhaps he heard my unspoken plea. At any rate, he was soon defending my position strongly. Then others joined him in supporting me.* They assured my father that things were not so bad as they seemed.[27]

From this excerpt, it is obvious to glean that everyone in the room had good intentions and wanted only the best for the young Martin. Moreover, history shows us that Daddy King's fears were well founded, and it is clear that he loved his son deeply. But Mays was a master teacher and mentor when it came to the work of helping students identify and live into their life-project. *Mays advocated for students doing their lifework.* Despite the threat to life and limb, his spiritual insight allowed him to see deeply into the soul of Martin Luther King and understand how failing to return to Montgomery

---

27. King, *Autobiography*, 86; emphasis added.

would represent a betrayal of his life-project and result in existential frustration and distress, which is defined by Frankl as "a man's concern, even his despair, over the worthwhileness of life."[28] And consistent with the definition that I have proposed for life-project, America as we know it would be materially different had Martin Luther King not returned to Montgomery and instead opted to betray himself and his life-project.

It is conceivable that among the reasons Mays was so good at mentoring students into their life-project was because he himself had experienced the real prospect of abandoning his lifework in an effort to appease the vision of his family and community of origin regarding who he should be, and more specifically, to secure the approval of his father. Said differently, Mays had firsthand experience with the pain of existential frustration and distress. In particular, Mays's father, Hezekiah Mays, was staunchly against Benjamin getting an education. He thought it was pointless. Instead, Hezekiah's vision for his son, this idea of what constituted a man, was that his son become a farmer or a preacher. Ostensibly, it was only within this narrow framework of life that Hezekiah had the capacity to affirm his son's humanity. Benjamin Mays recounts the following:

> My greatest opposition to going away to school was my father. When I knew that I had learned everything I could in the one-room Brickhouse School and realized how little that was, my father felt that this was sufficient—that it was all I needed. Weren't there only two honest occupations for Negro men—preaching and farming? My father must have repeated this dictum a thousand times.[29]

Benjamin Mays was well acquainted with the pain of seeking affirmation, admiration, recognition, and approval—all of which basic psychological needs are necessary for psychospiritual health—from a father who lacked the emotional equipment to provide as such. Benjamin Mays knew what it was *not to be believed in* by a primary caregiver or a community of origin. In another place Mays asserts, "When Father saw that I was determined to go to a better school, and knew that I had to have money in order to do so, *he angrily threw a ten-dollar bill at me. So I made my way to Orangeburg without Father's blessing but with my mother's prayers.*"[30] In these episodes, not only do we see Mays's pain associated with the futile effort to secure his father's admiration, but we also see a father, and perhaps a community, either refuse, or lack the capacity, to see him and recognize him as he desired to be seen

---

28. Frankl, *Man's Search for Meaning*, 96.
29. Mays, *Born to Rebel*, 35–36.
30. Mays, *Born to Rebel*, 38; emphasis added.

and recognized. Hezekiah Mays either refused, or lacked the psychic ability, to see his son, Benjamin Mays, on the terms and conditions of Benjamin's prospective life-project. This, in part, is symptomatic of internalized racism and self-flagellation: you identify with, and then comply with the racialized caricatures, archetypes, or lies projected on you by the racial imagination. According to Benjamin Mays, the lie that his father internalized and then projected onto his son was clear, but also very painful for the younger Mays to accept: the only honest profession for a black man—and by extension his son—was farming or preaching. Hezekiah's affirmation and recognition of his son was to be found only in Benjamin aligning his life according to his father's life-limiting vision. To be fair, one could argue that Hezekiah Mays was a product of his time. In an environment where the Jim Crow terrorism was a reality that black people had to contend with, it is conceivable that Hezekiah simply wanted his son to pursue a vocation that would maximize the likelihood of his physical survival by *staying in his place* within the racial caste system. But angrily throwing a ten-dollar bill at his son speaks to a deeper emotional ailment, a psychospiritual sickness whereby he lacked the capacity to see, love, and accept his son as an individual self-determining subject with agency. Said differently, Hezekiah Mays didn't believe in Benjamin Mays. In the most selfish way, Hezekiah Mays could be in a relationship with his son only to the extent that Benjamin functioned as an object of Hezekiah's imagination: *be who and what I want and need you to be, or you will not be with me at all.* The relationship between Benjamin and Hezekiah ultimately ran its course when Benjamin refused to delimit his schooling to four months out of the year in order to help his father on the farm for the other eight months. Mays recalls, "So the break with my father came and it was final. I disobeyed him without regret and with no pangs of conscience. It was now crystal clear to me that I must take my education into my own hands and that I could not and must not permit my father to dictate or determine my future."[31]

BLACK BOYS AND EXISTENTIAL FRUSTRATION

This episode between Benjamin Mays and his father, Hezekiah Mays, is a microcosm of a much larger systemic issue that is a product of the legacy of the slavocracy and the racial imagination: the internalization of the negative archetype of black boys in the Western psychic space. Hezekiah Mays didn't believe that Benjamin Mays could be anything more than what the social structure imagined his son could be—a farmer or a black preacher.

31. Mays, *Born to Rebel*, 38.

Hezekiah internalized this deleterious image of black boys and then projected it onto his own son. It is one matter for non-raced individuals not to believe in black boys and project all sorts of repugnant beliefs and stereotypes onto them. It is an entirely different matter when actors from within black and brown communities internalize those same repugnant beliefs and stereotypes and project them onto black boys. This practice effectively eclipses the individual and communal imagination to visualize what black boys could be, and it undermines the psychic capacity to recognize and affirm the full humanity of black boys. Staying out of prison becomes the measure of success for black boys. As they get older, for them to hold onto any job is seen as a life-achievement. Once internalized racism takes root in the collective communal psyche, the ability to recognize the subjectivity and full humanity of black boys—that is to say, to see and affirm that black boys are indeed beautiful—is replaced with harmful sociocultural myths and folklore like *you know how black boys are*, or *you know how black men are*, or *you are going to be just like your ole daddy*, or *black men ain't shit*. I think you get my point here.

Reducing the humanity of black boys to a perverse object of Western imagination reflects the observation made by the French West Indian psychiatrist Frantz Fanon who rightfully argued, "For not only must the black man be black; he must be black in relation to the white man."[32] To offer up an example of this claim, Fanon goes on to recount an episode where a white boy, upon seeing Fanon, reacts with astonishment to his mother and exclaims, "*Maman*, look, a Negro; I'm scared,"[33] with the mother offering a response of "Ssh, you'll make him angry. Don't pay attention to him, monsieur, he doesn't realize you're just as civilized as we are."[34] Mind you, this conversation between the mother and son is all occurring within earshot of Fanon. But it doesn't matter to them that Fanon hears them talking about him, as they experience Fanon as no more than an object to be acted upon. Fanon goes on to describe his interior world as this happens to him. I suggest his sentiments regarding this experience mirror that of the younger Benjamin Mays and many other black boys that have been *raced* in our society. They don't have the opportunity to write and co-create the narrative of their life-story, as the master narrative of *you know how black men are* was already inspired by the racial imagination and inscribed on the soul of a nation well before Benjamin Mays, Frantz Fanon, and millions of other black boys and men were even born:

32. Fanon, *Black Skin, White Masks*, 90.
33. Fanon, *Black Skin, White Masks*, 91.
34. Fanon, *Black Skin, White Masks*, 93.

My body was returned to me spread-eagled, disjointed, redone, draped in mourning on this white winter's day. The Negro is an animal, the Negro is bad, the Negro is wicked, the Negro is ugly; look, a Negro; the Negro is trembling, the Negro is trembling because he's cold, the small boy is trembling because he's afraid of the Negro, the Negro is trembling with cold, the cold that chills the bones, the lovely little boy is trembling because he things the Negro is trembling with rage, the little white boy runs to his mother's arms: "*Maman*, the Negro's going to eat me."[35]

Fanon is reflecting on what it is like to be objectified in the collective mind of the community. He is reflecting upon what it is like when his black male body is the marker that triggers an individual or collective narrative about who he is, what he is capable of doing (for better or worse), and on what basis he should be engaged with. This is also emblematic of the experience of black boys who experience existential despair, whether it be in the broader society, or perhaps even worse, when it occurs in their own community of origin or family system—similar to what Benjamin Mays experienced from his father. And even when speaking of delinquency that is so often profiled in the media, the point of course is not to say that delinquent actors do not exist among black boys. The point is that delinquency exists among the entire human race, and that black boys (and by extension black men) do not constitute a special subcategory of humanity that makes their mistakes, failures, and delinquency any more deleterious than that of white boys.

In a compelling quantitative study that examined the effects of dehumanizing black children, Phillip Goff and colleagues field-tested three hypotheses that theorized that black boys were perceived to be less "childlike" than white children, that the concept of childhood was associated less with black boys than white boys, and that the previously mentioned hypotheses were compounded in contexts where black boys were dehumanized through the practice of associating them with animals, particularly apes.[36] The findings are troubling to say the least, and point to wide disparities in how black boys in particular are socially perceived relative to white children. The authors conclude there is "evidence that Black children are afforded the privilege of innocence to a lesser extent than children of other races . . . [that] Black boys are seen as more culpable for their actions within a criminal justice context than are their peers of other races . . . [that] Black boys are actually misperceived as older relative to peers of other races . . . [and] that dehumanization of Blacks not only predicts racially disparate

---

35. Fanon, *Black Skin, White Masks*, 93.
36. Goff et al., "Essence of Innocence."

perceptions of Black boys but also predicts racially disparate police violence towards Black children in real-world settings."[37] Research findings like this emphasize how dangerous it is when people of goodwill, especially *non-raced people* in religious communities like the Christian church, function as passive bystanders when listening to family, colleagues, and friends use dehumanizing and debasing language when referring to black and brown people. While remaining quiet in such instances may provide an immediate sense of comfort and safety (by conforming to the status quo), such silence over the long run is an enabler of racial hatred and violence.

The intracommunal inability to believe in black children, and in this case black boys, in part reflects internalized racial hatred. Moreover, internalized racism and the practice of poor self-worth (often disguised as Christian humility) lead to a malignant form of self-flagellation that culminates in a psychospiritual death. Similar to a young Martin Luther King Jr., the prospective psychospiritual death that I refer to here reflects black boys experiencing existential frustration and distress because their community of origin does not believe in them enough to even recognize and affirm them as self-determining agents with the intelligence and capacity to craft their own life-project and to do their work. In a qualitative research project on how black boys in Chicago experience themselves in public spaces that are overrun with negative imagery and feelings towards black males, I examined the extent to which the boys were able to see and experience themselves in a life-giving way that transcended public perception contaminated by the racial imagination. In that article I lament "how can Black boys experience themselves in a life-giving way that is accretive to human flourishing when colonial fantasy, group-level racial delusion, and the death-dealing stereotypes have all but stamped out any substantive or life-giving symbols in the . . . public sphere . . . [and that] the insatiable media appetite for negative Black male imagery reflects a long history of colonial images that play out in the psyche and emotional field of Western civilization, effectively reducing the bodies of Black men and boys to objects of fear, suspicion, and abjection."[38] Perhaps among the most insightful takeaways from that experience was learning that for all of the boys interviewed, the idea of their role model was not some high-profile sports figure or entertainer. Instead, they identified older peers among themselves or in their schools, as well as teachers who took a special interest in them, as their role models. That is to say, *the boys gravitated towards those who believed in them.* I suggest that Mays carried elements of this existential pain with him

37. Goff et al., "Essence of Innocence," 539–40.
38. D. G. Gibson, "When Empathy," 618.

throughout his life. He knew the pain of having an important figure in his life who should have believed in him, but for whatever reason either lacked the capacity to or outright refused to believe in him. During his tenure as the dean of Howard University School of Divinity, both of his parents died. When his mother died, he wrote extensively about her influence on him in the divinity school's newsletter. But when his father died, he was publicly silent on the matter.[39]

The emotional pain Benjamin Mays incurred in the early years of his life informed how he cared for the boys who matriculated through Morehouse College and ultimately graduated as young men. The encounters of existential frustration and distress that Mays experienced as a young black teenager, the risk of a meaningless life of legalism that was misaligned from his life-project, all served as a source of deep empathy when he looked into the lives of young black boys and endeavored to mentor and mold them into young scholars, businessmen, theologians, educators, doctors, lawyers, or professionals in any other calling—*all of whom would be very capable black men equipped to do their work.*

Benjamin Mays helped to create a culture at Morehouse College where black boys and men could understand and articulate their life-project and begin the life-long practice of doing their work. While racial oppression is obstinate and pervasive in the American story, Mays knew that black people could not form their personal identity and life story around resisting the terror of racism. Over the long run, such a move is self-destructive, as it makes your life about redeeming the racial oppressor. While this may be a noble project, it is ill advised to make it a lifetime aspiration. Instead, Mays knew that embracing the life-project was perhaps among the best self-sustaining strategies against the racial injustice and oppression, as it compels the individual and community to reach beyond themselves to embrace the religious moment, to cast the narrative of their life-story in a larger eschatological plot, where self-love and then neighborly love are the governing life forces, and where doing your work is not optional, but nonnegotiable. Understanding his life-project and then doing his work is among the most salient psychospiritual themes in the life of Mays that I believe sustained him and defined him. Of his time at Morehouse College, he concludes:

> Twenty-seven years is a long time to stay on a job, and more than three score years is an incredibly long time to remain in the South, especially in the South at its worst, in the South that Sadie and I knew all too well... However, as far as we were concerned, to run away rather than face the always embarrassing, always

---

39. See Jelks, *Benjamin Elijah Mays*.

humiliating racial problems would be an act of cowardice. We wanted to be in the thick of the fight as long as there was a glimmer of hope that we could help ameliorate the racial problem by even the slightest degree, could change the Southern pattern of society by one whit. We believe that during our twenty-seven years *we helped instill in many a Morehouse student a sense of his own worth and a pride that thereafter enabled him to walk in the earth with dignity*. We believe that long before the current emphasis on pride in being black, the Morehouse student had already found his identity.[40]

Being an educator, theologian, and scholar was Benjamin Mays's life-project. Remaining in the South and serving as the president of Morehouse College was reflective of him doing his work. Mays knew that having one's identity grounded in their life-project, or doing their work, was perhaps the most potent weapon against the hegemony of the racial imagination. He knew that for Morehouse men, life had to be about more than battling the onslaught of racial domination and oppression, no matter how pervasive it was in the life of black and brown people. For black and brown people, identity cannot be understood only in terms of resistance to white supremacy, no matter how stubborn and ornery its presence. To do so would suggest that one really believes the lies of the racial imagination and that racism is about people of color, when in actuality, it is about the brokenness of those who have internalized and adhered to its dictates. Mays taught Morehouse students not to allow the racial imagination to define them, and that there was absolutely nothing to be gained by being defined—even in part—by the racial imagination. The racial imagination is wholly death-dealing and idolatrous.

This is how I understand the quotes by Nina Simone and Toni Morrison at the beginning of this chapter. Both of the black women's ideas point towards a self-identity that is grounded in doing your work, and not allowing others to define who you are, or engaging in the futile practice of attempting to secure the approval of those beholden to the racial imagination or trying to disprove its many lies. This governing philosophy of his life is perhaps best captured in the following reflection of Mays when he reminds us, "It must be borne in mind that the tragedy of life doesn't lie in not reaching your goal. The tragedy lies in having no goal to reach. It isn't a calamity to die with dreams unfulfilled, but it is a calamity not to dream. It is not a disaster to be unable to capture your ideal, but it is a disaster to have no ideal

---

40. Mays, *Born to Rebel*, 194–19; emphasis added, denoting what I believe was a key component of May's life-project.

to capture. It is not a disgrace not to reach the stars, but it is a disgrace to have no stars to reach for. Not failure, but low aim is sin."[41]

---

41. Mays, as quoted in "Quotable Quotes."

6

IDA B. WELLS ON WORKING THROUGH EXISTENTIAL DISAPPOINTMENT

The Power of Finding Your Voice

I am feeling so sorry for myself that the bitter tears have been coursing down my cheeks. I am wondering what a fool am I to sacrifice so much and suffer so much and work so hard for a race which will not defend itself or protect me in defending it. Not for myself alone do I weep. My heart aches for those of my race who are being immolated everyday on the alter of the white man's prejudice—hanged, shot, flayed alive and burned; over the widows and orphans made desolate; over the great bulk of the race which reads these things and whose hearts are not stirred to action of some kind on behalf of the victims; over the spirit of envy and jealousy which actuates those who can help to opposition instead of support; lastly and most of all, I weep because the manhood of the race knows itself slandered, its women and children slaughtered, its mothers, wives, sisters and daughters insulted and despoiled and traduced and still fails to assert its strength or extend its protection to those who have the right to claim it. Is mine a race of cowards?

—IDA B. WELLS

Ida B. Wells on Working Through Existential Disappointment

THE ABOVE PASSAGE PENNED by Ida B. Wells appeared in the *New York Age* on July 12, 1894. It is but one example of the intellectual, emotional, and spiritual complexity that permeates the individual and collective inner world of black subjectivity in the face of racial hatred and oppression. The multiplicity of subject matter outlined by Wells in just a few sentences is far too weighty and robust to be sustained and encapsulated by the simplicity of a racial reconciliation conversation posited by many institutions that make the decision to address issues around race and racism, but perhaps lack sufficient intellectual and spiritual capital, and even moral authority, to have effective dialogue. In this one passage, Wells expresses being overwhelmed by the human atrocities, feeling abandoned and misunderstood, isolated, morally outraged, disillusioned, and ultimately, clinically traumatized.

Ida B. Wells was arguably the leading public theologian and voice of the anti-lynching campaign at the turn of the twentieth century. Without her critical research on white racist terrorism and its nationwide campaign of lynching that propped up white supremacy, we might well be largely ignorant to this very day of the depth of the atrocities that occurred. Lynching remains a prominent historical symbol of white supremacy that was underwritten, in part, by the church in America, directly or indirectly. In the most essential expression of her personhood, Ida B. Wells was able to find her voice. Moreover, in finding her voice, she became a formidable opponent to be reckoned with, not only for those who were outright supporters of lynching (directly or indirectly through their silence), but for those who attempted to justify lynching through racist narratives of perverse black male sexuality (i.e., lynching was in response to black men raping white women).

In this chapter, I offer up a concise psychospiritual analysis of Ida B. Wells that emphasizes the strength of her authentic self in the context of racial violence and extremity. My analysis focuses on this vital question: *How did Ida B. Wells discover her authentic self and find her journalistic voice and moral protest against the public lynching of thousands of black people that became commonplace, a trend that swept the country towards the end of the nineteenth and well into the twentieth century in America?* This is an important question as many of Well's contemporaries were seduced into cooperating with the epidemic of lynching through silence, appeasement, or rationalizing and justifying its practice. How then can we look to Ida B. Wells and emulate a psychospiritual practice of living into our authentic self and finding our voice?

Before examining the psychospiritual journey that I suggest enabled Ida B. Wells to find her voice in the anti-lynching campaign, I will briefly provide a psychological profile of the culture and context of lynching in the late nineteenth and early twentieth centuries. While there is commendable research in this area, my emphasis here is more on the group psychological dynamics that gave way to public lynching. And to be sure, the prospect and reality of being lynched represented a clear and present danger that terrorized Ida B. Wells and thousands of black people. Its sole purpose was to keep black people subjugated in the American racial caste system. In the summer of 2022, I had the opportunity to visit the Legacy Museum and the National Memorial for Peace and Justice in Montgomery, Alabama, with a study group. As I walked through both exhibits and reflected on the lives of victims it sought to commemorate, as well as the history of terror that it seeks to remind us of, *it became clear to me that lynching was not carried out by individuals. Instead, lynching represented a sociopolitical apparatus that was maintained and perpetuated by entire communities.* As I shared with the group in a keynote that I delivered, *the museum and the memorial not only commemorate the past but are a current mirror into the collective soul of a nation.*

With this in mind, it is easy to imagine that the architects of lynching were monsters that we can easily identify in a crowd (either by their looks or their behavior) and then emotionally distance ourselves from them because of their vicious and evil deeds—deeds we imagine that we would never succumb to. But this is not the case. Those who were advocates of black lynching, whether by direct participation, by being a witness or silent bystander, or by passively accepting the unchecked lie that lynching was in response to black crime and, particularly, an epidemic of black men raping white women, could have represented anyone in the community. Said differently, many of those who actively or passively participated in the apparatus of lynching and torturing black people were *card-carrying Christians and supposedly upstanding citizens of the American democratic experiment. That is to say, they were regular people.* In another place, I give an example of the group psychology of lynching in America through the public dialogue between Jane Addams (hailed as one of the prominent figures in women' suffrage and social work in the early twentieth century) and Ida B. Wells. Jane Addams was against lynching and lynch mobs as an alternative to formal legal remedies. But she attempted to justify them on moral grounds, with her justifications clearly being a product of the racial imagination. Ida B. Wells publicly repudiated Addams's position.

> Jane Addams is (deservingly) recognized and celebrated for her work in women's suffrage, feminism, and the establishment of Chicago's Hull House—a settlement house for European immigrants. Nevertheless, Addams's notable regard for human experience falls short in her examination of lynching in the Jim Crow

South and her explanation of why so many Black men were being victimized. According to Addams, the epidemic of lynching was in reaction to an assumed rise in crime committed by Black males. She further argued that Southerners had a right to self-govern, to determine how to deal with this alleged rise in crime, that criminals should not be hanged without a trial by jury, and that the primary mistake of Southerners was the false assumption that "criminality can be suppressed and terrorized by exhibitions of brutal punishment; that crime can be prevented by cruelty." Her entire analysis stems from the implicit and unconscious criminalization of Black males. To support her position, Addams grants robust hermeneutical privilege to the supporters of lynching (participants, observers, and bystanders).[1]

Jane Addams is but one example (and common practice) of the psychological splitting—individually and collectively—that is necessary for a culture of lynching to flourish. Without a doubt, Jane Addams is a commendable public figure and upstanding citizen with a body of works to support her stature. Nevertheless, that same Jane Addams is apologetic towards the sentiments of those who partake in lynching. *That is to say, Jane Addams actually humanizes the lynch mobs.* But she lacks the capacity to humanize the black victims of lynching and the millions who live in fear of lynching. This is because the racial imagination is incapable of humanizing the people it has objectified, and bodies it has raced. Psychological splitting is an effective, albeit maladaptive way to address the cognitive dissonance caused by upholding human rights for one group of people and being empathic towards those who inflict human atrocities upon another group of people. No doubt there are many who would come to the defense of Jane Addams based on her work at Hull House and make the claim that she was a good person. And indeed, she was. But her goodness is beside the point being made here. Jane Addams is a perfect example of a good person beguiled by the racial imagination. Ida B. Wells's public rebuff of Addams's toxic rationale is clear, concise, and compelling:

> It is unspeakably infamous to put thousands of people to death without a trial by jury; it adds to that infamy to charge that these victims were moral monsters, when, in fact, four-fifths of them were not so accused even by the fiends who murdered them ... It is this assumption, this absolutely unwarrantable assumption, that vitiates every suggestion which it inspires Miss Addams to make. It is the same baseless assumption which influences

---

1. D. G. Gibson, "When Empathy," 614. Addams's quote comes from Addams, "Respect for the Law," 18.

> ninety-nine out of every one hundred persons who discuss this question. Among many thousand editorial clippings I have received in the past five years, ninety-nine per cent discuss the question upon the presumption that lynchings are the desperate effort of the Southern people to protect their women from black monsters, and while the large majority condemn lynching, the condemnation is tempered with a plea for the lyncher—that human nature gives way under such awful provocation and that the mob, insane for the moment, must be pitied as well as condemned.[2]

This represents the sociopolitical environment that Ida B. Wells found herself in. It was the environment that I was reminded of as I walked among the six-foot monuments at the National Memorial for Peace and Justice in Montgomery. We are reminded that it is not about an environment of monsters, but the human capacity to engage in monstrosities and crimes against humanity. It represents the telos of unchecked human animus in the form of racial hatred and oppression. And it was in this environment that Ida B. Wells labored to find her voice.

In this chapter, I suggest that Ida B. Wells found her voice through a process of de-idealization or what we can also understand as devaluation. The *New Oxford American Dictionary* defines idealization as "the action of regarding or representing something as perfect or better than in reality." Idealization is a psychological practice, consciously or unconsciously, that all human beings engage in, for better or worse. Davidson offers a helpful comparison between idealization and reverence, with the former representing more of an unrealistic projection of perfection or flawlessnes onto another, and the latter representing more of a bestowal of admiration upon an adorned person, place, or object. For Davidson, idealization and reverence are closely associated and even intertwined as "research on emotionality has indicated that reverence has mostly to do with a sense of awe in the presence of mystery, the so called 'numinous' . . . [and that] it also appears at times of contemplation in the meaning of life . . . [and that] in the presence of a wiser, so-called more realized, or more enlightened other, it manifests as regard or admiration."[3] According to Davidson, the clear risk and downside of idealization is that it "is an extension of one's own narcissism and search for a perfect self, and can in some cases become pathological."[4] Amy Schaffer juxtaposes idealization to what she refers to as a person's "dark

---

2. Wells, "Lynching and the Excuse," 1133–34.
3. Davidson, "Idealization and Reverence," 128.
4. Davidson, "Idealization and Reverence," 129.

side." According to Schaffer idealization is "a form of human relatedness in which the perception of another is characterized by the downplaying of the undesirable and the inflating of the positive. What is undesirable, the patient's dark side, may be comprised of traits deemed objectionable culturally and/or in the personal histories of the members of the therapy dyad." But Schaffer warns that taken in the extreme, "an over-benign view of a patient may do great harm . . . [and] in the most dramatic cases it can lead the analyst into overlooking severe pathology."[5] While both Davidson and Schaffer are referencing a clinical context, their observations are nevertheless valuable when we consider how idealization causes us to overestimate a person, place, institution, or even a life-script or presupposition that we have conformed our lives to. When the veracity of an idealization is compromised, it precipitates existential disappointment. And as we will shortly see, Ida B. Wells had to travail a series of disappointments in the journey towards finding her own voice.

Heinz Kohut perhaps offers the most vivid description of what idealizing achieves for us from and psychological and emotional perspective. According to him, we idealize cultural symbols and icons as well, For Kohut, the essence of idealization is:

> To have somebody strong and knowledgeable and calm around with whom I can temporarily merge [emotionally], who will uplift me when I am upset. Originally, that is an actual uplifting of the baby by the mother; later that becomes an uplifting feeling of looking at a great man or woman and enjoying him or her, of following in his or her footsteps, of a great idea being uplifting, or a wonderful piece of music, etc. That is extremely important. And when I talk about cultural selfobjects [i.e., a person, place, or thing], which is the replica of the culture for the group self of what occurs in individual development, I think that these two basic needs are also present [to be accepted or know you bring value to another, and to be uplifted], perhaps collectively.[6]

The importance of what Kohut is observing (as he reflects retrospectively on the role of individual and collective psychology in the Holocaust) cannot be overstated. For our purposes here, we see that cultural icons, symbols, organizations (sacred and secular), and institutions (religious organizations, denominations, colleges, universities, etc.), can all be idealized or revered by individuals and groups as a way to be emotionally uplifted, especially in times of despair. But as Amy Schaffer recognized, such idealizations can

---

5. Schaffer, "Analyst's Idealization of Patient," 604–5.
6. H. Kohut, *Self Psychology and Humanities*, 226–27.

go too far to the point of pathology: our idealization causes us to become enablers of intellectual sloth and moral depravity, and it can launch us into chronic despair and depression.

In my own project, I describe idealization as the externalization of our internal need to be associated with something *we perceive as greater than ourselves*. Sometimes in idealization, we will project onto another person (place or object) our personal desires for virtue, goodness, excellence, strength, courage, or uprightness, all areas we may perceive that we have deficits. The key to any idealization is that we form an emotional bond with the constructed image that we have projected onto another individual. It is this emotional bond, the attempt to associate with or psychically merge with the target of our projection, that becomes the source of the inevitable disappointment we will experience when the idealized object fails to deliver on what we imagined it promised. The opposite of this, de-idealization or devaluation, occurs when a person witnesses or experiences life in a way that reorients *more towards reality* distorted images or perceptions about people, worldviews, or life experiences. Said differently, devaluation reflects a psychospiritual process of working through spiritual and emotional disappointment. It is an indispensable form of self-work that leads to enhanced psychospiritual maturity.

Ida B. Wells found her voice as she worked through the disappointments she experienced, disappointment precipitated by the process of de-idealization. And in her quest to undermine the terror of lynching, her disappointments would be great. Working through existential disappointment, as opposed to repressing or ignoring them, is a consequential activity in the process of self-care and self-reflexivity that is necessary for healing and human flourishing. Minimizing or repressing existential disappointment(s) is not evidence of maturity. To the contrary, it reflects the fear of coming to terms with the loss of a dream, a mistaken worldview, or an idealization that has fueled a personal passion. Engaging in grief work that strives to come to terms with existential disappointment strengthens a person's core self and enables them to differentiate their noble ideas, values, and aspirations, from that of others they may have idealized, and then build up and strengthen those noble ideas, values, and aspirations. Ida B. Wells's autobiographical writings suggest she did just that: Wells worked through the inevitable disappointments and setbacks she would experience in the pursuit of her life-project in a way that enabled her to find her voice and live into her authentic self. The gradual untangling of all that we have idealized (people, culture, institutions, worldviews, life-commandments and scripts, etc.) represents a maturation of our psychospiritual growth process. As we divert psychospiritual energy away from the false images we have projected onto others, we are now in the position to channel such energy to the benefit of our own personhood, resulting in the capacity to form our own ideas, goals, values, and ambitions to strive towards.

Through the process of devaluation, Ida B. Wells engaged in a painful, albeit necessary process of recognizing, and then coming to terms with the shortcomings, failures, sins, and brokenness of those she had idealized as heroes in her own mind—heroes she sought to emulate. As with any human being, it can be argued that some of her idealizations of people in her immediate circle (i.e., religious leaders, Frederick Douglass, etc.) were unfair and represented only a projection of Wells's own need to be associated with perfection and greatness. In other instances, her idealizations were well within what could be considered reasonable and expectable, but she had to come to terms with human frailty and imperfection. As such, the excerpt from the article "Are We a Race of Cowards" must be seen, in part, through the lens of Wells working through existential disappointment—a process that all leaders, practitioners, and scholars of freedom must travail. For Wells, it represented a painful process of accepting the fact that those whom she had idealized as heroes—perhaps by way of possessing noble courage and virtue or being principled and ethical—in some cases fell woefully short and were instead only human. In the process of devaluation, Wells came to terms with the humanness (along with its brokenness and vices) of those she had idealized within her interior world. She could now divert the psychological and spiritual energy she expended to idealizing and believing in false images of others to now believing in herself, believing in the strength of her ideas and values, and now focussing on the beauty of becoming Ida B. Wells.

A BRIEF COMMENT ON IDA B. WELLS AND TRAUMA

An assessment of how Ida B. Wells *potentially* found her voice requires that we examine her first-person autobiographic accounts, in part, through a traumatological lens. Failing to account for the human element in the story of Ida B. Well, or for our purposes here, what we now can better understand as the psychological trauma she endured, predisposes us to romanticize her context and objectify her personhood by idealizing who she was. And in some sense, the component of the human situation we now understand as clinical trauma represents a critical aspect in the lives of each of the titans covered in this text. When viewed through the lens of trauma, we are compelled to not only be aware of the presence of tragedy and pain in the life and body of the protagonist of our historical analysis, but also to question the larger community and context in which the violence against the protagonist was fashioned and imposed. Viewing autobiography through the lens of trauma forces the reader to question and reassess versions of history that have been uncritically accepted in service to ideologies of Western innocence, exceptionalism, and divine election. This is perhaps one of the most notable innovations of Judith Herman in her work on psychological trauma: even as a scientific researcher, medical doctor, and psychiatrist, Herman recognizes the irreducible link between psychological trauma and the moral universe. In other words, while psychological discourse does not have a formal category that attempts to describe the nature evil, Herman does not deny the reality of evil that precipitates psychological trauma. Because of its relevance to interpreting the narratives of the titans through a traumatological lens, I quote Herman at length:

> To study psychological trauma is to come face to face with human vulnerability in the natural world and with the capacity for evil in human nature. To study psychological trauma means bearing witness to horrible events. When the events are natural disasters or "acts of God," those who bear witness sympathize readily with the victims. But when the traumatic events are of human design, those who bear witness are caught in the conflict between victim and perpetrator. *It is morally impossible to remain neutral in this conflict. The bystander is forced to take sides.*[7]

Yet the traumatological lens is often disregarded in the annals of anti-racism literature. This can lead to egregious romanticized interpretations of the life-narratives of historical personalities like Ida B. Wells, a mistake repeatedly made in the halls of the ivory tower. Idealizing historical figures and romanticizing their lives undermines the educative potential of the black autobiographic genre. Moreover, as observed by Judith Herman, when studying traumatizing topics like lynching and racial terrorism, the reader cannot emotionally remain as a bystander—a position many quietly (and comfortably) default to when presented with the spiritually redemptive opportunity to contend with the history and legacy of racial animus and violence within their own ranks and how it continues to affect the individual and collective world of the community. Instead, perpetual silence bolsters spiritual malady and undermines the potential for building moral agency:

> It is very tempting to take the side of the perpetrator. All the perpetrator asks is that the bystander do nothing. He appeals to the universal desire to see, hear, and speak no evil. The victim,

---

7. Herman, *Trauma and Recovery*, 7.

on the contrary, asks the bystander to share the burden of pain. The victim demands action, engagement, and remembering.[8]

Without a traumatological lens that compels the reader of Wells's autobiography to take sides when presented with human atrocity, the student of this history is potentially engaged in nothing more than the practice of vanity in the form of data consumption that ossifies the soul's capacity for moral agency. Engaging with the autobiographic, first-person accounts of Ida B. Wells demands that the reader-bystander take sides with those who were traumatized by the anti-black racial terror and lynching that swept the nation in the early twentieth century. Anything less represents a misreading of her work. Commenting on the arduous journey to write her seminal text *Beloved*, Toni Morrison warns of the pitfall of intellectual arrogance when a reader or writer has an abundance of data at their disposal but fails to use their imagination to personalize the data in a way to become intimate with it, and to expose the human element revealed by the data. For Morrison then, education that reflects integrity requires that "we move from data to information to knowledge to wisdom . . . [and] separating one from the other, being able to distinguish among and between them, that is, knowing the limitations and the danger of exercising one without the others, while respecting each category of intelligence, is generally what serious education is about."[9] She warns of the seductiveness of data for the sake of data, arguing that in an effortless way we can "assume that data is really knowledge . . . or that information is, indeed, wisdom . . . or that knowledge can exist without data . . . [and] we can forget that wisdom without knowledge . . . [or] wisdom without any data, is just a hunch."[10] Morrison's warning represents an ever-present danger in the halls of the ivory tower where the collection and consumption of data (history, narratives, biographies, etc.) about ethnic minority groups risks becoming a toxic form of narcissistic colonial surveillance and gazing designed to culturally subjugate those perceived as *the other*.

Especially within theological education (and by extension the church), there exists a notion that the mere consumption of historical or contemporary data about another person or group—in and of itself—translates to knowledge and wisdom capable of bridging the harmful psychospiritual gap created by the sinful intentional neglect of cultural, ethnic, and gender diversity. Data consumption about *the other* becomes the communal evidence and symbol of being multicultural when in actuality it reflects a

8. Herman, *Trauma and Recovery*, 7–8.
9. Morrison, "Source of Self-Regard," 307.
10. Morrison, "Source of Self-Regard," 307.

self-aggrandizing attempt at finding a *right way to continue wrongdoing*. Attempting to achieve diversity by merely reading about it, or by consuming intellectual resources written by black and brown authors and scholars, creates an illusion that a community is engaged in the work of anti-racism and diversity, and undermines the divine mandate for a Pentecostal community—not in the sense of the Pentecostal religious tradition but of a community that intentionally reflects the radical multiplicity we see on the day of Pentecost in Acts 2. This kind of thinking (that reading about diversity satisfies the moral mandate for diversity) is self-deceiving and a costly error for any institution, especially when that institution is the church. To be clear, engaging the work of anti-lynching was traumatizing work for Ida B. Wells. And if her work was traumatizing, then a traumatological lens requires us to *enter into history* with Wells and the victimized—*similarly to what Jesus did for humanity in the nativity event*—and side with the thousands who were tortured and lynched, as opposed to remaining outside of history in the abyss of mindlessness and spiritual sloth. This is the value of the traumatological lens in the enslaved narratives or the black autobiographical genres; it humanizes the protagonist and brings the reader into history.

Dehumanizing the victims of lynching by remaining outside of history and attempting either to rationalize the actions of lynch mobs and advocates of lynching or to humanize their motivations was in part what Jane Addams and many others were doing in responses to the terror on black lives: they were taking the side of the perpetrators of evil in claiming lynching was in response to black men—*en masse*—sexually assaulting white women and children. The unfounded claim represented the perverse sexualization of black bodies found in the unchecked racial imagination—an imagination that still runs amuck and animalizes black and brown people to this very day. And many of those taking the side of the lynch mobs were Christian. In one of his final public lectures that took place at the Metropolitan AME Church in Washington, DC, Frederick Douglass takes on the burgeoning terror of lynching, which in no small part was carried out by self-professed Christians. He laments, "We claim to be a Christian country and a highly civilized nation, yet, I fearlessly affirm that there is nothing in the history of savages to surpass the blood chilling horrors and fiendish excesses perpetrated against the colored people by the so-called enlightened and Christian people of the South."[11] But the scandal was not limited to the South (as many like to believe to this day). In the same lecture, Douglass goes on to quote the words of Frances Willard, the head of the Women's Christian Temperance Union (WCTU), as she perpetuated the same myths that

---

11. Douglass, *Lessons of the Hour*, 5.

fueled the epidemic of lynching. According to Douglass, Frances Willard says, "I pity the Southerner. The problem on their hands is immeasurable. The colored race multiplies like the locusts of Egypt. The safety of woman, of childhood, of the home, is menaced in a thousand localities at this moment, so that men dare not go beyond the sight of their own roof tree."[12] In her autobiography, Ida. B. Wells criticizes both Frances Willard and Rev. D. L. Moody for their appeasement, and in some cases outright defense, of lynching. Seldom do we hear of this side of Moody in modern reflections on his preaching. Nevertheless, when reflecting on the apathy of Willard and Moody on the topic of lynching, Wells claims that "neither of those great exponents of Christianity in our country had ever spoken out in condemnation of lynching, but seemed on the contrary disposed to overlook that fashionable pastime of the South."[13] In a more critical observation of Frances Willard after she had traveled in the South to promote the WCTU and then was interviewed about the trip by the New York Voice (a Northern newspaper), Wells writes about the interview observing of Willard that "she practically condoned lynching . . . [and that] every Negro newspaper in the South quoted and criticized that interview." Wells ultimately concluded that "I could not truthfully say that Miss Willard had ever said anything to condemn lynching; on the contrary, she had seemed to condone it in her famous interview after returning from her first visit in the South."[14] In the cases of both Wells and Douglass, they are protesting the silence, complicity, apathy, and appeasement of the church on the topic and practice of burning alive, lynching, and mutilating black people.

But more than this, Douglass and Wells are protesting the gullibility of the church to willingly internalize the myth that an entire group of people—namely black men—are innate sexual predators who represent an inherent threat to white women and children, and that white men—by necessity—have the right, and are justified, in summarily executing any black person they perceive as a threat. This delusional thinking, and by extension lynching, represents the death-dealing fallout of the racial imagination when left to its own devices. Evil thrives on silence and apathy. Moreover, one cannot help but see the irony of this racist delusion, as generations of black people who lived throughout the slavocracy were subjected women and children being raped and sexually abused, habitually, by the controlling power structure, and such actions were ignored, justified, and even religiously sacralized, as black people were seen either as nonhuman, the property of white people,

---

12. Douglass, *Lessons of the Hour*, 7.
13. Wells, *Crusade for Justice*, 123.
14. Wells, *Crusade for Justice*, 124.

or the objects of white gratification. From a psychodynamic perspective, at a group level, this myth of black men raping white women and children (as the justification for lynch mobs) represents notion of projection, where the individual or group psychically projects onto another person (or group) unwanted or deplorable elements they know (consciously or unconsciously) to be within themselves. Said differently, the evil that the lynch mob (or those sympathetic to the cause of lynching) perceived as coming from *the other* (i.e., black people) actually represented a psychospiritual cancer that resided within the psyche of the lynch mob, and by extension, those who were sympathetic to the fears of the communities involved in lynching. Even in their writings, Douglass and Wells were sure to point out that this does not mean there were no bad actors in black culture. But there are bad actors in every culture. The myth that underwrote the regime of lynching terror in the first half of the twentieth century—that lynch mobs were in response to an epidemic of sexual assault against white women and children by black men—was nothing more than racial delusion.

As alluded to earlier in this work, the power of psychohistory is that it invites us to consider the psychospiritual condition of the individual-self and the collective-self that gave rise to the historical events in question. Consequently, while many could look at Ida B. Wells's body of work—both activism and scholarship—and claim that because lynching occurred in the past, studying Wells is irrelevant for today (an asinine but common claim that is often levied towards black history), psychohistory compels us to ask if the psychospiritual condition of the collective-self that precipitated lynching is still present with us today, and if so, in what manifestation. How does the presence of black and brown bodies arouse abject emotions in the psychic space of groups, institutions, and the collective psychic space of the democratic experiment? It's naïve to believe that the church has magically moved beyond the racial stereotypes and psychospiritual state that fueled terror in the twentieth century, and that the racial imagination does not continue to plague the Christian psychic space. Without the intentional recognition of the collective psychospiritual sickness of racism and an intervention for healing, restitution, and justice, *the passage of time does not heal all wounds and cure the sickness of racial hatred and animus.*

WHY GROUPS RESONATE WITH EVIL: A TRAUMATOLOGICAL EXPLANATION

Why was it so easy for people to sympathize with the passions of the lynch mobs in the early twentieth century? Why is it so natural for individuals and groups either to justify or sympathize with the position of the violent? Why are the rationalizations or moralizations of those who oppress and inflict violence more readily believed and accepted than the protests, reactions, and rage of those who have been injured and maimed by the former? These questions become more disturbing when they are asked of those who profess Christian faith. We are compelled to ask why it was so easy for Christians to function as bystanders and align themselves with the passions and fears of the proponents of lynching? Today, the word *victim* has been stigmatized and levied at people who dare to protest evil and injustice, as if their personal character and integrity is somehow lacking or flawed. Moreover, from the perspective of those who have been injured (i.e., victimized), the ability to repress or deny the resulting pain and injury is seen as a mark of maturity—a red badge of courage. It is akin to being shot with a gun, being victimized by the resulting wound, and then being criticized by the onlookers for bleeding, or being upset with oneself for bleeding. How should we understand the affinity towards perpetrators of violence, especially when this affinity emanates from the church?

In part, I suggest this historical propensity of the church to be sympathetic to systemic transgression is psychologically compensatory in nature, resulting in the entrenchment of apathy within the Christian imaginary. To put it another way, in striving to look above the suffering of those whom Scripture declares are our neighbors reflects a group attempt to maintain the illusion of a pure Christianity, and a safe and ordered universe—an illusion propped up by the ideology of Christian triumphalism. In another writing, I go so far as to suggest that Christian triumphalism is the antithesis of trauma recovery.[15] To support this argument, I reflect on the passage of Scripture in the book of Job, suggesting that the question posed by Satan to God of *does Job fear God for nothing* is an existential question for all Christian to grapple with. Even for the most altruistic self-sacrificing adherent of the faith, it is ego intertwined with naïveté to think that people are committed to God or religion with no expectation of some temporal advantage or benefit—even if that benefit has nothing to do with wealth and material, but simply to circumvent, to some degree, human suffering or misfortune. This entitled presupposition is at the heart of Christian triumphalism. Then, borrowing from the parable of the good Samaritan, I suggest that while the religious leaders may have bypassed the injured man on the road because of misaligned priorities, it is more likely that they crossed the road to avoid the beaten man because they didn't want to get too close to human suffering. That is to say, the closer we get to the suffering of others, the more we are

---

15. D. Gibson, "Christian Triumphalism."

reminded of our own human frailty and finiteness, as well as the arbitrary nature of the cosmos. Close proximity to evil and suffering runs the risk of undermining the ideology of Christian triumphalism, as it compels us to consider if we really serve God for nothing (whether or not we are ready to answer the question with integrity).

Individuals who have experienced psychological trauma and are suffering from PTSD can often find themselves being unwelcomed neighbors in the church, as the traumatological lens compels the church community to grapple with the ideology of Christian triumphalism and to expose its false promises. Being in close proximity to fellow adherents who suffer from PTSD reminds the larger community of its own finiteness and human frailty and that being a Christian does not offer us any competitive advantage when it comes to circumventing human suffering and tragedy. Similarly to the narrative of Job, righteousness and human suffering or tragedy are not mutually exclusive categories; they are frightfully independent. As a consequence, what many victims of trauma and PTSD run the risk of experiencing from their immediate faith community, and then the larger Christian community, is *psychological pressure to behave and exist as if the evil that precipitated the trauma, or the very trauma itself, does not exist.* In many cases, this results in the local faith group, or the larger Christian community, emotionally sympathizing with the perpetrators of violence or rationalizing the supposed necessity of systems of oppression, rather than sympathizing with the victims of trauma. The communal action is psychologically compensatory. That is to say, pressuring the victims of trauma to just get over it indemnifies the church community from having to acknowledge the false promises of triumphalism, and to own up to the fact that our faith is not as pure and altruistic as we would like to imagine. Responding to the question the Satan posed to God—*perhaps we do fear God for something.* I capture these thoughts in the conclusion of the article:

> Individuals who have been traumatized (such as military veterans, survivors of rape, or refugees fleeing terror and violence) will generally say that there are two types of people in the world: those who have been traumatized, and those who have not been traumatized. In the Church, traumatized individuals typically discover that they have a narrative that is antithetical to the non-traumatized narratives of Christian triumphalism (i.e., the stories with good endings that we like to hear on Sunday morning). Whereas the traumatized Army veteran is living in a world where she has first-hand experience of people being shot or even blown up, her narrative runs counter to uninterrogated

> narratives and platitudes in a faith community that argue God protects those that God loves.
>
> Often, victims of trauma will hear questions like "do you want to be a victim forever?" or "do you want to be a conqueror?" However, if the community of faith actually knew what it was like to suffer from PTSD, they would know that victims of trauma were doing their best to recover. Religious platitudes and loaded questions aimed in the direction of trauma victims suggests that in many ways, the Church does indeed fear God for something—and that something (albeit an illusion) is the expectation of safety and orderliness . . . These actions taken by an uninformed faith community imply that for those who have been traumatized (like victims of sexual assault in the Church) can no longer be neighbors, but simply visitors entertained by cursory expressions of hospitality. The reality and lived experiences of the traumatized represents a frightening narrative that destabilizes the drama of Christian triumphalism. And the hallucinogenic power that triumphalism has over a church can make it an unsafe place for those suffering from trauma.¹⁶

In part, I suggest this was the nature of psychosocial malaise that Ida B. Wells contended with in the church, where the ideology of Christian triumphalism seduced religious figures like D. L. Moody and Frances Willard into remaining indifferent about the epidemic of lynching, or to sympathize with the fears and passions of the mob, as both choices were easier than coming to terms with the reality that the church itself was intertwined with (and in some cases the architect of) the history and ongoing legacy of the slavocracy and racial terror. When leadership or power structures within the church summarily reject anti-racism literature on a broad and often uninformed basis that such literature is not Christian (as if they have a monopoly on who gets to claim that title), it is code for *the text makes them uncomfortable* or that it was not written by someone within their accepted ranks (i.e., *it was not written by one of ours*). It reflects the individual and group practice of denial and self-deception, refusing to recognize that racial animus is not merely tangential to the history of the church, but has been central to its existence in America. Moreover, it fails to recognize the death-dealing intersection between Christian triumphalism and the ongoing legacy of racism that continues to exist in the church. As a matter of pastoral psychology, the group failure to accept this truth undermines healing and any meaningful chance of spiritual freedom.

16. D. Gibson, "Christian Triumphalism," 10–11.

Judith Herman's observation of the link between society, culture, and trauma remains an underappreciated component of her groundbreaking work in crystallizing the nature of trauma and PTSD. As a psychiatrist, her insight into the connection between the perpetrators of evil, bystanders, and trauma recovery in the broader society are especially useful in helping us to imagine what Ida B. Wells may have been contending with. Herman's observation remains relevant today. I quote her at length to demonstrate how a traumatological lens aids us in understanding how groups and institutions sympathize with perpetrators and shun the traumatized:

> In order to escape accountability for his crimes, the perpetrator does everything in his power to promote forgetting. Secrecy and silence are the perpetrator's first line of defense. If secrecy fails, the perpetrator attacks the credibility of his victim. If he cannot silence her absolutely, he tries to make sure that no one listens. To this end, he marshals an impressive array of arguments, from the most blatant denial to the most sophisticated and elegant rationalization. After every atrocity one can expect to hear the same predictable apologies: it never happened; the victim lies; the victim exaggerates; the victim brought it upon herself; and in any case it is time to forget the past and move on. The more powerful the perpetrator, the greater is his prerogative to name and define reality, and the more completely his arguments prevail . . . [Consequently, the] perpetrator's arguments prove irresistible when the bystander faces them in isolation. Without a supportive social environment, the bystander usually succumbs to the temptation to look the other way.[17]

In order to understand Ida B. Wells, we must understand the psychosocial milieu in which she was entrenched. Otherwise, we run the risk of misunderstanding the affective state that informed her writings, such as the emotional excerpt at the beginning of this chapter. Bearing witness to the horror of lynching, coupled with laying the intellectual groundwork for the anti-lynching campaign, was traumatizing work for Wells. Moreover, challenging religious and secular power structures that had come to sympathize with the cause of lynching either by internalizing the myth of nefarious black male sexuality or by becoming indifferent to black suffering under the regime of white supremacist terrorism would prove to be an impossibly disappointing journey for Wells—as it would be for any freedom fighter. Judith Herman's description of the interplay between the perpetrators of evil, the victims of trauma, and the bystanders who witness it accurately depicts

---

17. Herman, *Trauma and Recovery*, 8.

the psychosocial environment in which Ida B. Wells was entrenched, and the context in which we must understand her personhood and her body of work. Decades before the concept of psychological trauma began to appear in the literature, Wells understood the irreducible connection between apathetic bystanders and the outgrowth of the gratuitous evil of lynching when she argued that "the men and women in the South who disapprove of lynching and remain silent on the perpetration of such outrages, are particeps criminis, accomplices, accessories before and after the fact, equally guilty with the actual law-breakers who would not persist if they did not know that neither the law nor militia would be employed against them."[18]

Perhaps the most compelling evidence that Wells was afflicted with psychological trauma and its post-traumatic effects was when she gave a public address at Lyric Hall on October 5, 1892. At this event, sponsored by her fellow black female contemporaries in New York, Wells recounts (in her public lecture) the horror of her friends being lynched in Memphis, and the destruction of her newspaper business by the lynch mob. What Wells describes as "an exhibition of weakness" when she was overcome with tears of grief during the lecture is perhaps what is clinically understood today as post-traumatic intrusion. In psychological trauma, the shock of the traumatic event is imprinted on the psyche of its victim, where the emotional memory of the event has a tendency to intrude (like an unwanted burglar) without warning on the person who has suffered the trauma.

> *Although every detail of that horrible lynching affair was imprinted on my memory*, I had to commit it all to paper, and so got up to read my story on that memorable occasion. As I described the cause of the trouble at home and my mind went back to the scenes of the struggle, to the thought of the friends who were scattered throughout the country, a feeling of loneliness and homesickness for the days and the friends that were gone came over me and I felt the tears coming.
>
> *A panic seized* me. I was afraid that I was going to make a scene and spoil all those dear good women had done for me. I kept saying to myself that whatever happened I must not break down, and so I kept on reading. I had left my handkerchief on the seat behind me and therefore could not wipe away the tears which were coursing down my cheeks. The women were all back of me on the platform and could not see my plight. Nothing in my voice, it seemed, gave them an inkling of the true state of affairs. Only those in the audience could see the tears dropping. At last I put my hand behind me and beckoned even as I

18. Wells-Barnett, *Southern Horrors*, 21.

> kept reading. Mrs. Matthews, the chairman, came forward and I asked her for my handkerchief. She brought it and I wiped my nose and streaming face, but I kept on reading the story which they had come to hear.
>
> *I was mortified that I had not been able to prevent such an exhibition of weakness. It came on me unawares. It was the only time in all those trying months that I had so yielded to personal feelings. That it should come at a time when I wanted to be at my best in order to show my appreciation of the splendid things those women had done!* They were giving me tangible evidence that although my environment had changed I was still surrounded by kind hearts. After all these years I still have a feeling of chagrin over that exhibition of weakness. Whatever my feelings, I am not given to public demonstrations. And only once before in all my life had I given way to woman's weakness in public.[19]

Well's recounting of her experience at Lyric Hall perfectly fits the clinical understanding of intrusion in PTSD. And similarly to how many victims of trauma experience their traumatic symptoms, Wells unfortunately experienced her symptom as "an exhibition of weakness." But it was not weakness. Wells was being human. Moreover, I suggest that in Lyric Hall, Wells experienced a welcoming community that was affectively attuned to her personhood and the world of terror in which she lived. She was surrounded by like-minded black women who could empathize with her experience. This was perhaps one of the first environments in which Wells found herself where she didn't have to expend inordinate amounts of emotional energy simply to justify her womanhood and humanity or prove the veracity of her body of work and her view of the world. An empathic community is an essential component of trauma recovery.

Articulating trauma through the matrix of the larger community, in part, represents the innovation of Judith Herman's work on trauma. A discussion of trauma is inseparable from the narrative that describes the traumatic event, and the subsequent response of the larger community. Herman describes elements of post-traumatic stress disorder in a manner that better prepares caregivers to empathically care for those who suffer from the ailment. What is often overlooked in her work, however, is her systematizing of trauma. Instead of locating trauma and the hope of recovery exclusively in the experience of the victim, Herman calls for us to recognize the culpability and responsibility of the broader community. For Herman, traumatological discourse not only reflects a dialogic between victim and perpetrator, but necessarily reflects a tripartite engagement between victim, perpetrator, and

---

19. Wells, *Crusade for Justice*, 95–96; emphasis added.

community. The resulting narrative from this tripartite engagement is what is important as it relates to trauma recovery. Herman argues:

> Sharing the traumatic experience with others is a precondition for the restitution of a sense of a meaningful world. In this process, the survivor seeks assistance not only from those closest to her but also from the wider community. The response of the community has a powerful influence on the ultimate resolution of the trauma. Restoration of the breach between the traumatized person and the community depends, first, upon public acknowledgment of the traumatic event and, second, upon some form of community action. Once it is publicly recognized that a person has been harmed, the community must take action to assign responsibility for the harm and to repair the injury. These two responses—recognition and restitution—are necessary to rebuild the survivor's sense of order and justice.[20]

Ida B. Wells experienced elements of this when she gave her public address at Lyric Hall to hundreds of her fellow black sisters.

WORKING THROUGH EXISTENTIAL DISAPPOINTMENT

My contention in this chapter has been that Ida B. Wells was able to find her voice and personhood by working through the existential disappointment in her life as opposed to ignoring or repressing it. That disappointment, in part, stemmed from the process of de-idealization (or devaluation). Wells, like any person, demonstrated a propensity to idealize people, institutions, or various cultural symbols. As human beings, all of our idealizations reflect the externalization of our internal need to be close to what we perceive as perfection or ideal. The object of our idealizations will inevitably fail to deliver on what we perceived they promised to deliver in terms of our expectation of greatness and perfection. Sometimes the idealization we impose on others (be it a person or an institution) is unreasonable and unfair, as it reflects our own enfeebled self and our need to be associated with a perfection we have not attained or are unwilling to work towards. In other instances, our idealizations of others fall within the realm of reason and reflect legitimate expectations, but still lack an element of reality, as our ideals fail to take into consideration the human condition, sin, and depravity. Because both of her parents died of yellow fever when she was just a teenager, and she took on the responsibility of caring for her younger siblings in a racially

---

20. Herman, *Trauma and Recovery*, 70.

oppressive environment, it would not be unreasonable for Wells to manifest idealization needs as a way of calming her own internal anxiety. Any person in Well's position would yearn to connect with something beyond a profound acquaintance with tragedy, loss, grief, and the traumatizing legacy of the slavocracy. In some measure, idealization represented a path towards alleviating the threat of despair. Here, I suggest that Ida B. Wells was compelled to work through existential disappointment in three categories: (1) disappointment related to idealizing the human spirit's capacity to be guided by a moral compass, (2) disappointment related to idealizing religious institutions, and (3) disappointment related to idealizing prominent people in her life.

Ida B. Wells's idealization of the human capacity to be governed by a moral compass took a major blow during her anti-lynching work. Her body of work in terms of advocacy, education, speeches, and writings is voluminous, and reflected a commitment to building up the human spirit, not only for black people but for people of all races and backgrounds. Her writings in relation to ant-lynching was extensive. Based on this, it is not beyond the pale to assume Wells believed that by appealing to reason, facts, and logic, she could compel the democratic experiment towards rejecting the bold-faced lie that black men raping white women was the reason for mob violence and lynching. Objectifying black sexuality was (and remains) a sweet spot in the racial imagination. Even Frederick Douglass, who was very selective in using his own name and reputation to affirm others, publicly commended, in writing, the veracity and comprehensive nature of Wells research, stating that while "I have spoken [about lynching] . . . you give us what you know and testify from actual knowledge . . . [and] have dealt with the facts with cool, painstaking fidelity and left those naked uncontradicted facts to speak for themselves."[21] In the first lines of her publication *The Red Record*, Wells is clear that she is appealing to students of sociology. She is often overlooked as being a trailblazer of contemporary research in the field of sociology.

It is suggested here that Wells idealized the capacity of the human spirit to act morally and justly by way of being educated with facts and truth. She believed that if the public was armed with the factual truths about lynching, it would respond with a modicum of morality and justice. Instead, Ida B. Wells was met with indifference and gaslighting from her political and religious contemporaries. She was made to believe that she was somehow misguided in her understanding of the situation and that the lynching of black people was morally justified. Like many freedom fighters and lovers

---

21. Wells, *Red Record*, 1.

of humanity (both past and present), Wells believed that the tolerance of racial terrorism was, in part, due to lack of knowledge, and that if people were given incremental knowledge, they would not tolerate mob violence and lynching. But this did not happen, and it was a source of major de-idealization and existential disappointment for Well—a frustration that she had to work through.

There are several examples of Wells de-idealizing the notion of the human spirit to act morally. For example, after her friends in Memphis were lynched for no other reason than being successful businessmen, and then her newspaper business burned to the ground because of her anti-lynching work, Wells was among those community leaders who encouraged black residents to flee Memphis. She had given up on appealing to common sense and morality among the racist establishment in Memphis. Moreover, it was after her devaluation of an idealized notion of human altruism that she began to get a clearer understanding of the nature of lynching. Herein is the power of de-idealization: if one works through the disappointment as opposed to repressing it, one is more able to find their voice. This is precisely what Ida B. Wells was doing in her recounting of the murders of her friends:

> But Thomas Moss, Calvin McDowell, and Lee Stewart had been lynched in Memphis, one of the leading cities of the South, in which no lynching had taken place before, with just as much brutality as other victims of the mob; and they had committed no crime against white women. *This is what opened my eyes to what lynching really was. An excuse to get rid of Negroes who were acquiring wealth and property and thus keep the race terrorized and "keep the nigger down." I then began an investigation of every lynching I read about. I stumbled on the amazing record that every case of rape reported in that three months became such only when it became public.*[22]

In another example of devaluing the idea that she could appeal to common sense and the human spirit, and then working through the ensuing disappointment when she couldn't, Wells surmises the following conclusion in the wake of her newspaper outfit being burned to the ground by a lynch mob seething at her published critique of the murder of her friends in Memphis:

> The more I studied the situation, the more I was convinced that the Southerner had never gotten over his resentment that the Negro was no longer his plaything, his servant, and his source of income. The federal laws for Negro protection passed during

22. Wells, *Crusade for Justice*, 81; emphasis added.

> Reconstruction times had been made a mockery by the white South where it had not secured their repeal. This same white South had secured political control of its several states, and as soon as white southerners came into power they began to make playthings of Negro lives and property. This still seemed not enough to "keep the nigger down."
>
> Hence came lynch law to stifle Negro manhood which defended itself, and the burning alive of Negroes who were weak enough to accept favors from white women. The many unspeakable and unprintable tortures to which Negro rapists (?) of white women were subjected were for the purpose of striking terror into the hearts of other Negroes who might be thinking of consorting with willing white women. I found that in order to justify these horrible atrocities to the world, the Negro was being branded as a race of rapists, who were especially mad after white women.
>
> I found that white men who had created a race of mulattoes by raping and consorting with Negro women were still doing so wherever they could, these same white men lynched, burned, and tortured Negro men for doing the same thing with white women; even when the white women were willing victims.[23]

De-idealization liberates the imagination from the burdensome task of propping of fantasies of human virtue and perfection, thus allowing the liberated idealizer to better assess the context, hear their own voice, discover their own sensibilities, and to pursue their own intrinsic modus operandi. For Wells, the murder of her friends and the destruction of her newspaper triggered this path of psychospiritual growth.

Perhaps the most compelling autobiographic evidence of Ida B. Wells de-idealizing the altruistic human capacity for justice and morality is found in the chapter entitled "Self Help" in her seminal publication *Southern Horrors*. She laments, "The appeal to the white man's pocket has ever been more effectual than all the appeals ever made to his conscience . . . [and] absolutely nothing, is to be gained by a further sacrifice of manhood and self-respect [by black people]."[24] Based on this de-idealized observation, Wells diverts the inner eros she has formerly used to prop up the idealization of human altruism and instead refocuses it to an inner eros that fosters images of self-help and self-love:

> Of the many inhuman outrages of this present year, the only case where the proposed lynching did *not* occur, was where they

---

23. Wells, *Crusade for Justice*, 87–88.
24. Wells, *Southern Horrors*, 22.

men armed themselves ... and prevented it. The only times an Afro-American who was assaulted got away has been when he had a gun and used it in self-defense.

The lesson this teaches and which every Afro-American should ponder well, is that a Winchester rifle should have a place of honor in every black home, and it should be used for that protection which the law refuses to give. When the white man who is always the aggressor knows he runs a great risk of biting the dust every time his Afro-American victim does, he will have greater respect for Afro-American life. The more the Afro-American yields and cringes and begs, the more he has to do so, the more he is insulted, outraged and lynched.[25]

Ida B. Wells experienced existential disappointment in religious life as well and had to work through the disappointment of de-idealizing fantasies of perfection and goodness she had projected—to some degree—on the institutional church and its religious leaders. Wells's disillusionment with well-known personalities like D. L. Moody and Francis Willard has already been noted. In another example, Southern Methodist bishop Atticus G. Haygood, who was arguably more vocal than the average Southern white minister as it pertained to matters of slavery and racism, was perhaps idealized by many as being a religious personality who was an advocate for black people. But this idealization came crashing down when Haygood seemed to lend support to lynching and the myth of black sexual deviance. Wells makes the following observation of Haygood:

Dr. Hass, editor of the leading organ of the Methodist Church South, published in its columns that it was his belief that more than three hundred women had been assaulted by Negro men within three months. When asked to prove his charges, or give a single case upon which his "belief" was founded, he said that he could do so, but the details were unfit for publication. No other evidence but his "belief" could be adduced to substantiate this grave charge, yet Bishop Haygood, in the Forum of October, 1893, quotes this "belief" in apology for lynching, and voluntarily adds: "It is my opinion that this is an underestimate." The "opinion" of this man, based upon a "belief," had greater weight coming from a man who has posed as a friend to "Our Brother in Black," and was accepted as authority.[26]

25. Wells, *Southern Horrors*, 22.

26. Wells, *Red Record*, 59–60. *Our Brother in Black* was the title of a book written by Haygood.

Further evidence of religious idealization can be seen in her description of missionaries from the North who came to the postbellum South to assist in educating formerly enslaved children. Wells's description entails a hint of excessive ennoblement. She claims, "The bishops I had known were scholarly, saintly men in the Methodist Episcopal church and most of the pastors we had were the same. All my teachers had been the consecrated white men and women from the North who came into the South to teach immediately after the end of the war. It was they who brought us the light of knowledge and their splendid example of Christian courage."[27] In another place, Wells attends an AME conference in Philadelphia and describes how she was "unimpressed" with what she saw at the conference, but then juxtaposes her assessment of the proceedings when describing a brief interaction with one of the AME bishops, saying, "It was my first and last meeting with Bishop Daniel A. Payne, who fulfilled my every ideal of what I thought a Negro bishop ought to be."[28] Again, she uses a somewhat grandiose accent to describe an otherwise uneventful interaction with another person.

Perhaps the most vivid example of de-idealization for Wells came when she accepted an invitation from a group of AME ministers in Philadelphia to discuss her anti-lynching work. Prior to this meeting, Wells had already met with other groups of ministers from the Methodist, Baptist, and Congregationalist churches, where they extended commendation and appreciation for her crusade against lynching. Wells expected to receive the same commendation from the AME ministers, as she thought this was the purpose of the meeting. Instead, she was met with suspicion, doubt, and contempt. I quote Wells at length here in order for the reader to get a better sense of the complex psychosocial web of the context in which Wells was embedded and the complexity of the existential disappointment she had to navigate:

> I told them that I had cut out one of the four meetings to which I had been invited that Monday morning in order to show my appreciation of the courtesy they had extended me. That at every meeting in which I had appeared that morning, the announcement of my presence had been greeted with applause, and I had been instantly given opportunity to appeal to them to use their influence to help put a stop to lynching in this country. First, by giving me a chance to address their congregations; second, by passing the resolutions against lynchings which had been passed in every one of my meetings in Great Britain.

27. Wells, *Crusade for Justice*, 21.
28. Wells, *Crusade for Justice*, 52.

> This, I said, had been immediately done and glowing words of commendation had come from every one of those white gatherings on the work they said that I had done; *it had remained for the ministers of my own race to bring me before them to hear them discuss whether they could afford to endorse me.* "Why, gentlemen," I said, "I cannot see why I need your endorsement. Under God I have done work without any assistance from my own people. And when I think that I have been able to do the work with his assistance that you could not do, if you would, and you would not do if you could, I think I have a right to a feeling of strong indignation. I feel very deeply the insult which you have offered and I have the honor to wish you a very good morning." With that I walked out of the meeting and left them sitting with their mouths open. That was the beginning of a great deal of the same sort that I received at the hands of my own people in the effort to follow up the splendid work which the English people had begun for us.[29]

Wells had fallen victim to the sort of sexism and subjugation that black women in African American religious tradition have been subjected to for generations. Her established body of work and commendations from around the globe were no match for entrenched male chauvinism. And this is but one example of the sexism and misogyny that she would be subjected to.

The most vivid example of idealization and existential disappointment in the life of Ida B. Wells is arguably to be found in her relationship with Frederick Douglass. Her description of him reflects a tone of romanticism as she reflects back on their relationship.

> Frederick Douglass came from his home in Washington to tell me what a revelation of existing conditions this article had been to him. He had been troubled by the increasing number of lynchings, and had begun to believe it true that there was increasing lasciviousness on the part of Negroes. He wrote a strong preface to the pamphlet which I afterward published embodying these same facts. This was the beginning of a friendship with the "Sage of Anacostia" which lasted until the day of his death, three years later. I have never ceased to be thankful for this contact with him, *the greatest man our race has produced in this "land of the free and home of the brave."*[30]

---

29. Wells, *Crusade for Justice*, 188; emphasis added.
30. Wells, *Crusade for Justice*, 62; emphasis added.

But as in every healthy relationship, idealizations are eventually challenged, as illusions of grandeur and perfection are tainted, and even replaced with images of realism. For Wells, her idealization of Douglass would soon be cut down when he failed (or refused) to adequately respond to a relatively innocuous request put forth by Wells and her allies during her travels in Europe. While visiting Douglass's home, Wells received a letter from a group in England extending an invitation to her to come over and do a series of lectures to raise awareness in Europe of the lynching of black people in America. News of Wells's extraordinary work had reached England to groups and individuals who were also friends of Frederick Douglass. The proposed lecture circuit would be fully funded. Ida B. Wells's reputation preceded her. But when she arrived in Europe, through no fault of her own, the prospective funding fell through. Her constituents in England suggested she secure a letter of introduction and commendation from Douglass (who was highly regarded throughout Europe) to help with possibly securing more funding and to better ensure she would be well received during the tour. However, in Douglass's initial response, he chastised Wells and suggested that she had not received an invitation to England, and instead had gone of her own volition and self-ambition. Wells was both humiliated and crushed by the accusation from Douglass. In her response, she wrote in part:

> *Your letter which I received this morning has hurt me cruelly.* With all the discouragements I have received and the time and money I have sacrificed to the work, *I have never felt so like giving up as since I received your very cool and cautious letter this morning*, with its tone of distrust and its inference that I have not dealt truthfully with you. The thought never occurred to me that I would need letters of introduction as I was coming as I did before—on invitation. I thought to come here, fill dates made out for me and restore home after the work was done ... *However, I have found some friends for the cause, who without a single letter of introduction have gone on arranging meetings and getting me changes to be heard in the churches* ... While my heart bleeds that you should class me with that large class who have imposed upon your confidence, *I still love you as the greatest man our race has yet produced* and because of what you have suffered and endured for the mass's sake.[31]

The accusation of dishonesty from Douglass was rather odd given that Wells had received the invitation while visiting Douglass and had even shown him the invitation. It is suggested here that in reading the letter,

---

31. Wells, "Letter to Frederick Douglass" (Apr. 6, 1894); emphasis added.

Douglass may have experienced a degree of narcissistic injury—that is to say, a bruising of his ego—as the author of the invitation inferred that Douglass was too old to travel, and that Wells should come in his place. Douglass was compelled to concede to Wells. But more pertinent to the analysis here, it is noteworthy to point out that while in their relationship Wells may have been deferential to Douglass, and while she may have benefited from their collegiality, she did not depend on him or even need him for her success. It was Ida B. Wells who enlightened Douglass to the real reasons behind lynching. She writes, "Frederick Douglass came from his home in Washington to tell me what a revelation of existing conditions . . . [my] article had been to him . . . [and that even] he had been troubled by the increasing number of lynchings, and had begun to believe it true that there was increasing lasciviousness on the part of Negroes."[32]

As such, by the time they met, Wells was well established in her own right as a scholar, journalist, and businesswoman. This observation then highlights the power of idealization: its task is to satisfy an emotional need, not necessarily an actual material need. Several points should be emphasized in Wells's response to Douglass. First, *disappointment from a major de-idealization is akin to catatonic shock and is emotionally devastating.* This is evident in Wells's claim of Douglass's words hurting her cruelly, with the result being that she feels like giving up. De-idealization has the potential to take the emotional wind out of its victim. But secondly, and perhaps more importantly, once the idealization has been ruptured, the individual is no longer blinded by the illusion that any one person or institution is indispensable. De-idealization frees the human imagination to explore endless possibilities and to fall back on one's own genius. The need for a hero dissipates. This is evidenced in Wells's connecting with other people who arranged meetings for her without letters of introduction from Douglass. Lastly, idealizations die hard, as evidenced in Wells's assertion that even after he has deeply wounded her, she still loves him as "the greatest man our race has yet produced." But even after her heartfelt response to Douglass, Douglass apparently still fell short of what Wells and others were expecting of him in a subsequent letter, perhaps evidence of his narcissistic injury.

> Your letter directed to Manchester has followed me all around till it reached me here. I am indeed glad to get it. Then I wrote to you I had not seen your letter to Mr. Aked; since seeing it I know from what he and others said, that while they did not expect "gush" (may they pay you the same compliment I do, in knowing you to be incapable of such a thing) still *they would have been*

---

32. Wells, *Crusade for Justice*, 62.

better satisfied if you had spoken more positively regarding me and my work. Mr. Aked thought that since the Society had failed so miserably and I was thus left to vouch for myself, you would not hesitate to vouch for me. We cannot go thro the country telling people about this personal quarrel and why I am unaccompanied by the persons who brought me over.[33]

Apparently in his follow-up letter, Douglass still fell short of the mark in his endorsement of Wells.

FINAL THOUGHTS ON WORKING THROUGH EXISTENTIAL DISAPPOINTMENT

The abundance and rawness of Ida B. Wells's writings and reflections on the epidemic of lynching reflects her *working through* her ruptured idealizations and existential disappointments as opposed to ignoring the pain within her interior world, repressing it, or *not talking about it* as she was admonished by so many persons to do. She didn't keep silent about the truth or turn a blind eye to the gratuitous evil of lynching and racial terrorism—a practice that is valorized today. Merely declaring that Ida B. Wells had faith is not enough to adequately capture the significance of her life. Platitudes and euphemisms romanticize her life, as they fail to take a much fuller account of the context of extremity in which she was embedded, and the significant psychospiritual work she practiced in becoming Ida B. Wells.

It is in this context that we must understand her comments at the beginning of the chapter when she poses the question "is mine a race of cowards." This question should be understood as rhetorical. She asks this question in a context where black people must consider the cost of even defending themselves against mob violence and lynching. Wells's question captures the depth of evil and depravity the nation found itself in by tolerating racial violence. Her question expresses the profoundness of black suffering. Perhaps James Cone best captures this dialectic between mob violence, lynching, and racial terrorism; black suffering; and the notion of cowardice that Ida B. Wells pondered, as he considers what few options black people had in terms of counter-hegemonic strategies. Because of his profound insight on this, I quote him at length:

> [Few] blacks in the South could fight back with pen or gun and survive. "You couldn't do nothing about those things," Mississippi bluesman Willie Dixon said, as he reflected back on the

---

33. Wells, "Letter to Frederick Douglass" (May 6, 1894); emphasis added.

lynching era in his autobiography. "The black man had to be a complete coward." *Yet cowardice is not the right word to describe the black response to lynching and white mob violence*; even Willie Dixon had the courage to leave Mississippi for Chicago, where he joined other bluesmen and women, like Muddy Waters, Howlin Wolf, and Etta James, together creating a musical response to lynching that told the world about the cultural power of blacks to preserve and protect their humanity.

Blacks knew that violent self-defense was tantamount to suicide; even affirming blackness in a world defined by white power took great courage. Whites acted in a superior manner for so long that it was difficult for them to even recognize their cultural and spiritual arrogance, blatant as it was to African Americans. Their law was not designed to protect blacks from lynching, especially when blacks acted as if they were socially equal to whites. Should a black in the South lift his hand or raise his voice to reprimand a white person, he would incur the full weight of the law and the mob. Even to look at white people in a manner regarded as disrespectful could get a black lynched. Whites often lynched blacks simply to remind the black community of their powerlessness. Unemployed blacks passing through an area with no white man to vouch for them could easily find themselves on a prison chain gang or swinging from a lynching tree. There were many "sundown towns" in the South and the North—some with signs warning, "Nigger, don't let the sun set on your head," and others with no signs but which could be fatal to blacks who happened to be passing through.

How did southern rural blacks survive the terrors of this era? Self-defense and protest were out of the question, but there were other forms of resistance. For most blacks it was the blues and religion that offered the chief weapons of resistance. At the juke joints on Friday and Saturday nights and at churches on Sunday mornings and evening week nights blacks affirmed their humanity and fought back against dehumanization. Both black religion and the blues offered sources of hope that there was more to life than what one encountered daily in the white man's world.[34]

The work of Ida B. Wells must be interpreted then—in part—through a traumatological lens. Wells must be understood as a person who musters the courage to *work through* the trauma of what she has witnessed and to *work through* the existential disappointments that are an inherent part of

34. Cone, *Cross and Lynching Tree*, 11–12; emphasis added.

one's life-project when you choose not to be a bystander, but a participant in the work of love, justice, and freedom. She does this by not remaining silent. Being vocal about lynching was her form of resistance. It would be a mistake to interpret the rawness of Ida B. Wells's writings as cynicism. To the contrary, her body of work represents a sacred and therapeutic prose that seeks to indict white supremacy and redeem the value of black life. That is to say . . . Ida B. Wells should be understood as doing God's work.

7

FANNIE LOU HAMER AND THE CASE FOR LOVE

What Does Love Look Like?

We are not fighting against these people because we hate them, but *we are fighting these people because we love them and we're the only thing can save them now.* We are fighting to save these people from their hate and from all the things that would be so bad against them. We want them to see the right way. Every night of my life that I lay down before I go to sleep, I pray for these people that despitefully use me. And Christ said, "The meek shall inherit the earth." And He said before one-tenth—one jot—of His word would fail, heaven and earth would pass away. But His word would stand forever. And I believe tonight, that one day in Mississippi—if I have to die for this—we shall overcome.

—Fannie Lou Hamer

This chapter identifies the performance of the love ethic as the next critical move—beyond empathy—that is necessary to redeem the soul of a nation. As such, this chapter seeks to address a pivotal question: What does love look like? While we are well acquainted with the vestiges of indifference, incivility, and ultimately violence, as a nation, we seem to be less acquainted with, and even suspect of, the look of love. The democratic experiment is becoming immunized to human suffering imposed by radical evil and callousness. To compensate for this ongoing loss of empathy, compassion, and tenderness towards each other, the lust of busyness, entertainment, conspicuous consumption, and capital accumulation have become opiates that numb the conscience, dictate what constitutes morality, and project illusions of value and self-worth. In the wake of a global COVID-19 pandemic that devastated the lives of millions, coupled with sociopolitical unrest and a racial reckoning not witnessed in the United States since the 1960s, the performance of the love ethic is especially critical for pastoral leaders, practitioners, and caregivers. In this chapter, I argue that Fannie Lou Hamer demonstrated love—the ethic, capacity, and practice that is indispensable, even constitutional, to what it means to be human. She showed the nation what radical love looks like and what it entails. Through her body of work, Hamer answered the question "what does love look like." She modeled love in action.

In the passage that begins this chapter, Hamer is clear that the love ethic is what governs her actions to undermine individual and systemic structures of white supremacy and racial hatred. The ethic of love is a theme that runs consistently throughout her body of work. For Hamer, the ongoing legacy of the slavocracy and the nation's struggle with racism—at its core—is a spiritual sickness that plagues the heart of the country. The etiology of this sickness reflected the absence of a praxis of love. For Hamer, the praxis of love is not merely incidental, but absolutely essential to how we both understand and practice democracy. She understood that the love ethic was not delimited to a sacred or religious category to be used only for the purposes of being politically correct. Instead, for Hamer, love was a matter of epistemology that governed the production of knowledge and how we understand what it is to be human. As such, she understood that love called for an overhaul of how we educate citizens of the republic if we are to have any chance at deconstructing generations and systems of racial animus and reconstructing a beloved community. On this point I quote Hamer at length:

> And I don't want you to think that you have to pick out a way for me to exist in this society. You know, black people is caught a lot of hell too. We first ben told that we wasn't fit into—we got the kind of education to fit into this society. *But as sick as it is, I wonder do I want the kind of education that's going to really rob me of having real love and compassion for my fellow man? We got to start, we got to start in every institution in this country because the history that we been getting, baby, had never happened and it*

> never will. *And we got to change some curriculum and in making the change, we can have more peace, and real democracy* when we bring the boys home and some of the billions of dollars that's being spent in Vietnam can go into rural areas like Mississippi.[1]

For Hamer, the connection between a praxis of love and education, the health of the democracy, and justice and equality represented an interlocking and reciprocating interchange that was self-evident and irreducible. That is to say, you cannot have one without the other. Perhaps in her most damning critique of a racialized America, Hamer uses the praxis of love to challenge the normalization of racial hatred, arguing that if equal rights meant internalizing and adopting (as that which is morally right) the values of a racist power structure, then she will not aspire to any such equivalency. It is clear then that when she uses the phrase "white America," she is not referring to people of European descent, but those who adhere to the social construct of white American supremacy. While current scholarship understands this centuries-old binary as racism vs. anti-racism, for Hamer, it is love vs. hate:

> But what I'm trying to say to you tonight, we are faced with some difficult days ahead. *And I hope white America learns to love, before they teach every one of us to hate.* This is what is happening in this country. And you see I couldn't tell anybody in my right mind that I am fighting for equal rights because I don't *want* any. I am fighting for human rights, because I don't want to be equal to the people that rape my ancestors, dead, kill out the Indians, dead, destroyed my dignity, and taken my name.[2]

This chapter is not a biographical interpretation of Fannie Lou Hamer. There has been significant and commendable scholarship done in this area.[3] The goal here is to profile a salient psychospiritual practice embodied by Hamer that lends itself to redeeming the soul of the nation. In this case, that psychospiritual practice is the ethic of love—emphasizing what a praxis of love entails. We know what violence looks like. But as a matter of both pastoral theology and practical theology, the fundamental question remains, how do we know love when we see it? I suggest we see the praxis of love embodied in the life of Hamer. Perhaps one of the pivotal moments in the life of Fannie Lou Hamer was the unimaginable evil she suffered at

---

1. Hamer, *Speeches*, 102. Speech at the Vietnam War Moratorium Rally in Berkeley, California, on Oct. 15, 1969; emphasis added.

2. Hamer, *Speeches*, 117. Speech at Loop College in Chicago on May 27, 1970.

3. See Blain, *Until I Am Free*; Brooks, *Fannie Lou Hamer* and *Voice That Could Stir*; Larson, *Walk with Me*; Lee, *For Freedom's Sake*; and Mills, *This Little Light*.

the hands of prison officials and other inmates at the Winona, Mississippi, jail on June 9, 1963. Having traveled throughout Mississippi to encourage black people to vote, Hamer and her colleagues were arrested when their bus arrived at Staley's Café in Winona. The beating that Hamer endured at the jail was nothing short of savage. Her testimony at a federal trial (on December 2, 1963) of what she and her colleagues suffered . . . the screams . . . the physical brutality . . . the sexual assault . . . is but one example of the depravity of the racial imagination and how it corrupts the souls of all those seduced by it: the perpetrators of racial terror and brutality, benefactors of white supremacy, and bystanders alike.

Nevertheless, it was the suffering she experienced in Jim Crow South, and the suffering she witnessed among her black and brown contemporaries, that served as the crucible of human experience, from which she drew her public theology and social ethics. For Hamer, it was only common sense that her personal experiences and the oppressive experiences of her community should inform how she understood Scripture, and how she constructed her social ethics and public theology. She bore witness to her personal suffering, and that of her community in Mississippi, and that witnessing fueled her life-project and her body of work. To do otherwise—that is, to behave as if black suffering was inconsequential to the American story and the democratic experiment—would have been an act of self-flagellation. Contemporary practical theology's claim to be organized around a thick description of the human situation is neither innovative nor pioneering.[4] It is basic common sense that indigenous scholars of black and brown descent have understood for generations. Hamer understood this implicit methodology when on the evening of May 8, 1969, at an elections rally for the Mississippi Freedom Democratic Party in Lexington, Mississippi, she told the crowd:

> We've had quite a bit of very beautiful talks tonight, and I want you to know something; honey, *don't nobody feel comfortable* when I leave the building because *I'm going to tell you where it's at*. I don't want you to start thinking that you're going to *feel comfortable* around here with me talking, and I don't want you to think that I'm going to stop talking about black folks and where we are today because I'm going to tell you where it's at, children . . . now, some of you all is going to be scared because you was scared when you got here. That's all right, too. *I'm going to tell it like it is.*[5]

---

4. See Miller-McLemore, *Wiley-Blackwell Companion*.

5. Hamer, *Speeches*, 87. Speech at the Mississippi Freedom Democratic Party Municipal Elections Rally in Lexington, Mississippi, on May 8, 1969; emphasis added.

At first glance, it would be easy to dismiss Hamer's words as being no more than southern vernacular. *But if she is taken seriously as a human being*, a closer look reveals that Hamer is making a connection between our desire for personal and collective comfort with our capacity to make a rich and authentic appraisal of the human condition and the sociopolitical context. Said differently, it doesn't take much to talk about a context or situation in a manner that is disingenuous and is constructed to maintain the comfort of the speaker and the audience. More often than not, this kind of witnessing or telling is designed to maintain the racial status quo and to justify the apathy and inaction of the bystander. But it is altogether another matter to talk about a context or situation and have the capacity and courage to tell it as it really is—no matter how uncomfortable it makes the speaker and the listener, and no matter the implications of what is then required in terms of action and praxis. This is the meaning of Hamer declaring, "I'm going to tell you where it's at . . . [and] I'm going to *tell it like it is*." What is the point of a *thick description* in practical theology if such description lacks integrity and authenticity, or if the *thickness of what is being described* (more often than not) centers the Western Eurocentric human experience as that which is fit for determining what it means to be human and for constructing theology, while implicitly subordinating black and brown human experiences as merely elective?

In her project that brilliantly unpacks the genius of Fannie Lou Hamer's theology, Karen Crozier makes a very power argument for religious and theological educators learning from Hamer's approach to practice, theological reflection, and social ethics. According to Crozier:

> Hamer's leadership in rural, local, contextual, and national public religious thought was replete with practical knowledge and sound theological sociopolitical messaging without the privilege of a formal theological education. The substance of Hamer's faith and the way she lived and practiced faith, religion, and beliefs suggests that *her non-academic practical theology could assist and enhance theological education and the discipline of practical theology instead of the other way around*.[6]

For Crozier, Fannie Lou Hamer's capacity for this sociopolitical messaging stemmed, in part, from her motivations to love and care for the people she represented. According to Crozier, "Hamer was not motivated by the need to identify Christian insiders and outsiders . . . [or to identify] theologically laden practices that could be traced back to an essential Christian beginning

---

6. Crozier, *Revolutionary Practical Theology*, 69–70; emphasis added.

of beliefs and practices."[7] I suggest that what Crozier observes as the difference in motivation between Hamer and religious scholars in the ivory tower is the tribalism of theological education. It is a tribalism with high (if not insurmountable) barriers to entry that creates an in-group and an out-group, and ultimately serves as a gatekeeper that determines whose religious heritage and life-experience is most fit to interpret theology, spirituality, and faith.

HAMER KNEW THAT EMPATHY WAS NOT ENOUGH

For our purposes here, I suggest that Hamer's motivation for her public theology and social ethics emerged out of a praxis of love. Her work teaches us that transformative, prophetic, redemptive scholarship must be imagined, informed, and constructed by the crucible life. The night she was abused and tortured in a Winona, Mississippi, jail forever changed and informed her thought-life. In light of this, theologians and religious scholars are compelled to ask: What is the cost of transformative and prophetic scholarship? What price are theologians and religious scholars willing to pay for what they write? The authority and imagination for Hamer's body of work was underwritten by the despised and dejected of Mississippi who were impoverished (including white people), and the black and brown community terrorized by racial violence and the culture of Jim Crow. Hamer was acquainted with that racial terror.

In an attempt to emulate Hamer's methodology and praxis of love, and in an effort to respond to the question of what does love look, I now turn to another often-despised group whose voice I endeavor to captured in my own work: *black boys in public spaces*. We don't readily think that black boys could provide us with an answer to the question of how love is embodied. As a society, and especially in the church and theological education, we are more ready to consider what lessons we can teach or impose upon black boys. But in this case, I turn to black boys to teach us what love might look like.

The idea of the performance of the love ethic stems from research I conducted on the self-experience of black boys in public spaces.[8] During my brief time with the boys in a school setting on the south side of Chicago, something unexpected occurred, actions and behaviors that I have since come to understand as the love ethic, or a praxis of love. I learned from the boys that empathy in and of itself is insufficient for caregiving and healing.

7. Crozier, *Revolutionary Practical Theology*, 53.
8. D. G. Gibson, "When Empathy."

Empathy, alone, does not necessarily lead to moral, corrective, or restorative action. Fannie Lou Hamer understood this, as evidenced in her tireless efforts to bring justice, equity, healing, and a since of dignity to the poor, disenfranchised, and dejected of Mississippi. The boys that I interviewed during this research understood this as well. The boys offered up what I believe are images of love.

Here, I suggest that the lessons learned in that research are useful for understanding caregiving, healing, and restoration in the current environment of social unrest, calls for political violence, rising hate crimes and the increasing risk of normalizing them, and a racial reckoning not witnessed since the mid-twentieth century. To develop this argument, I briefly address the problem of empathy and love that my study on the self-experience of Black boys in public spaces uncovered. Secondly, using the thought of Martin Luther King Jr., I point towards a practical theological definition of a praxis of love. Next, I briefly highlight possible psychosocial obstacles in the movement from empathy to performances of love. Lastly, I highlight images of love created by the boys who participated in this research project. I imagine how such performances of love could be useful for pastoral leaders, caregivers, and practitioners in the quest for self-care and healing in the current social context.

THE PROBLEM WITH EMPATHY: IT DOESN'T MEAN THAT I GIVE A SHIT!

In recent years, when conversations about racism, hate crime, anti-Semitism, mass shootings, xenophobia, or any other form of human atrocity take center stage in the media, a common reaction has been to emphasize the need for empathy. The ostensible perception is that empathy will curtail hostile manifestations of human animus. More specifically, there is a common belief that if the political, social, or cultural power structures were more empathic, then there would be fewer incidents of violence. While this proposition is not entirely misguided, it represents an uninterrogated assumption about the efficacy of empathy. As a clinician and scholar, this assumption troubles me. Even the most developed capacity to imagine oneself in the place of another human being in an effort to better understand them, or to feel with them, does not guarantee (not even in the least) the result of moving on behalf of another, or being motivated to work in the best interest of another person or group. While empathy may be a condition precedent to acting with justice and mercy, it is not a guarantor of such actions.

My interest in reflecting on *what comes after empathy* stems from a previous research project where I examined the self-experience of black boys in public spaces. One of the group interviews occurred in a high school. In reviewing the qualitative data and my initial reflections, provocative observations made by several of the faculty and administrators who participated in the research project caught my attention:

> When asked about what it took to do their jobs, one of the teachers lamented, "We can equip younger teachers and staff with certain skills that will allow them to be relatively successful, but we cannot teach younger teachers *how to give a shit. You have to give a shit.*" Another senior faculty member added, "*You have to love them and be willing to do things outside of your official job description.*"[9]

What then does a pastoral theology of giving a shit entail? What does a clinical picture of giving a shit look like? As a black scholar, these questions have compelled me to contemplate the efficacy of empathy—in isolation—as it relates to caring for black boys who commonly experience the devaluation of their personhood and humanity in the public spaces of the American polis. While the concept of the empathic has captivated the academic guild of pastoral care, after my engagement with the boys, I have since questioned the category of empathy and its ability to dismantle structures of inequality and racism that subjugate black boys in public spaces. More importantly, as it relates to the overarching theme of when empathy is not enough, *it seems we are compelled to ask if a person or group can have empathy for those at the margin (black boys in this instance), but at the same time not give a shit about their well-being? Is it possible to be empathic towards the plight of a person or group, but not give a shit about their overall well-being?*

Since my interactions with the boys and faculty members at that school on the south side of Chicago, these questions have haunted me even more, especially in the current sociopolitical global context characterized by gratuitous human suffering and the normalization of wanton violence. While the concept of empathy has long represented a critical epistemological category in academic guild of spiritual care and the broader professional field of caregiving, seldom do we talk about the limits of empathy. That is to say, *how do we understand human interaction within caregiving when we lack adequate intrapsychic and soul capacity to empathize?*[10] When endeavoring

9. D. G. Gibson, "When Empathy," 625.

10. It is important to note that this question is not one about compassion fatigue. If understood as an epistemological category, then the question is about the limits of one's capacity to understand another human being or group, while also preserving the integrity of another's alterity.

to function as agents of hope in the life of another, awareness of empathic limitations is a matter of pastoral ethics in order to avoid self-delusion and narcissism in the engagement with careseekers. While developments in how we understand empathy over the past several decades are immense, commendable, and additive to pastoral ethics and praxis, failure to acknowledge empathic limitations (and how to understand and engage those limits) threatens to undermine the entire spiritual care enterprise. There are some gaps in culture, social location, and understanding that empathy will not be able to bridge, no matter how well intended we may be. In those situations, how do we then understand our moral obligation?

During the encounter with the boys and their teachers, there was something else I experienced in the room that was beyond empathy. There was clearly an intimate and endearing connection between the boys and the teachers. On the one hand, it could be argued that I was exposed to the inevitable emotional contagion precipitated by the interview questions I asked the boys, along with the overall objective of our gathering (to better understand the self-experience of black boys in public spaces). But there was another element in play. I witnessed an affective exchange between the teachers and students that I could not partake of, where I was clearly an outsider looking in. The conversation between the faculty and students was casual, yet pertinent. The interactions between the boys and teachers in the room was fluid and familial, with everyone involved displaying an element of adoration for the other. In play was something that seemed to go beyond empathy. *It was as if these boys were creating visions of love.*

Empathy does not beget moral action. A common adage in Western folklore is that the more a person suffers or finds themselves in trouble, the lesser friends and family are available to be with them. People don't like to be close to the pain of others, as it may remind them of their own vulnerability to such suffering. If empathy is understood as the capacity to *imagine oneself in the situation or shoes of another*, then in some respects it could lead to the social isolation of the afflicted, as close proximity to human suffering reminds individuals and groups of the fragility of their own lives, or their complicity (directly or indirectly) in structures of oppression. The result is social distancing and separation from the source of suffering. It is conceivable that empathy could lead to what James Dittes refers to as being a *player* in the life of another. When a caregiver becomes a player in a careseeker's life, the caregiver's empathy (the capacity to imagine oneself in the place of another while still maintaining healthy boundaries) disintegrates into emotional enmeshment and contagion. The unfortunate result is that the caregiver will inappropriately use time with the careseeker to selfishly address their own unmet emotional needs.[11] An example of this is seen in the biblical narrative of Job, where initially, the empathy of his friends enabled them to grieve with Job in silence. However, because they were players (i.e., close friends with porous emotional boundaries) in his life, their empathy quickly devolved into *impatience and emotional brutality*, as *they had an emotional need* for Job to accept an idea that personal immorality caused his own suffering. Such a narrative would prop up a common life-script of the orderliness of life (i.e., good things happen to good people, etc.). Bloom, in his critical analysis on empathy and its capacity for moral action, states:

> People often cross the street to avoid encountering suffering people who are begging for money. It's not that they don't care (if they didn't care, they would just walk by), it's that they are bothered by the suffering and would rather not encounter it. Usually, escape is even easier. Steven Pinker writes: "For many years a charity called Save the Children ran magazine ads with a heartbreaking photograph of a destitute child and the caption 'You can save Juan Ramos for five cents a day. Or you can turn the page.' Most people turn the page."[12]

The question of the limits of empathy is not altogether new. This is an issue that Hannah Arendt wrestled with in her work throughout a significant part of the twentieth century, as she bore witness to the devastation of the Shoah, the rise of modern totalitarianism, and the emergence of the Cold War. According to Matthiesen and Klitmoller, for Arendt, there was no clear path from empathy to moral agency or a person's will to act in accordance with an ethical framework. She, probably more than any twentieth-century thinker, understood the limitations of empathy and the potential for its false promises. Empathy was not the condition precedent to moral agency. According to Arendt, preserving the alterity of the other and resisting the human propensity to be mindless about the sociopolitical spaces we inhabit are more meaningful steps that contribute to moral agency.[13] Instead of engaging empathy as an epistemological category to better understand another person, *Arendt proposes an ontological posture of visiting the other person as a superior antecedent to fostering the will to act*, as empathy is inevitably reduced to the empathizer's self-experience and self-conception of the world. While useful, empathy has the propensity to turn on itself in the pursuit of comprehension. Failure to acknowledge empathic

---

11. See Dittes, *Pastoral Counseling*.
12. Bloom, *Against Empathy*, 74–75.
13. See Matthiesen and Klitmoller, "Encountering the Stranger."

limitations risks *essentializing the felt experiences of dominant cultures* at the expense of the subaltern. Matthiesen and Klitmoller suggest that:

> Visiting is an aspect of understanding the other. For Arendt, understanding ... does not totalize and cannot reach conclusions ... Understanding has to do with coming to terms with the world, with the other, and reconciling oneself to a world where experiences, perspectives, values, opinions, etc. that differ from my own are possible ... Empathy, when defined through a propensity to sameness, is one mode of explaining the other by drawing on such familiarities. So, rather than comprehending the other in any full and totalizing way, understanding has to do with coming to terms with the reality that the other experiences and inhabits our shared world differently than I.[14]

For Arendt then, it was not that she questioned the legitimacy for empathy, but just that taken alone, empathy was inherently unreliable in the quest for the moral agency needed to challenge the evils of the twentieth century. Instead of empathy being a means to an end of creating moral agents and lovers of people, if misunderstood, empathy can become an idol that represents the end goal. This unfortunate outcome works to absolve individuals and groups of guilt (and even shame) related to silence and inaction, because in part, the emotional goal of empathy has been met. Ultimately, after reaching the erroneous end goal of empathy (instead of it being a means to a higher end), it yields a state of inactivity, moral paralysis, mindlessness, and silence. That is to say, as a matter of pastoral ethics, "a time comes when silence is betrayal ... [as] some of us who have already begun to break the silence of the night have found that the calling to speak is often a vocation of agony, but we must speak."[15] And it is this misplacement of empathy that seems to be a commonplace error today when it is suggested that empathy is the antidote to gratuitous incivility, violence, and human callousness. But this is a grievous epistemological error that could prove to be deadly. To be clear: *because empathy, even done correctly, provides an individual with a felt understanding of another person does not mean that the empathizer is now less inclined to harm the other individual, nor does it mean that the empathizer will be more inclined to take moral action on behalf of another's suffering.* That is to say, as the participant observed in my research, empathy doesn't necessarily mean that I *"give a shit."* Nelson captures the aversion to empathy in Arendt's body of work when she reflects on

---

14. See Matthiesen and Klitmoller, "Encountering the Stranger," 192.

15. See Dr. Martin Luther King's speech at Riverside Church, Apr. 1967, in King, *Testament of Hope*, 231.

how both Arendt and Mary McCarthy were often misunderstood as being apathetic to many of the progressive social movements in the mid-twentieth century. But Nelson counters this public sentiment when she asserts:

> They [Arendt and McCarthy] sought not relief from pain but heightened sensitivity to what they called reality. Perversely or not, they imagined the consolations for pain in intimacy, empathy, and solidarity as anesthetic. Their toleration of pain—indeed, their insistence on its ordinariness—is a part of their eccentricity. In discourses where pain is a serious ethical and political question . . . the explanatory authority of trauma has rendered unintelligible both ordinary suffering and the ordinariness of suffering. "Facing reality" was an inflexible mandate to their readers for two reasons . . . First, they saw the reluctance to look directly at the unpleasant facts of experience as a potentially fatal form of self-delusion . . . and as amorally crippling one . . . Second, they believed that facing reality set in motion a process of alteration and self-alteration that was a precondition of social change.[16]

As an alternative to empathy, Arendt believed that intentional thoughtfulness was a superior antecedent to moral agency and social action. For her, it is the temptation to be mindless that is the real problem. Recall in chapter 1 where it was established that mindlessness (while perhaps emotionally satisfying) was akin to the sin of sloth. Clinically speaking, the mindlessness that Arendt witnessed in her context was probably comparable to the coping mechanism of dissociation, where a person may dissociate in response to experiencing intolerable affect caused by cognitive dissonance, or simply having to come to terms with truths and realities that may undermine individual and collective identities propped up by illusions of innocence or virtue or a safe and orderly world. In her observation of Adolf Eichmann at the Nuremberg trials, Arendt reflects on the mindlessness of Eichmann as he unwaveringly blamed his crimes against humanity to those who had seniority over him. She postulates:

> *He was not stupid. It was sheer thoughtlessness—something by no means identical with stupidity—that predisposed him to become one of the greatest criminals of that period.* And if this is "banal" and even funny, if with the best will in the world one cannot extract any diabolical or demonic profundity from Eichmann, that is still far from calling it commonplace. It surely cannot be so common that a man facing death, and, moreover, standing

---

16. D. Nelson, "Virtues of Heartlessness," 88.

beneath the gallows, should be able to think of nothing but what he has heard at funerals all his life, and that these "lofty words" should completely becloud the reality of his own death. That such remoteness from reality and such thoughtlessness can wreak more havoc than all the evil instincts taken together which, perhaps, are inherent in man—that was, in fact, the lesson one could learn in Jerusalem. But it was a lesson, neither an explanation of the phenomenon nor a theory about it.[17]

In similar fashion today, it is mindlessness when millions are seduced into claiming that a nationwide election was stolen, even when state audits, legal proceedings, or independent scientific analysis (even from the incumbent's own political party) substantiates the legitimacy of the votes. It is mindlessness when millions deny scientifically proven evidence of a global coronavirus pandemic. The cost of such mindlessness is the needless deaths of hundreds of thousands of people because of a selfish refusal to adhere to appropriate public health policy. It is mindlessness when nearly half of a federally elected body is willing to overturn the votes of an entire nation for the sake of following a demagogue. It is mindlessness when religion, faith, culture, and political ideology are conflated such that there is no distinction among them, and loyalty to nationalism becomes the determinant of morality. Mindlessness is not due to a lack of data that would otherwise cause someone to act in an alternative way, nor is mindlessness about a lack of intellectual acumen or education. Instead, mindlessness is a mechanism of psychic defense designed to reduce guilt or cognitive (and moral) dissonance. *It is a refusal to think, not an inability to think.* Arendt is clear on this point.

Alternatively, being mindful, which is the antidote to mindlessness and a more reliable antecedent to moral action, is not about having "a highly developed intelligence or sophistication in moral matters, but rather the disposition to live together explicitly with oneself, to have intercourse with oneself, that is, to be engaged in that silent dialogue."[18] The culture of mindlessness reflects a refusal to think critically about—and then engage with—the tension of current sociopolitical moment. Mindlessness is at the core of the so-called accusation of being woke: any protest, conversation, or argument that dares to disturb an entrenched status quo is repudiated and rejected. The fallacious logic of mindlessness is that if you don't think about it or talk about it, then it doesn't exist. Moreover, in the church and

17. Arendt, *Eichmann in Jerusalem*, 287–88; emphasis added.
18. Hannah Arendt, as quoted by Matthiesen and Klitmoller, "Encountering the Stranger," 194.

theological education, mindlessness can become an idol, whereby the community becomes inundated with a superficial engagement with abstraction and propositions that work to maintain the status quo. Case in point: *mindlessness and silence in the church about the Capitol insurrection on January 6, 2021, and what it means in terms of revealing the true condition of the collective soul.* Indeed, the task of effective pastoral theology and spiritual care is more pertinent than ever since the 1960s.

By now, it should be clear as to why I am proposing that empathy is insufficient for the current sociopolitical situation, and that a praxis of love is the next logical psychospiritual move beyond empathy, as a matter of individual self-care and providing care for others and the larger community. Fannie Lou Hamer understood the logic of love perhaps better than any of her contemporaries. She was clear about this when at the University of Wisconsin, she claimed, "You can't legislate love. That's the one thing that you can't do. And what America and the rest of the world need today—some kids put out a song some time ago is what the world need now is love—but today people is not seeking and trying to find love, one of the greatest things of survival on earth, but seeking for more power and power corrupt."[19]

The current social, political, and cultural situation demands that we know what love looks like, and then engage in practices of love as a matter of survival. As suggested in my research with the group of boys, a person or group can be empathic towards those at the margin or those who are suffering and at the same time (in the nomenclature of one of the teachers) *not give a shit about their ongoing well-being and flourishing.* Moreover, I suggest that what I witnessed and encountered with the group of boys signaled a move beyond empathy. That is, beyond empathy is the *courage and strength to love.* There is no demilitarized zone between love and that which is not love. The alternative is a terminal situation of apathy, incivility, violence, and ultimately death. Hamer knew this all too well, which is why she suggested that love is about survival. Perhaps Martin Luther King captured it best in a Palm Sunday sermon in 1959 when he asserted, "Today it is no longer a choice between violence and nonviolence; it is either nonviolence or nonexistence."[20]

---

19. Hamer, *Speeches*, 184. Speech at the University of Wisconsin, Madison, on Jan. 29, 1976.

20. West, *Radical King*, 37.

BUT WE STILL NEED EMPATHY, RIGHT?

Over the past several decades, the concept of empathy has become a staple in pastoral theology and caregiving discourse at large. Teaching and training students, pastoral caregivers, and other care practitioners in the development of empathic capacity remains a crucial pedagogical element in theological education, chaplaincy, pastoral counseling and psychology, social work, and other areas in the social sciences and humanities. It is suggested here that empathy is best understood as an epistemological category—a way of knowing—as a person suspends their way of knowing and experiencing the world for the sake of attempting to know and experience the world through the lens of another person, all the while maintaining their own sense of self-awareness and perspective. In contemporary ecclesiology and pastoral theology, empathy is indispensable, and is a key determinant in the efficacy of the care of souls and the integrity of the spiritual care enterprise.[21]

Perhaps Heinz Kohut, more than any other contemporary psychoanalytic thinker in the latter half of the twentieth century, has advanced the concept of empathy, referring to it as "vicarious introspection . . . [reflecting the] capacity to think and feel oneself into the inner life of another person." Being far more than a one-time event, Kohut describes it as "our lifelong ability to experience what another person experiences, though usually, and appropriately, to an attenuated degree."[22] But Kohut is also clear to highlight the neutrality of empathy, that is, a capacity for empathy does not transform one into a moral agent. Instead, empathy is only one tool, albeit an important tool, that is used to understand or enhance relationality with another. Kohut is forceful on this point when outlining the use of empathy in psychoanalytic culture, noting that "it is a *value-neutral tool of observation* which (a) can *lead to correct or incorrect results*, (b) can be used in the service of either compassionate, inimical, or dispassionate-neutral purposes, and (c) can be employed either rapidly and outside awareness or slowly and deliberately, with focused conscious attention."[23]

Nevertheless, we find that empathy is commonly mistaken as *the end*, as opposed to a *means to an end*. Moreover, as a matter of pastoral theological ethics, it begs the question then of *what that end should be*, and *what other human faculties are required—in addition to empathy*—to achieve that end. This misunderstanding is especially prevalent in contexts where the concept of empathy is mistaken for politically correct social etiquette or

---

21. See McClure, "Pastoral Care."
22. H. Kohut, *How Does Analysis Cure*, 82.
23. H. Kohut, *How Does Analysis Cure*, 175; emphasis added.

simply an appeasing way to communicate to others. Here, empathy is often referred to (whenever it is invoked) as a kind of *check-the-box* requirement that must be fulfilled when interacting with others. But even in the more so-called progressive areas of church and society where empathy is often taken for granted (as if people are born with it), the notion of empathy can cause individuals or institutions to become desensitized and blind to their own biases or empathic deficiencies. This is because the psychic need to *be identified as an empathic person or institution outweighs the difficult work of developing a capacity for empathy*. In such instances, assigning empathy to individual or group identity becomes almost ideological in nature. Said differently, it is one thing to be progressive on paper and in word, and another thing to be progressive in deed, context, and culture. Moreover, what about the limits of empathy? Is there an epistemological limit to what vicarious introspection can reveal? Unchecked hubris within an institution about its self-proclaimed progressive culture often creates the illusion that with empathy, they can comprehend and interpret the entirety of human experience. Especially as it relates to the enterprise of caregiving, such arrogance puts caregivers and institutions of care in the dangerous position to potentially do harm to others—even while having the best of intentions. Failure to recognize one's empathic limitations can lead to emotional brutality towards others.

The work of Hall, Matz, and Wood (2010) on the positive (and surprising) correlation between religious involvement and racism offers up a compelling example as it relates to the misunderstanding of empathy, and what it means to be empathic on paper, but to lack empathic capacity in culture. Referring to what they termed as religious racism, the authors argue that because "religious group identity organizes social perception in the same way as political, national, and other social identities, then religious people are likely to respond to others based on whether they are in-group or out-group members."[24] Of all of the categories of religiosity the authors examined such as intrinsic, extrinsic, fundamentalism, or agnosticism, they found that those who were agnostic were more universal in their thinking and, as a result, more racially tolerant. The other categories were positively correlated to racial intolerance. The authors recognize the incredible irony of their research given that, according to them, "all major religions preach love and acceptance, and many religious people experience their faith as oriented towards social welfare."[25] *It is not beyond the pale to suggest that for those who participate in religions that preach love and acceptance, and*

---

24. Hall et al., "Why Don't We Practice," 127.
25. Hall et al., "Why Don't We Practice," 128.

are oriented toward social welfare, those same participants and groups also believe that they are empathic towards individuals of another race or ethnicity. Yet the authors of this study conclude that "religious motivations tend to be linked to a circumscribed form of humanitarianism that is *expressed primarily to in-group members* . . . [and that] highly religious people endorse benevolent values of humanitarianism, which reflect selflessness in relations with close others, *but not universalism, which involves accepting diversity and expressing concern for the welfare of all people and nature*."[26]

As Kohut indicated in his work, the use of empathy does not necessarily produce the right outcome, although it is generally needed to generate the right outcome. Empathy is but one tool. Doehring offers up a much-needed step in the right direction when she makes a clear distinction between empathy and other human faculties—compassion in this instance. Describing a pastoral care spectrum upon which to imagine human faculties such as emotional fusion, emotional disengagement, and empathy, she locates empathy in the middle—alongside compassion. While it is a little distinction, it is very important to note that Doehring uses empathy to define compassion. She doesn't make the common mistake (often made by scholars and practitioners alike) of using the words interchangeably. For Doehring, "compassion involves empathically experiencing the other's pain and being moved to help . . . empathy is about stepping into the religious world of another while monitoring what is going on in one's own world; compassion is about stepping into the worlds of pain and reaching out to those who are suffering."[27] It is here that I would argue that many scholars and practitioners don't make the next step: to enter the world of those who are suffering. Empathy is not enough.

Perlitz takes a similar approach to Doehring, suggesting that what he has termed "affectionate understanding" is just as pertinent as empathy to the therapeutic encounter. Empathy should not serve as an umbrella term that encompasses the full range of emotion in human experience.[28] The fact that the psychoanalytic field has not significantly explored how the other affective states of the caregiver impact the therapeutic encounter is rather odd given the inordinate amount of literature on erotic transference. According to Perlitz, "Valorizing and exploring empathy without also exploring the analyst's specific emotions therefore unduly truncates the fullness of the intersubjective field of patient and analyst."[29] He goes on to conclude that

26. Hall et al., "Why Don't We Practice," 128; emphasis added.
27. Doehring, *Practice of Pastoral Care*, 42–43.
28. Perlitz, "Beyond Kohut."
29. Perlitz, "Beyond Kohut," 250.

affectionate understanding, which is "comprised of both being understood and also affectionately felt about by the understanding other, is a more accurate and comprehensive term to describe a process that enables a patient to both feel understood and validated."[30] To this end, what Doehring and Perlitz refer to as compassion and affectionate understanding, respectively, in this book I refer to as *practices of love*. And it was this evidence and demonstration of love—a vision of a beloved community—that left the deepest impression upon me, when I met with the group of black male students in the research project.

ANTI-LOVE AND THE MESMERIZATION OF EVIL: THE ALTERNATIVE TO THE PRAXIS OF LOVE

Practices of love, and the proliferation of violence and hatred, are mutually exclusive. Practices of love and practices of violence are not independent. That is to say, there is no demilitarized zone between practices of love and practices of violence. Admittedly this proposition is Augustinian in nature when Augustine claims, "Evil has no positive nature; but the loss of good has received the name 'evil.'"[31] Yet, this is crucial in our understanding of love being the next step beyond empathy, and when it is abandoned, how it relates to the accrual of violence and evil. *When practices of love are abated or interrupted, forms of violence necessarily are put in motion. There is no space between practices of love and the mobilization of animus, evil, and violence. To stress this point, I suggest the binary of love vs. anti-love. There is no demilitarized space between practices of love and practices of hatred, hence the proposed dualism of love and anti-love.* The writer in the first chapter of John speaks in mutually exclusive terms with the announcement of the arrival of Jesus, saying that "in him was life, and the life was the light of men ... the light shines in the darkness, and the darkness has not overcome it" (John 1:4–5 ESV). That is to say, the redeeming light that radiates from the love ethic cannot at the same time entertain the darkness that emanates from violence and hatred. Again, in another place, the writer in 1 John continues with the language of mutual exclusivity when he posits, "If anyone says, 'I love God,' and hates his brother, he is a liar; for he who does not love his brother whom he has seen cannot love God who he has not seen" (1 John 4:20 ESV). Hence, the long tradition of attempting to justify American violence through Scripture is indicted in this one statement. The mutually

---

30. Perlitz, "Beyond Kohut," 250.
31. Augustine, *City of God*, 303.

exclusive nature of love and violence is firmly established when the writer claims:

> For this is the message that you have heard from the beginning, that we should love one another. We should not be like Cain, who was of the evil one and murdered his brother. And why did he murder him? Because his own deeds were evil and his brother's righteous. Do not be surprised, brothers, that the world hates you. We know that we have passed out of death into life, because we love the brothers. Whoever does not love abides in death. Everyone who hates his brother is a murderer, and you know that no murderer has eternal life abiding in him. (1 John 3:11–15 ESV)

Because of this mutually exclusive nature between love and hatred/violence, I will also refer to hatred and violence as anti-love. In invoking the term of anti-love, I seek to create a binary that better clarifies the mutually exclusive nature of human love and human animus, and that also challenges the erroneous perception of a disinterested space between the two.

Perhaps one of the greatest misunderstandings (and tragedies) of the civil rights movement is that it was interpreted as giving concessions to black and brown people based on the sympathies and moral progress of white institutions and the American power structure. Since then, that interpretation has expanded to incorporate a presumptuous attitude of *enough is enough*. But this sordid form of romanticizing history has done significant damage to the soul of the nation. It blinds us to the true condition of a soul-sick nation, and then leaves us in shock by events like January 6, 2021, that threaten to upend the democratic experiment. The fact is, while the oppression of black and brown people was dramatized during the mid-twentieth century, that period in history was not about giving anything to a people that was in need. Instead, it was the latest example in human history of domination, hatred, contempt, and oppression, where the oppressed people endeavored to stir the collective conscience and repair the soul of a nation; a collective soul that had been ossified through the toleration of hatred, which, in this case, represented the indulgence of racial animus and white supremacy for generations.

Understood in this manner, we can understand how in the voluminous work of Fannie Lou Hamer and Martin Luther King, the mutually exclusive nature of love and violence was never separated. King understood better than most at the time (and probably still today) that because America was founded on violence (i.e., evidence of anti-love), then intentional practices of love in the form of nonviolence were the only way to heal the degenerative heart of the nation. He sought to offer an alternative vision to the violence that we have become mesmerized by, and then seduced into believing is unavoidable. He warned that "the aftermath of nonviolence is the creation of the beloved community, while the aftermath of violence is tragic bitterness."[32] For King, an understanding of love and the beloved community is inseparable from an understanding of human suffering and violence. He understood that the logic of love connected us all, and that the salvation of a nation could not transcend any group that was oppressed and marginalized, especially when it occurred for the benefit of the rich and powerful:

> All life is interrelated. We are caught in an inescapable network of mutuality; tied in a single garment of destiny. Whatever affects one directly, affects all indirectly. As long as there is poverty in this world, no man can be totally rich even if he has a billion dollars. As long as diseases are rampant and millions of people cannot expect to live more than twenty or thirty years, no man can be totally healthy, even if he just got a clean bill of health from the finest clinic in America. Strangely enough, I can never be what I ought to be until you are what you ought to be. You can never be what you ought to be until I am what I ought to be. This is the way the world is made. I didn't make it that way, but this is the interrelated structure of reality.[33]

Consequently, to understand love and violence as anything but mutually exclusive is to render the logic of love so unintelligible that its efficacy for individual and collective metanoia is eviscerated. There is no middle space between practices of love and acts of violence and human suffering. Over the long run, the absence of a praxis of love fosters communities of hostility, malice, suspicion of *the other*, bigotry, emotional brutality, and violence. Practices of love are essential to life-giving political, economic, and social policy. They are the last line of defense in saving the democratic experiment. We either labor to form a praxis of love or suffer the consequences of anti-love over the long run. Both Hamer and King understood the formidable undertaking of fostering the beloved community over and against the normalization of violence and hostility in the American psyche. Both leaders also knew that a praxis of love represented an intergenerational project that would be costly. King knew all too well that:

> There is no easy way to create a world where men and women can live together, where each has his own job and house and

---

32. See King, "An Experiment in Love," in *Testament of Hope*, 18.

33. See commencement address, King, "The American Dream," given at Lincoln University, in *Testament of Hope*, 210.

where all children receive as much education as their minds can absorb. But if such a world is created in our lifetime, it will be done in the United States by Negroes and white people of good will. It will be accomplished by persons who have the courage to put an end to suffering by willingly suffering themselves rather than inflict suffering upon others. It will be done by rejecting the racism, materialism, and violence that has characterized Western civilization and especially by working toward a world of brotherhood, cooperation and peace.[34]

It is foolhardy then to interpret the violence and human suffering witnessed in the aftermath of the first black presidency as only incidental to American culture. If we interpret as only incidental several hundred thousand needless deaths related to the coronavirus pandemic all because of individualism, selfishness, and a refusal to make even a token effort at complying with public health recommendations; or if we interpret the violent insurrection on the US Capitol on January 6, 2021 as only an anomaly; or if we believe that the murders of George Floyd, Breonna Taylor, or Ahmaud Arbery (just to name a few) are insignificant and not connected to the long-standing legacy of systemic racism; then we interpret and internalize all such thinking at our own peril. The common claim offered up by many that *this is not America* is a gross miscalculation that reflects idealism used to prop up group identity. *To be clear, this is America. All of these events represent the cessation of practices of love in the Western polis. They are symptoms of the accrual of anti-love over the long run.* In their study on hate crime trends in the United States as of 2020, Levin et al. note that black people are most often targeted in hate crimes by a wide margin (35 percent of all cases). The next closest community is the LBGTQ+ community at 13 percent. According to the authors of this study, race and ethnicity reflect the most common bias, representing nearly 60 percent of all reported hate crimes. When interpreting the data for 2020, the authors assert, "These hate crimes, which consist mostly of threats and assaults, rose to the highest level since 2001. Person-directed crimes accounted for over two-thirds of all 2020 FBI enumerated hate crimes."[35] Yet, despite the increase in hate crime, as a society, we continue to deny the reality of racial violence and hatred. In her research on the capacity for state and local governments to simply acknowledge the existence of hate crime, Jeannine Bell laments, "America is failing victims of bias-motivated violence. The vast majority of police departments, more than 80%, report that not a single hate crime occurred in their jurisdiction.

---

34. King, *Testament of Hope*, 61.
35. Levin et al., "U.S. Hate Crimes Trends," 769–70.

When hate crimes are recognized by the police, prosecutors are reluctant to prosecute. Despite the presence of hate crime laws in the vast majority of states, American law enforcement, with its refusal to acknowledge the presence of hate crimes by investigating and prosecuting, acts by and large as if hate crimes were not happening."[36]

An honest psychospiritual assessment demands that we take a long view when contemplating the soul-condition of the nation. In the balance between love and nonviolence vs. apathy, malice, and violence, what is the pastoral prognosis of the future? In a study commissioned by the Anti-Defamation League, two surges of violence were observed in the last quarter century: the first occurring in the mid- to late 1990s and then another sharp increase since 2005.[37] The ADL correlates the former surge to events like the standoffs in Waco, Texas, and Ruby Ridge, Idaho; the election of Bill Clinton; the passage of NAFTA; and tighter gun control in connection to the Brady Law. The latter surge is correlated to the election of Barack Obama, the global economic collapse in the first decade of the new century, and the foreclosure debacle. Since 1970, there have been at least 111 school shootings (K–12) where 202 people have been killed and 454 injured. The common demographic of the school shooters is young white males who were former or current students inspired by previous shootings.[38] In another study by Grinshteyn and Hemenway as it relates to violent death in the United States, the findings are compelling, but ominous. That work deserves special treatment here. Comparing the United States to other countries regarding gun violence, the authors observe that:

> *The United States has an enormous firearm problem compared with other high-income countries.* Americans are 10 times more likely to die as a result of a firearm compared with residents of these other high-income countries. In the United States, the firearm homicide rate is 25 times higher, the firearm suicide rate is 8 times higher, and the unintentional gun death rate is more than 6 times higher. Of all firearm deaths in all these countries, more than 80% occur in the United States.[39]

And in terms of general homicide:

> *The United States has a serious homicide problem.* The overall homicide rate in the United States is 7 times higher than in these

---

36. Bell, "Pick the Lowest," 725.
37. See Anti-Defamation League, *Dark and Constant Rage*.
38. Cai and Patel, "Half-Century of School Shootings."
39. Grinshteyn and Hemenway, "Violent Death Rates," 270.

> *other countries*. Men in the United States are approximately 9 times more likely to be a homicide victim than their male counterparts in these other high-income countries, and women are 4 times more likely to be a homicide victim than women in these other countries. The homicide rate is fueled by the firearm homicide rate in the United States. More than two-thirds of the homicides in the United States are firearm homicides; by contrast, firearm homicide accounts for less than 20% of homicides in the other high-income countries.[40]

And when connecting homicide and ethnicity, the authors observe:

> Nonwhites in the United States have far greater rates of homicide victimization than whites, but even the white homicide rate is greater than the total homicide rate of any of the other countries in our study. The white homicide victimization rate in the United States is 4 times higher than the average rate in the other high-income countries, driven in part by a white firearm homicide victimization rate that is 13 times higher.[41]

Violence against religious institutions has gained momentum in recent years as well. In the first half of 2019, three black churches were burned in a southern Louisiana parish, sparking traumatic memories in the community of a violent Jim Crow South. The perpetrator who killed Lori Kaye and wounded three others at the Chabad of Poway Synagogue on April 28, 2019, justified his actions using Reformed evangelical theology. In 2018, a gunman killed eleven people and wounded six others at the Tree of Life Congregation in Pittsburgh. Twenty-six people were killed at First Baptist Church in Sutherland Springs, Texas, in 2017. This followed on the heels of the massacre at Emanuel African Methodist Episcopal Church in Charleston, South Carolina, in 2015 when the gunman entered a Bible study and killed nine people.

Ultimately, this trending of attacks against vulnerable populations such as schools and religious institutions, coupled with the seeming national infatuation with guns, is a sobering reminder of how this Western republic was founded through the justification and use of violence, and of the rationalization and moralization of radical evils perpetuated against those existing on the underside of modernity. It is not uncommon in such instances for political and community leaders, or religious scholars and clergy, to become defensive and attempt to distance themselves from the words and actions of the workers of evil, arguing that those who use religious ideology

---

40. Grinshteyn and Hemenway, "Violent Death Rates," 270–71.
41. Grinshteyn and Hemenway, "Violent Death Rates," 271.

to underwrite violence are illegitimate. In some instances, we must be willing to acknowledge that many of the architects and workers of this extremist violence are also card-carrying Christians.

Religious institutions must do the soul-searching work to acknowledge and own their violent (albeit embarrassing and shameful) histories in order to increase the probability that such actions will not repeat themselves in the present or future. Self-reflexive work on an individual and group level must be done to uncover latent biases, bigotry, and hatred that lie dormant in theory, scholarship, theology, and culture. Juergensmeyer outlines the ease with which far right-wing groups are able to appropriate theology and God-talk for their purposes. Adherents of various strands of dominion theology (the belief that Christian ideology should govern all aspects of creation) and postmillennial theologies employ theologians such as John Calvin, Dietrich Bonhoeffer, or Reinhold Niebuhr to justify their violence against what they perceive to be mainstream liberalism. Making the connection of religion to violence, Juergensmeyer argues this is possible because of "the nature of religion and its claims of power over life and death"; the symmetry of violence and politics that "bases its own legitimacy on the currency of weapons and can be challenged successfully only on a level of force"; and the intrinsic disposition of violence, which is "a destructive display of power, and in a time when competing groups are attempting to assert their strength, the power of violence becomes a valuable political commodity."[42]

Over the long run, the abatement of practices of love, which necessarily precipitates the individual and collective toleration of unnecessary human suffering, violence, or the conditions and practices that cultivate it, causes us to become immune to its material effects—generally until something much worse occurs in close proximity to us or to someone close to us. Over time, we cultivate a collective propensity to be mesmerized by the prevalence of evil and injustice, essentializing it—both as actors and bystanders—in a manner that renders it against a backdrop of invisibility. A cursory review of social media and a twenty-four-hour news cycle certifies the observation being made here. More often than not, unless something is related to violence, scandal, or brutality—physically, verbally, or emotionally—it does not make the headlines. Referring to the concept of "consensus trance" or the "sleep of everyday life" coined by Charles Tart,[43] Jeffrey Means puts forth a compelling argument for how violence has become intrinsic to the Western psychic space.[44] We have become so accustomed to violence and incivility that it has

---

42. Juergensmeyer, "Christian Violence in America," 99.
43. Tart, *Waking Up*.
44. Means, *Trauma & Evil*.

become normalized in what we perceive to be acceptable benchmarks in a civilized society. The ongoing inability to pass legislation for gun control, even in the wake of heinous massacres that could have been avoided, is but one example. The collective intrapsychic race to forget about the violent insurrection on the Capitol on January 6, 2021, and the refusal of many institutions (including the academy and Christian organizations) to engage in a critical analysis of what the insurrection reveals about the American democratic experiment, is symptomatic of another example of the consensus trance. For Means, "awakening from the consensus trances in which we are stuck as a result of living in a violent society is rare."[45] *Overall, our toleration and enchantment with violence and brutality suppress practices of love and ossify the human heart in a way that immunizes it against what should otherwise be emotions of anger, horror, and even rage, in the face of violence.*[46]

WHAT'S LOVE GOT TO DO WITH IT? A BIPOLAR RELATIONSHIP WITH LOVE

Why is it so difficult to talk about love? Why is it a topic that many people shy away from? In the public sphere, why is love often perceived as being inappropriate or irrelevant? These are but a few questions that I have begun to reflect upon more—especially as they relate to pastoral ethics and praxis. On one end of the spectrum in our cultural understanding of love, we timidly engage the topic of love from the idea of *tough love* (and I have never been sure what this means). Nevertheless, from this vantage point, one can already see that the understanding of love is predisposed to weakness, and those who use the qualifying adjective *tough* believe that some form of abrasiveness is conducive to, and perhaps even necessary for, interpersonal and group relations. Talk of love is considered suspicious, representing a threat to whatever is deemed normative or acceptable within the subculture. The justification of emotional brutality is rationalized with this understanding of love. At the other end of the spectrum of our cultural understanding of love, to even discuss love (at least openly) is considered contrary to social etiquette, unprofessional, perhaps even unscholarly, and ineffectual to the performance and productivity goals and objectives of the community or organization. In such places (which will often include the public sector, ivory tower culture, and even the religious guild and academy, and by extension the church), aloofness, suspicion, zero-sum competitiveness, clique culture, and even practices of social abrasiveness are often preferred over

---

45. Means, *Trauma & Evil*, 31.
46. See D. Gibson, *Frederick Douglass*.

manifestations of vulnerability, trust, compassion, self-sacrifice, hope, commitment, risk-taking, and kindness—all of which represent character traits we tend to idealize in prominent religious figures such as Gandhi, Dorothy Day, Fannie Lou Hamer, Martin Luther King, or Teresa of Calcutta, etc., but for some reason, we shy away from these various manifestations of love in our personal lives.

Occasionally during my classroom introduction to pastoral care courses, I ask students a simple question: What is God? More often than not, the initial responses I get back reflect how we have trained students and future leaders in theological education (and the church) for generations: descriptions of the Divine that are overrun with statements of theological complexity, abstractness, and historical creeds and confessions. After the class has labored with the question (which is a good thing), or after I have offered up a few hints, someone might eventually refer to love. Even within theological education we tend to struggle with one of the most profound ontological statements about the nature of the Divine: God is love. No matter the theological or philosophical position regarding the source and hermeneutical authority of the canon, no matter where one resides on a spectrum of liberalism or conservatism, the ontological statement offered up by the Johannine witness is profound: the Divine is love and love is of God. Consequently, when we see love, we see *an image* of the Divine. *This begs the question then of what love looks like.* We know what violence and brutality look like given their normalization in our collective psychic space. We know what violence and brutality look like when we see it, whether interpersonally, interculturally, or internationally. But how does love look? Do we know love when we see it? Moreover, why do we struggle with a coherent understanding and language of love?

In reflecting on this dilemma, I briefly turn to the liberal arts, and more specifically, the musical arts. The liberal arts and culture tend to maintain a robust capacity to illuminate the psychic space of groups and societies.[47] Here, I use the musical arts to showcase the collective bipolar struggle we have with love in public spaces. More specifically as it relates to the questions around public practices of love, I am reminded of two songs that, ironically, came out in the same year of 1984. To the extent that we accept the premise that the arts are reflective of society and culture in a given context and time, I believe these two songs reflect a kind of bipolar relationship Western culture struggles with when it comes to love. On the one hand, we deny the importance of love. In its place is a predilection for busyness and

---

47. Said, *Orientalism*. Refer to his commentary on culture, Westernism, and the Orient.

productivity, which often serve as markers of personal importance and human value. Physical human interactions are deemed unnecessary luxuries that hamper productivity, thereby limiting relational affect and human connectivity to mere happenstance. Massive amounts of *anxiety-based energy* are expended to repress the fear of being vulnerable to another. The result is *affective exhaustion*, which stems from the ongoing denial of love. On this side of the polarity (of the bipolar relationship with love), cognition, intellection, and disembodied discourse are valorized—and even sacralized. This relation to love is captured in the song performed by Tina Turner entitled "What's Love Got to Do with It." But in a moment during the song—when the unconscious becomes conscious—Turner's words betray the main theme of the song: the thought of giving love a try frightens her, so for the sake of emotional protection she shys away from it.[48]

This ballad, in brilliant fashion, captures in song and melody our *annihilation anxiety related to being lost in love*. The futility of love is put on full display such that it renders it unintelligible. *She puts into words and song the coping mechanisms and compensatory actions we take to protect our core-self from being disappointed by love*.[49] While there are many lenses through which we could examine this musical refrain that succinctly captures our collective propensity to deny love, Erikson is especially useful in describing how we have learned, early in life, to be mistrustful of relationships when the experience of love is hurtful, or even devastating or traumatic.[50] We have no fundamental capacity to trust ourselves and life, let alone anyone else. Imagine how this looks when pastors and caregivers go into their given vocations lacking the basic capacity to trust. According to Erikson, this "characterizes individuals who withdraw into themselves in particular ways when at odds with themselves and with others . . . [such that] they sometimes close up, refusing food and comfort . . . [and become] oblivious to companionship."[51] But in a moment during the song—when the unconscious becomes conscious—Turner's words imply that while she has been

---

48. Lyle and Britten, "What's Love Got."

49. The coping mechanism regarding love is the rationalization that what is being felt or experienced in human connectedness is akin to conspicuous consumption and therefore unnecessary because it represents nothing more than physicality and logic. It is the valorized rationalization that closeness is unnecessary if that closeness is expendable. Another way of saying this is "who needs a heart when a heart can be broken." The compensatory mechanism reflects the effort to repress the possibility of intimacy, or to put it another way, "you must try to ignore that it means more than that." Over the long run, repressing the possibility of intimacy, and ultimately love, results in other psychospiritual maladies. There is no replacement for love.

50. Erikson, *Identity and Life Cycle*.

51. Erikson, *Identity and Life Cycle*, 58.

thinking more about giving love a try, she also has to think about protecting herself, and that the combination of these thoughts frightens her. Even in the midst of coping and compensatory functions, probably through the psychological defense of splitting, Turner vocalizes what many people know, but are afraid to name and own: *that suppressing and denying love is not an emotionally healthy way to live, but we choose it over being devastated by love.*

On the opposite side of the love-polarity is the ever-present desire *to love* and *be loved*. Yet, it represents a *frustrated desire*, as the felt and embodied memories of either one's love not being good enough or the experience of love itself being traumatic makes individuals and/or groups become ambivalent (at best) about love. Such memories could go back to childhood. Yet, ambivalence does not abate the desire for love. This is captured brilliantly in the song performed by British-American band Foreigner in the song entitled "I Want to Know What Love Is."[52] While there is certainly more than one interpretation that could be applied to the lyrics of the song, it is clear that the singer is thinking more critically about the practice of meaning making and love as he grows older. This is a normative process that many people go through in the latter life cycle stages: negotiating what love will mean in my life going forward. Yet, the traumatic memories of love make the singer doubt that he can love again. Nevertheless, this doubt about love does not make the desire for, and pursuit of love go away, and the *frustrated desires* of the singer are made manifest in the chorus and title of this best-selling song. Again, we cannot overstate the irony that this song is released in the same year of Tina Turner's platinum hit. It reflects a culture's struggle with love. Could it be that the love-polarity described herein is in part the reason behind the brutality, violence, incivility, and *suspicion of the other* that have become normalized and intrinsic within the collective psychic space of the Western democracy? In another place where I take up the effects of emotional trauma, or what I refer to as trauma of the heart, I discuss the deleterious health effects related to the frustrated desire of love. In that case, the implications were related to HIV/AIDS, but can be transferred to any situation of unhealthy coping and compensatory functions when love is frustrated. While my observations in that article were informed by my therapeutic work in black and brown communities, they also reflect an element of the broader human condition when we are deprived of love:

> The spread of HIV/AIDS in the African American community, I am suggesting in part, is a reaction to affective or emotional disillusionment, or what I have termed *trauma of the heart*. Trauma of the heart is conceptualized as emotional devastation that

52. Jones, "I Want to Know."

stems from the experience of infidelity in any intimate relationship where a covenant, not just marriage, has been established. The covenantal, interpersonal intimacy need not be limited to sexual relationships, but could include close friendships, or any other relationship with a partner, family member, or person whereby the nature of the relationship in and of itself was based on its exclusivity and an expectation of fidelity. The violation of such relationships can be traumatic. In my clinical and pastoral experience with persons with HIV/AIDS, a narrative of emotional and relational betrayal by family, friends, and lovers was a common theme [that led to reckless practices that contributed to infection].[53]

A DESCRIPTION OF THE LOOK OF LOVE

Martin Luther King Jr. offers a compelling glimpse as to what love looks like, and what I believe I witnessed in my research with the group of black boys. For King, a robust life is multidimensional and reflects human interconnectedness. He likens life to three dimensions where its length is characterized by personal achievement and self-concern, its breadth reflects concern for others, and the height is connectivity with God. King further likens the breadth-dimension to the parable of the good Samaritan, where the priest and the Levite look beyond the needs and suffering of a person who was brutalized during a robbery. It was the Samaritan passerby that offered assistance. It is important to observe that the parable suggests it was the *religious other*, the one whose religious tradition was considered subordinate to that of the Jews, who offered assistance. This compels us to ponder the role that religion plays in fostering apathy. King's commentary on this episode is compelling, and I quote him at length here as we ponder a prospective image of what love looks like:

> So often we say that the priest and the Levite were in a big hurry to get to some ecclesiastical meeting and so they did not have time. They were concerned about that. I would rather think of it another way. I can well imagine that they were quite afraid. You see, the Jericho road is a dangerous road, and the same thing that happened to the man who was robbed and beaten could have happened to them. *So I imagine the first question that the priest and the Levite asked was this: "If I stop to help this man, what will happen to me?"* Then the good Samaritan came by, and

53. D. Gibson, "Trauma of the Heart," 49.

by the very nature of his concern reversed the question: "If I do not stop to help this man, what will happen to him?" And so this man was great because he had the *mental equipment for a dangerous altruism.* He was great because he could surround the length of his life with the breadth of life. He was great not only because he had ascended to certain heights of economic security, but because he could condescend to the depths of human need.[54]

According to King's commentary on the parable, the Samaritan was compelled to social action, or moved to become involved with the injured victim after engaging in thoughtful reflections with himself (i.e., *mental equipment for a dangerous altruism*). For King, the Samaritan asked a more compelling question that resulted in a will to act on behalf of another, compared to the more inconsequential self-centered questions that the priest and Levite entertained. The type of interior questioning exercised by the Samaritan is akin to Arendt's position that mindfulness (as opposed to empathy) is the more excellent condition precedent to social action. King refers to it as possessing "mental equipment for a dangerous altruism." In similar fashion, Arendt says that mindfulness is the "disposition to live together explicitly with oneself, to have intercourse with oneself, that is, to be engaged in that silent dialogue."[55]

To this end, combining the thought of Hannah Arendt and Martin Luther King Jr., *I suggest love looks like a person's intentional willingness to get involved with another person for the sake of that person's well-being and humanity. Love is my willingness to get involved with you, on behalf of you, for the sake of you. Love is the courage of vulnerability and to get involved with you, on behalf of you, for the sake of you. Love is action, and that action is getting involved with you. Love is having an affair with you, for the sake of you.* This look of love is precisely what we see in the life and work of Fannie Lou Hamer. I suspect that some may find this suggested definition of a praxis of love uncomfortable, as it may come across as too provocative. The immature, insecure, or uninitiated may try to sexualize the proposal. Yet, while the sex act may represent one of many expressions of love, it is ill advised to sexualize what is being put forth in this suggestion of a praxis of love. To sexualize this proposition of an image of love and subsequently reject it runs the risk of rendering our understanding of love so abstract that it requires no ethical mandate and as such, renders it so unintelligible that it becomes one of the few Christian ethics that *requires no proof of life.* Moreover, this is

---

54. King, *Measure of a Man*, 44–45; emphasis added.

55. Hannah Arendt, as quoted by Matthiesen and Klitmoller, "Encountering the Stranger," 194.

precisely what God decided to do for us: get involved with us, for the sake of us, at great cost to God's self.

It is this proposed image of love that I witnessed when I met with the group of black boys and their teachers, and when I posed the original question *what does a theology of give-a-shit entail.*[56] I suggest that what the teachers were in effect saying is that while they can give new faculty members the tools and techniques to teach in the classroom, *they cannot teach new faculty how to love the students*. In their nomenclature, *they cannot teach how to give a shit*. That is a lesson that was not only relevant for that high school, but is irreducibly relevant to theological education, personal life, interpersonal and intercultural relationships, and church and society at large. A practical theology of giving a shit means practices of love that suggest I am willing to get involved with you for the sake of you. Love must be practiced. And it is only after arduous practice that we can imagine and develop a praxis of love that is capable of transforming and healing a democratic social experiment that was founded, in large part, on the backs of enslaved black people, the genocide of Native American people, and continues to be overrun with anti-love and violence because we refuse to acknowledge our true soul-condition.

Herein is a picture of love: the black boys that I met with demonstrated that despite whatever pain and heartache they may have experienced in their personal lives (and to be sure, some of their stories brought the teachers to tears), the boys still fostered the courage to show vulnerability and affection to their peers and the teachers in the room during the interview. The boys were straightforward in communicating that they decided to volunteer to be a part of the research project because they wanted to be with the teachers and peers who were also involved. That is to say, they were there because the others were there. They wanted to be involved with the others. When asked about who they admired or wanted to be around, they referred to each other with a strong sense of endearment. There was not one mention about admiring a famous actor or rich athlete. The boys demonstrated courage to be vulnerable with their peers, the teachers, and to vocalize that they wanted to be involved with their comrades. As I observed the faculty in the room, there was not a dry eye.

When asked about who they wanted to be, and what they wanted to do in the future, all of the responses pointed back to loving their communities, and a vision of love for the larger society. There was a movement from the individual practice of love to imagining a larger praxis of love that transcended their individual goals or ambitions. Here is how I describe what I

---

56. D. G. Gibson, "When Empathy."

experienced in that moment, and the deep impression that was left on me: *the pain of love from many of their past experiences did not deter the boys from assuming the risk of love in the present and embracing the hope of love in the future.* Admittedly, I was initially concerned (and remain concerned) that with such responses, the boys were being forced to grow up too fast. Instead of allowing them to be boys, there was a risk that they were being thrust into spaces of psychospiritual maturity that even adults resist and shy away from. Nevertheless, this concern does not have to be mutually exclusive to using my experience with the boys as a viable source for theological and psychospiritual reflections. The love that the boys demonstrated was consistent with King's connection of courage and love. Borrowing from Paul Tillich's understanding of courage, King asserts that courage "is self-affirmation in spite of death and nonbeing, and he who is courageous takes the fear of death into his self-affirmation and acts upon it . . . [this courage] is not selfishness, for self-affirmation includes both a *proper self-love* and a *properly propositioned love of others.*"[57] To be clear, in this instance, instead of society and culture arrogantly assuming that they possess all knowledge and supposition to teach black boys—in this instance, it is black boys who have much to teach us.

In my observation of the teachers, they were willing to take the risk of displaying affection to the boys, not knowing how or if their affection would be received. For anyone, it can be emotionally painful and disorienting when one's love and affection is not received, let alone reciprocated. But in my estimation, the teachers assumed the risks of love, in part, through their tears. They displayed embodied affection, not knowing if it would be received or belittled. Moreover, they demonstrated that they *took the boys seriously*, and that they *believed in the boys*, both of which are critical to practices of love, but not necessary as they relate to empathy. To be sure, a person can be empathic towards another human being and, at the same time, not believe in them. Here, the lesson is that whether we are engaging in the individual practice of love or daring to imagine a larger praxis of love capable of transforming a community, *there is no such thing as riskless love.* There is always the risk that we can suffer the emotional consequence of our love not being received or good enough. If there is no risk, there is no love. Moreover, unlike empathy, you cannot love people you don't believe in. *Empathy has limitations and boundaries that love dares to transgress.*

The teachers' engagement with the boys reminded me of James Baldwin's engagement with his nephew through a letter he wrote to him and placed in the preface to "The Fire Next Time." In this letter, he *takes his*

---

57. King, *Strength to Love*, 123; emphasis added.

nephew seriously by not devaluating his appearance, presentation, subjectivity, or his persona. Telling his nephew that he reminds him of his father (i.e., Baldwin's brother), he observes "like him, you are tough, dark, vulnerable, moody—with a very definite tendency to sound truculent because you want no one to think you are soft."[58] Perhaps at this point, many would have presumed to tell Baldwin's nephew how to change those character traits and to become *more normalized* according to social etiquette. But Baldwin doesn't engage in this demeaning behavior. *This is because he takes his nephew seriously.* He believes in his nephew. That is, he loves his nephew. Consequently, instead of paternalistically depreciating this young boy, Baldwin follows his observation by suggesting his nephew's way of being is because "you want no one to think you are soft."[59] Viewed through his nephew's perspective, empathy demands that Baldwin must consider the repercussion for being thought of as "soft" in the world of his nephew. Instead of rebuffing his nephew's subjectivity, Baldwin affirms and honors it—he embraces it.

Similarly, I found the teachers that were present with the boys that I interviewed *took the boys seriously*. They didn't rebuff, challenge, or trivialize the personhood of the boys. Instead, they loved on the subjectivities that were presented to them. Lastly, in another place in the letter, Baldwin refers to his nephew as "my dear namesake," a reference of endearment that carries the connotation that Baldwin believes in his nephew. Baldwin suggests that he will live on through his nephew in a way that separation or death cannot thwart. For Baldwin, love is forever. To love another is to also suggest that you believe in them. And I witnessed this in the teachers' interactions with the boys that I interviewed, and I witnessed this in several of the senior boys as they talked about some of their younger peers (who were present). It was unequivocally clear that all of the faculty members had the earnest expectations that the boys would move forward beyond high school and be successful in their endeavors and pursuits. The boys knew that others *believed in them*. It was evident that the boys knew they were loved. From the perspective of the teachers, it was a foregone conclusion. The boys fed off the confidence that was psychically invested in them.

I have resisted offering up a concise definition of love. For bell hooks, love does not represent just one human faculty or expression. She suggests that love is both simultaneously a concern about one's personal, spiritual welfare and growth, and another's spiritual welfare and growth. In her definition, spiritual is not delimited to the religious realm, but related to the core realm of each human being. I believe such a paradigm opens the boundaries

---

58. Baldwin, "The Fire Next Time," in *Collected Essays*, 291.
59. "The Fire Next Time," in *Collected Essays*, 291.

we erect in how we love others. According to hooks, "To truly love we must learn to mix various ingredients—care, affection, recognition, respect, commitment, and trust, as well as honest and open communication . . . [but] learning faulty definitions of love when we are quite young makes it difficult to be loving as we grow older."[60]

LEARNING TO RESPECT THE POWER OF LOVE

Fannie Lou Hamer understood all too well that there was an inextricable link between a robust praxis of love and the welfare of the democracy. In the summer of 1968, just after the assassination of Martin Luther King that sent shock waves across the country, Hamer addressed an audience in Kentucky where among the many issues of racial hatred that she spoke to, she also suggested that the death of King was not limited to an actor in Memphis, but in many respects, was reflective of the racial animus of the nation. It represented yet another instance of death and destruction when anti-love has run its course. But Hamer maintained an irreducible respect for the power of love. It was the ethic through which she interpreted her social ethics and her body of work. With much of black America still in traumatic shock over the death of King, Hamer boldly exclaimed to her Kentucky audience:

> *You don't want to hear the truth—I know you're upset, but we just going to upset you more. I love you, the reason I'm upsetting you.* And we going to have to face the problem that we have in America today and stop going to church acting this big lie because we know the most segregated hour in America is eleven o'clock church service . . . We have a grave problem that's facing us today in this country and if we're going to make democracy a reality, we better start working now.[61]

Empathy is not enough to save the democratic experiment from the death throes of the racial imagination. A praxis of love is the next move after empathy to redeem the collective soul of the nation. Caregivers and faith leaders across the board are experiencing burnout at record levels that I suggest, in part, reflects the absence of reciprocal practices of love in our communities. No matter how we may attempt to professionalize, moralize, justify, or rationalize practices of anti-love, over the long run, it will only yield the fruit of self-delusion and death. All are in need of love, and all have

---

60. hooks, *All About Love*, 5.
61. Hamer, *Speeches*, 82. Speech in Kentucky during the summer of 1968; emphasis added.

a responsibility to give love. The democracy is in need of love affairs—that is to say—practices of love that will enable them to experience their own sense of humanity, to reaffirm to them that their love is good enough, and to remind them that they too are lovable. But this vision of a new Jerusalem, or of a beloved community, requires that we be willing to get involved with each other. As evidenced in the social ethics and body of work we see in Fannie Lou Hamer, *love is not what you say to me—love is what you do to me*. Perhaps, the vision of love offered up by the black boys I interviewed is a good start for love. After it is all said and done, perhaps the current situation simply means that we have to start *giving a shit about each other*.

8

PLAYING WITH JAMES BALDWIN'S FIRE
Vestiges of Backlash, Redemption, and Hope

Everything now, we must assume, is in our hands; we have no right to assume otherwise. If we—and now I mean the relatively conscious whites and the relatively conscious blacks, who must, like lovers, insist on, or create, the consciousness of the others—do not falter in our duty now, we may be able, handful that we are, to end the racial nightmare, and achieve our country, and change the history of the world. If we do not now dare everything, the fulfilment of that prophecy, re-created from the Bible in song by a slave, is upon us: *God gave Noah the rainbow sign, No more water, the fire next time!*

—JAMES BALDWIN

SINCE CHILDHOOD I HAVE possessed a rather vivid and active imagination. My imagination spanned from the fictional to the nonfictional, from fantasy to reality. I had an appetite to dream, to play with my thoughts, to drift away, to lose myself in liminal spaces, in the world of possibilities. I loved to ponder my thoughts. It seemed like I could never turn them off. During my years of pastoring a church, I would periodically tell the congregants that part of my sermon preparation included running several miles before I entered the pulpit on Sunday morning. But it was not the running that was important. It was what the running afforded me: a time to myself where I could imagine. Before I would preach, I had to imagine the sermon and the preaching moment. Even in academia, before I enter the classroom to engage with students, I need space to imagine the pedagogical event, to imagine the learning moment. The practice of imagining is therapeutic for me. Spending time alone with my thoughts was indispensable to my sense of self. It remains indispensable to my core being.

I recall my imagination being especially incited as a child when my parents would watch the television miniseries *Roots*.[1] Or, if they were not actually watching the miniseries, it would be playing in the background on the television. *Roots* frightened me. The images terrified me. To this very day, there is one scene that I have never forgotten. I recall a black man attempting to escape his enslavement. He was running across a vast field of what appeared to be grain or wheat. There were two white men, each on their respective horse, chasing this man. The two white men were holding what appeared to be a net that was spread out between the two of them as they were riding their horses. The pursuers eventually caught the fleeing man, entangling him in their net. After they caught him, I vividly recall the next scene where they restrained him and subsequently positioned an ax just above his toes, preparing to sever this portion of his feet, presumably to thwart another escape attempt. Mind you, I have not watched this television series since I was a child. Yet the scene remains etched in my memory.

But more than my recollection of this, I recall my imagination. Specifically, I thought to myself, *How could something so horrible as slavery happen? What made this possible?* Mind you, I was no more than six years old when I pondered these questions. Perhaps some would think that this is too much for a child to ask, but for me it was not. I recall asking myself, *Was it something in the water or the air that caused slavery to happen?* Then I began to imagine, *Could this happen again today? Could a people be re-enslaved? In what manner or fashion could this historical atrocity reemerge in the twenty-first century? What's to keep this from happening again?* Yes, as a child, my imagination prompted such questions. I suppose these questions remained lost somewhere in my preconscious, but they never left me. I was never satisfied with the inconclusive nature of the attempted responses to myself. And it was not until decades later, well into adulthood, that I began to formulate an acceptable answer for myself. Yes, crimes against humanity can and will repeat themselves when individuals and communities turn a blind eye to radical evil. When practices of silence, indifference, and apathy are valorized and then religiously sanctioned—all in service to capitalism and wealth accumulation, hedonism, conspicuous consumption, productivity,

---

1. *Roots* is a 1977 made-for-television miniseries based on Alex Haley's 1976 novel *Roots*, a biopic of his own family history.

and individualism—the body politic, over time, becomes primed for the next human atrocity.

As detailed in this text, psychohistory and psychobiography work to derail the fallacy that historical events are far removed from us (and as such are irrelevant). Instead, psychohistory invites us to consider the psycho-spiritual condition of the historical individual and group that constructed and enacted historical events—for better or worse. It is the psychospiritual condition of the human project that represents the common thread that connects the past, present, and future. While technological innovation may progress, it is only hubris that leads us to believe that the human condition (and morality) progresses in the same fashion such that past atrocities could never be repeated. In my lifetime I had not anticipating witnessing a brazen attack on the Capitol building to overturn a presidential election, with nearly half of a sitting Congress refusing to certify the results of a legal presidential election (even after countless audits and legal proceedings verified the legality of the state's results), or witnessing the attempted kidnapping of a sitting governor and the rise in brazen political violence. More disturbing has been the complicity of the church by way of its near silence, indifference, and apathy as it relates to these matters. It is the sin of sloth that culminates in idolatry.

We have been here before as a nation. And we are playing with fire. In the excerpt from "The Fire Next Time" at the beginning of this chapter, James Baldwin warns that silence and passivity will not resolve the sins and practices of *racial anti-love* and terror. Apathy creates an illusion of psycho-spiritual health in the democratic experiment. The wages of indifference—cloaked by celebrations of progress—lead to death and destruction. The fallout of the racial imagination, when ignored, gets only worse over time, leading to wanton injustice, violence, and terror. As a nation, this represents a collective soul-sickness that is repeated after a movement towards human equality in the democracy.

Historians and scholars have long pointed to the reversal of progress as a nation when the Civil War had broken the back of legal slavery, and the democracy—being a fragile experiment on life support—had the opportunity to redeem itself from the evil of the slavocracy through the Reconstruction era, but ultimately succumbed to the death-dealing grip of the lesser-known Redemption era, which represented a foray into the Jim Crow period of the early twentieth century. The Redemption era reflects the collective racial imagination seeking to reestablish itself at the center of democratic experiment through the use of racial terror, disenfranchisement, and revisionist history as it relates to the realities of the slavocracy. It sought to reinstate an emotional caste system whereby formerly enslaved human beings could be collectively experienced as inferior by the architects and benefactors of the slavocracy. According to Gates, the motivation behind the Redemption movement was "to demonstrate to the North, in seductive, easily digestible language that the South—though it had nothing for which to apologize, and most certainly not the institution of slavery—had reinvented itself following the war and had now achieved 'the perfect democracy,' precisely as it was aggressively dismantling the advances in rights that black people had enjoyed during Reconstruction."[2] Lemann describes the nuance of how the Redemption period materialized in response to Reconstruction. What began as an insignificant word used by Southerners to describe what they felt they lost post-slavery in the wake of the Civil War soon took on a life of its own—religiously, culturally, and politically:

> Among the seemingly endless cruelties the South visited upon . . . [advocates of Reconstruction] was one of nomenclature: "Redemption" was just the word that white Southerners chose to denote the bloody events of the mid-1870s; and the leaders of the successful campaign of political violence, defiance of the national government, and local repeal of part of the Constitution called themselves "Redeemers." The name implied a divine sanction for the retaking of the authority the whites had lost in the Civil War, and a heavenly quality to the reestablishment of white supremacy in the post-Reconstruction South. "Reconstruction," the North's word, was sturdy, purposeful, and optimistic. "Redemption," the South's, was empyrean.
>
> In the heat of battle in 1875, respectable white Mississippians were uncomfortable about the [violent] particulars of how they were winning back political control of their state . . . But as time passed and the goals of the Redeemers were enshrined in law, the political risk of offending public opinion in the North disappeared, and the South became much more unapologetic. *The Redemption story became a durable, emotionally stirring defining myth, informally passed along on front porches and, later, openly celebrated with monuments and commemorations.*[3]

Frederick Douglass was very much aware of the capacity of the nation to reverse course in its progress of repenting from the intergenerational practices of oppressive hegemony and anti-love, and moving forward toward the freedom found in love and recognizing the full humanity and equality of all people, including the black, brown, and Native American peoples who had been enslaved, brutalized, or murdered, in the furtherance of the

---

2. Gates, *Stony the Road*, 3–4.
3. Lemann, *Redemption*, 185–86; emphasis added.

American imperial democracy. Douglass was well aware of the human capacity to *become weary in well-doing*. He recognized the human capacity to engage in what we now refer to as psychological splitting. Here, splitting is used as a coping mechanism to maintain the status quo or to block out anxiety-provoking realities of human existence. If done well enough, individuals or groups are able to hold incompatible values and beliefs within their individual (or collective) self by engaging in psychological denial, rationalization, or repression. For example, in one place, Douglass asserts, "Opposing slavery and hating its victims has become a very common form of abolitionism."[4] The paradox and irony of what Douglass was witnessing in abolitionist circles manifests itself on a national level as well.

Douglass challenged this form of collective splitting in a speech he gave on April 14, 1876, at the unveiling of the Freedmen's Monument in Washington, DC, to commemorate Abraham Lincoln's efforts to emancipate enslaved black people in the Southern states that had defected from the Union. *The events on this day were meant to celebrate national progress.* And in part, Frederick Douglass's speech commended the progress of Abraham Lincoln and the nation. But then in brilliant fashion, Douglass challenged the nation's propensity to engage in splitting—that is to say, to celebrate progress all the while tolerating the underpinnings of Redemption and what would eventually give way to Jim Crow. In his challenge, Douglass undermined the psychic need to make Abraham Lincoln a hero. Instead, Douglass, through the practice of truth-telling, chose to humanize Lincoln:

> *Truth is proper and beautiful at all times and in all places*, and it is never more proper and beautiful in any case than when speaking of a great public man whose example is likely to be commended for honor and imitation long after his departure to the solemn shades, the silent continents of eternity. It must be admitted, truth compels me to admit, even here in the presence of the monument we have erected to his memory, Abraham Lincoln was not, in the fullest sense of the word, either our man or our model. In his interests, in his associations, in his habits of thought, and in his prejudices, he was a white man.
>
> *He was preeminently the white man's President*, entirely devoted to the welfare of white men. He was ready and willing at any time during the first years of his administration to deny, postpone, and sacrifice the rights of humanity in the colored people to promote the welfare of the white people of this country. In all his education and feeling he was an American of the Americans. He came into the Presidential chair upon one

---

4. Frederick Douglass, Apr. 5, 1856, as quoted in Gates, *Stony the Road*, 11.

principle alone, namely, opposition to the extension of slavery. His arguments in furtherance of this policy had their motive and mainspring in his patriotic devotion to the interests of his own race. *To protect, defend, and perpetuate slavery in the states where it existed Abraham Lincoln was not less ready than any other President to draw the sword of the nation. He was ready to execute all the supposed guarantees of the United States Constitution in favor of the slave system anywhere inside the slave states. He was willing to pursue, recapture, and send back the fugitive slave to his master, and to suppress a slave rising for liberty, though his guilty master were already in arms against the Government.* The race to which we belong were not the special objects of his consideration. Knowing this, I concede to you, my white fellow-citizens, a preeminence in this worship at once full and supreme. First, midst, and last, you and yours were the objects of his deepest affection and his most earnest solicitude. You are the children of Abraham Lincoln. *We are at best only his stepchildren; children by adoption, children by forces of circumstances and necessity.*[5]

At the time Douglass gave this speech in 1876, we are arguably looking at the pinnacle of Reconstruction. Unbeknownst to Douglass and his contemporaries, they had gotten as much out of Reconstruction as they were going to get and were on the brink of losing it all. Indeed, the idealism of human progress juxtaposed against the concept of total depravity represents a philosophical conundrum worthy of further inquiry. At that time, there were more black people holding political office at a federal, state, and local level than we have ever seen since Reconstruction—and that includes today. The upcoming reversal of fortune for Douglass and millions of other black people would be epic, lasting for generations.

Back on April 14, 1876, when Douglass rehearsed the *facts* about the *actual words* that came out of Lincoln's mouth, he was signaling the necessity of truth-telling for the purpose of de-idealizing a tragic and violent history that a large segment of the American public was attempting to romanticize. In 1876, it was precarious (and dangerous) work for a black man to publicly utter such scathing, but true words about a beloved figure among Northerners and the abolitionist community. Moreover, Douglass was faced with growing social fatigue among Northern abolitionists about Reconstruction efforts. Similar to what we have witnessed in contemporary times, the public can grow weary in its efforts to turn away from a history of racial violence and indifference. There was a growing public sentiment for things to *get back to normal*, and to emotionally reunite with the South. A period

5. Douglass, *Oration*, 4–5.

of redemption, or backlash, tends to follow a season of forward movement in justice and equity. Douglass was faced with social sentiments like "haven't we done enough for black people" or "black people should show more appreciation for what we have done," as if violating and oppressing others is a God-given right that certain people are entitled to. Obviously, such sentiments miss the point of turning away from evil and pursuing righteousness, and instead reveal the deep sickness of the collective American soul, as if America was entitled to slavery, and that ending it was not the God-given inalienable right for black people, but a privilege. For sure, the inability to comprehend—or outright refusal to acknowledge—that *black life matters just as much as white life matters* stems back to the founding of the republic.

Frederick Douglass spent the remaining years of his life—actually until the very day of this death—engaged in the activity of truth-telling in an effort to undermine the romanticization of history. He knew all too well that the alternative practice of repressing the truth or distorting the facts for the sake of restoring *so-called normalcy and emotional comfort* would be catastrophic to the democratic experiment and the material gains of Reconstruction. But the human desire to internalize a good (albeit false) historical narrative that covers over the truth about the collective sins and the tragic condition of the American soul can represent a formidable force to be reckoned with. The practice of *historical revisionism* was in the air, and this greatly troubled Frederick Douglass. For example, he publicly chided his Republican contemporaries for referring to the actions of the Southern Democrats as anything but breaking the law and a rebellion against the union. Douglass criticized President Rutherford B. Hayes for striking a deal with Southern Democrats to prematurely remove federal troops from the South—which ultimately proved to be the death knell in Reconstruction.

Douglass understood better than most that there was nothing to be gained in sacrificing the precarious work of truth-telling for a romanticized and fallacious revisionist history—just for the sake of the illusion of *peace and a return to normalcy*. At the unveiling of the Freedman's Monument in DC, the façade of reconciliation and peace covered over the malignant and metastasizing cancer of racial hatred and terror that the nation was founded upon. This was the psychosocial environment and sentiment surrounding Douglass's speech at the unveiling of the Freedman's Monument. It illustrates the courage and audacity he possessed when he humanized the memory of a President Lincoln who had been depicted in a statue of him touching the head of an enslaved black person presumably kneeling before Lincoln in a show of gratitude—a scene that reeks of the racial imagination. By de-idealizing Lincoln through truth-telling, Douglass enhanced our capacity for moral agency. The ability for truth-telling didn't just happen automatically for Douglass. He had practiced this all of his life through the writing of his autobiographies. It was dangerous work. The implications of Douglass's work for Christian praxis are immense.

While Douglass didn't live to see it, his fears were not misplaced. Not even a decade after his death, and in the absence of truth-telling, we witness: (1) the reversal of Reconstruction-era voting rights for black people, which led to the disenfranchisement of a majority of the black population throughout the South; (2) the emergence of Jim Crow culture designed to enforce white supremacy and racial apartheid in culture and society via racial terrorism, mob violence, and lynching; (3) the emergence of the KKK—a historically irrefutable product of Protestant Christianity; and (4) the creation of "the lost cause" narrative, an invention of the racial imagination—created by the Daughters of the Confederacy—designed to recast the terror of the slavocracy as a perverted fantasy about Southern life and grandeur. According to this hegemonic imagination, the Civil War represented a moral defense of Southern innocence. "The lost cause" narrative was fine-tuned by Thomas Dixon's novel *The Clansman*, popularized by D. W. Griffith's movie *The Birth of a Nation*, and politically sanctioned by President Woodrow Wilson's screening of it in the White House. The legacy of "the lost cause" romanticized the sins of the nation. Instead of repentance and metanoia, we witnessed a full-scale effort to replace *truth-telling, justice, and righteousness with revisionist history*, all in an effort to maintain the status quo of white supremacy and the racial imagination. Historian and scholar John Hope Franklin describes in compelling fashion the sentiment and motivation of the postbellum proponents of the American slavocracy. Franklin's description underscores the danger of romanticizing history:

> Those who resist change are reminiscent of the ex-Confederates who, in the years following the Civil War, preferred to dream of a South that never was and never could be rather than accept one that was within the reach of all, if they would join together and make it so. But many whites in the post–Civil War South saw change—any change—as unsettling and dangerous, and they wanted no part of it. Surely they wanted no part of an uncivilized, uncultured South in which their former slaves would enjoy the vote and equal rights in all aspects of educational, social, and economic life. To move in such a direction would be catastrophic as well as tragic. Retreating to a safer, more secure past was infinitely more attractive and desirable than proceeding into a reckless future that seemed to offer the revulsive prospect of "social equality." *The history of the South in the 1880s and*

> 1890s is essentially the history of a search for a past so attractive that many regarded it as a nirvana.
>
> All of this was accelerated by the determination of Southern whites to replicate the slave period in everything but name. Their attack on the Civil Rights Act of 1875 found success in the 1883 decision of the United States Supreme Court that declared the act unconstitutional. In 1890, Mississippi found a way in its new constitution to disfranchise blacks effectively, and by the end of the century a trend had set in that led South Carolina and Louisiana to follow in creative and ingenious ways. The temptation to segregate blacks and whites was encouraged further by the 1896 Supreme Court decision of Plessy v. Ferguson.[6]

The group psychology and emotive sentiments detailed by John Hope Franklin in his description of the postbellum and Redemption culture can be said of any historically non-raced institution propped up by the racial imagination. Romanticizing fantasies of historical innocence and purity over and against the reality of ethnic, cultural, and social multiplicity represents a dangerous practice that cannot be merely reduced to benign utopianism. *While idealizing historical personalities or romanticizing history may not be sinful in and of itself, it prepares the individual and community for sin and evil.*

In an *institutional redemption culture*, the mere suggestion of the divine mandate for ethnic, cultural, or gender diversity in society, and especially in the work of the global church, often becomes a source of intense communal anxiety—sometimes referred to as annihilation anxiety in psychodynamic literature. Theological education—along with its abundance of guilds—is especially susceptible to the *institutional redemption culture* detailed by John Hope Franklin. Institutional redemption culture reflects a community spiritually and psychologically overrun with fear and anxiety. Consequently, the telos of biblical and theological reflection is the justification—and in some cases a glorification—of religious segregation and the creation of an us-versus-them religiosity. The product of the institutional redemption culture is often reflective of establishment theology that sets out to rationalize and justify inaction and the maintenance of the status quo in the face of (or wake of) racial terror and violence, or systemic injustice and oppression. The silence and indifference within the church is rationalized and given religious sanctioning. Ultimately, delusions of exclusivity and purity are often exposed for what they truly are: psychospiritual compensatory mechanisms that seek to cover over the sins and brokenness of the *in-group* by projecting

---

6. John Hope Franklin, "Foreword," in Cecelski and Tyson, *Democracy Betrayed*, 8–9; emphasis added.

unwanted or undesirable elements of the individual and group self onto an *out-group* (i.e., scapegoating the other), all for the sake of subscribing to the death-dealing notion of racial superiority. It bears emphasizing again that all such practices represent idolatry and are contrary to the heart and mind of God. Moreover, they represent a potentially deadly practice, as communities will attempt to achieve façades of exclusivity and purity by any means necessary, including psychological brutality or physical violence.

What we are experiencing in the second and third decades of the twenty-first century is not unlike what Frederick Douglass saw during the Redemption era in the final decades of the nineteenth century: (1) systematic efforts at voter suppression and (2) indifference towards wanton violence aimed at restoring the perceived loss of a social order whereby racial violence and nationalism are normalized and cast as the invisible backdrop upon which the democratic experiment is performed. Such violence can take the form of mass murders and hate crimes targeting black and brown communities, or the January 6th mob violence. Akin to the sociocultural cycle that Frederick Douglass witnessed during his lifetime, where he escaped the death bonds of slavery; and then played an pivotal role in helping the nation take a step forward towards divine righteousness and divine love by ridding itself from its death-dealing dependency on the slavocracy (along with the violence and terror enacted to maintain the evil system); and then witnessed a brief period of the country engaging in the process of sociopolitical metanoia, encountering the *intergenerational opportunity to be born again* by *bearing fruit consistent with repentance*, but ultimately abusing that opportunity, only to relapse back to the death throes of white supremacy, racial terror, and racial apartheid; we too are experiencing sociopolitical backlash and redemption.

Again, herein rests the analytical power of psychohistory; it does not allow us to assume moral progress and become dismissive of shameful history because of the mere passage of time, but instead compels us to consider the psychospiritual state of the individuals and groups that underwrote the historical events we now study in the present. We cannot say that the Redemption era, disenfranchisement, and racial terror via mob violence and lynching are a thing of the past to move on from. We must reflect on the psychospiritual condition of the nation that led to such a pathologically regressed state, and how does that compare to the current psychospiritual condition of the democracy. In one of his final lectures just before his death, Douglass laments the state of the Union as it approaches the turn of the century. In relation to racial mob violence and lynching, he asserts:

> *We claim to be a Christian country and a highly civilized nation,* yet, I fearlessly affirm that there is nothing in the history of savages to surpass the blood chilling horrors and fiendish excesses perpetrated against the colored people by the so-called enlightened and Christian people of the South. It is commonly thought that only the lowest and most disgusting birds and beasts, such as buzzards, vultures and hyenas, will gloat over and prey upon dead bodies, but the Southern mob in its rage feeds its vengeance by shooting, stabbing and burning when their victims are dead.[7]

Then in relation to efforts to disenfranchise black people from their right to vote, Douglass laments:

> I have no confidence in the truthfulness of men who justify themselves in cheating the negro out of his constitutional right to vote. The men, who either by false returns, or by taking advantage of his illiteracy or surrounding the ballot-box with obstacles and sensuosities intended to bewilder him and defeat this rightful exercise of the elective franchise are men who are not to be believed on oath. That this is done in the Southern States is not only admitted, but openly defended and justified by so-called honorable men inside and outside of Congress.[8]

Finally, in what comes across as existential exhaustion, and even a bit of disillusionment, being compelled to come to terms with the rollback of the progress he labored and fought for throughout his life, Douglass laments:

> I have sometimes thought that the American people are too great to be small, too just and magnanimous to oppress the weak, too brave to yield up the right to the strong, and too grateful for public services ever to forget them or fail to reward them. I have fondly hoped that this estimate of American character would soon cease to be contradicted or put in doubt. But the favor with which this cowardly proposition of disfranchisement has been received by public men, white and black, by Republican as well as Democrats, has shaken my faith in the nobility of the nation . . . *When the moral sense of a nation begins to decline and the wheel of progress to roll backward, there is no telling how low the one will fall or where the other may go* . . . The Supreme Court has surrendered, State sovereignty is restored. It has destroyed the civil rights Bill, and converted the Republican party into a party of money rather than a party of morals, a party of things

---

7. Douglass, *Lessons of the Hour*, 5; emphasis added.
8. Douglass, *Lessons of the Hour*, 10.

rather than a party of humanity and justice. *We may well ask what next?*[9]

If it seems that many of Frederick Douglass's words that were uttered over 125 years ago could be spoken today, it is not because history necessarily repeats itself. Instead, it is because the psychological and spiritual state of the collective democracy remains unchecked and unchanged—without any sort of substantive pastoral and spiritual intervention—and as a result is predisposed to yield similar sociopolitical results in the public sphere. As such, akin to what Douglass experienced, we too are experiencing a similar historical and cultural moment, where the first black presidency in the history of the nation is now followed by a racial reckoning and social backlash unseen since the mid-twentieth century. In 2021 alone, the push to make it more difficult for black and brown Americans to vote took shape with state legislative bodies across the country introducing in excess of 440 bills aimed at complicating the voting process for citizens. By the end of the calendar year "19 states had passed 34 restrictive voting laws . . . [and] these laws made mail voting and early voting more difficult, imposed harsh voter ID requirements, and made faulty voter purges more likely."[10] Former US Attorney General Eric Holder captures the rollback of black voting rights in the wake of the Obama presidency succinctly, arguing that:

> From the moment President Obama took office, states began restricting voting rights—signing into law photo ID bills to combat nonexistent voter fraud and then closing the offices where you could get those forms of identification in low-income neighborhoods. After Republicans won a historic landslide victory in the 2010 midterms, taking over state legislatures and governor's mansions across the country, they boxed Black Americans out of political power through gerrymandering and introduced close to two hundred bills aimed at reducing access to the ballot across forty-one states.

While Holder does not use the terminology of the racial imagination, his description of why state legislatures across the country would make it more difficult for its citizens to vote (despite the absence of any evidence to support the allegations of voter fraud) is a clear example of how the racial imagination, left unchecked, can brazenly and unapologetically manifest itself in the democratic experiment.

---

9. Douglass, *Lessons of the Hour*, 23–24; emphasis added.
10. Brennan Center for Justice, *Democracy Can't Wait*, 23.

> The motivation behind this legislation was no secret, but it was clarified by an embarrassment of a congressman named Steve King, who lamented the passing of "a time in American history when you had to be a male property owner in order to vote." And then, in 2013, the Supreme Court gutted the Voting Rights Act, opening the floodgates for suppression . . . [with the result being that] state legislatures and local officials have closed nearly 1,700 polling places across the country. Voters have been unnecessarily and inexcusably stricken from the rolls—with purge rates 40 percent higher in states that were previously covered by Section 5. Over the past decade, a total of twenty-five states have instituted draconian anti-voting laws that clearly and intentionally have a disproportionate impact on communities of color.[11]

The same racial imagination that gave way to the voter suppression Frederick Douglass witnessed in the midst of the Redemption era is the same racial imagination that continues to underwrite voter suppression in the first half of the twenty-first century. It is an act of redemption in the wake of the election of the first black president. It bears repeating—we have been here before and continue to engage in the same practices. Unless the psychospiritual state of the individual and collective self is addressed, as a democracy, we will continue to engage in the same death-dealing behavior. Moreover, the church does not represent an exception to this pastoral diagnosis of the democracy. Its liability is joint and several in the construction and maintenance of the racial imagination. Through its silence and theological stonewalling, it has provided implicit religious sanction to the ongoing tenets and legacy of white supremacy.

DEATH OF THE HEART: A SOCIAL PSYCHOSPIRITUAL ASSESSMENT

Perhaps the January 6th insurrection at the US Capitol is the most compelling evidence that we are playing with *James Baldwin's fire* when we appease the racial imagination and engage in practices of indifference and apathy. Again, similar to how Frederick Douglass witnessed the disenfranchisement of black voters during the Redemption era, we have also seen a previous incident of an insurrection on November 10, 1898, in Wilmington, North Carolina. Only this time, deadly insurrection to overturn a legal election was successful. The cavalier and apathetic attitude that many politicians and Christian leaders have taken as it relates to the violence of January 6

---

11. Holder and Koppelman, *Our Unfinished March*, 10–12.

is dangerous, reckless and reflects a failure of moral leadership. In 2000, the North Carolina state legislature established the Wilmington Race Riot Commission (WRRC) to research, study, and craft an official account of the violent overthrow the city of Wilmington experienced in 1898. The Commission's primary findings concluded that the overthrow of a legally and legitimately elected municipal government was achieved through racially motivated mob violence and terror that had been sanctioned by a statewide political ideology grounded in white supremacy. The state and local government response to the coup d'état proved to be impotent.[12] The racist mob violence reflected the typical backlash in response to black and brown sociopolitical progress and, in this instance, black progress connected to Reconstruction.[13] The goal of the insurrection was to reinstate—by any means necessary—a racial caste and apartheid system that reestablished a social order governed by white superiority.

But it would be a mistake to believe that the violent overthrow of government in order to restore racial order was delimited to North Carolina. John Haley, in his research on Wilmington, describes how the city became a blueprint for other states to follow. Wilmington—similar to the January 6th insurrection—became a source of pride for the racial imagination. Because of its importance on this point, I quote Haley at length:

> White supremacists were so proud of their political success that they commended "the North Carolina Way" to those states that had not disfranchised blacks. When Georgia made a second attempt at disfranchisement in 1906, North Carolina governor Robert B. Glenn, U.S. senators Lee S. Overman and Furnifold Simmons, and former governor Charles B. Aycock—all elected for their leading roles in the white supremacy campaign of 1898—assisted the Peach State's white leaders by sharing their experiences. Senator Overman advised Georgians to be well armed and prepared to use violence similar to that in Wilmington. He extolled black disfranchisement as salutary for whites because it produced a "satisfaction which only comes of permanent peace after deadly warfare." *Governor Glenn testified that no respectable white man in North Carolina "either Democrat or Republican" would choose to reverse the results of the white supremacy campaign. "You can say to the people of Georgia that I believe it to have been the brightest day in our history when we adopted the constitutional amendment," Glenn declared, "and if they adopt a similar one, they will never have cause to regret it."*

---

12. See 1898 Wilmington Race Riot Commission, *1898 Wilmington Race Riot*.
13. See Umfleet, *Day of Blood*.

Overman advised white Georgians to look at the results of the white supremacy campaign in North Carolina, where only 5 percent of blacks voted. The Georgia audience was impressed, and the white supremacists, led by Hoke Smith, agreed to deal with blacks "as they did in Wilmington" and make the woods "black with their hanging carcasses." Indeed, the Atlanta riot of 1906 and the subsequent disfranchisement of black Georgians closely followed the North Carolina model.[14]

It bears repeating: the acts of insurrection on January 6 were not new to the US democratic experiment. The propensity to resort to falsehood and fiction in order to justify voter suppression and the disfranchisement of black and brown people, or to use terror and mob violence to secure a social order devised by the racial imagination, all resides deeply within the collective psyche of the republic and should not be considered beyond reach merely because it is assumed that the passage of times is automatically accompanied by moral progress. While this may be a common assumption in the shared memory of the nation's history, it does not necessarily mean that it is true. The nation has been here before. We must address the *psychospiritual condition of the individual and collective soul of the democracy if we are to break the death-dealing legacy of the slavocracy and the racial imagination.*

Whether considering the Wilmington insurrection in 1898, Jim Crow racial terrorism in the twentieth century, or the Washington, DC, insurrection on January 6, each incident is arguably the long-term result of indifference at best, or tolerating at worst, the racial imagination and its deadly manifestations. It is what happens when the citizenry of a society appeases and passively cooperates with any form of systemic oppression, dehumanization, and injustice, all for the sake of maintaining the racial apartheid status quo, along with its illusions of normality and social tranquility. It is ill advised to cast the aforementioned acts of brazen social violence—with the clear intent to overthrow a government, or to murder, maim, and terrorize innocent civilians as a means of control and domination—as mere happenstance in the history of the democracy, just to sustain a fraudulent master narrative of Western innocence and exceptionalism. These occurrences of social violence are symptomatic of a much deeper psychospiritual sickness whereby "the toleration of [racial] . . . evil anesthetizes and eventually denigrates the internal moral compass that leads humanity to communal love and justice."[15]

---

14. Haley, "Race, Rhetoric, and Revolution," 220; emphasis added.
15. D. Gibson, *Frederick Douglass*, 23–24.

In his 1963 interview with Kenneth Clark, James Baldwin refers to the psychospiritual condition I am referring to as "the death of the heart" or as "moral monsters."[16] The *death of the heart of the democratic experiment* is when a society has spiritually descended to the place where certain bodies—in this case black and brown bodies—are deemed inconsequential to the story of America. When black history, heritage, and bodies become inconsequential to the collective narrative, the domination of black and brown life becomes normalized, with moral apathy being entrenched in the collective psychic space. This degenerative state of collective spiritual decay is indicative of Achille Mbembe's description of necropolitics when he observes that "the ultimate expression of sovereignty largely resides in the power and capacity to dictate who is able to live and who must die . . . [as] to kill or let live thus constitutes sovereignty's limits, its principal attributes . . . [and] to be sovereign is to exert one's control over mortality and to define life as the deployment and manifestation of power."[17]

When considering Mbembe's account of necropolitics, one need only think of people like George Floyd, whose death was akin to a public lynching, or Breonna Taylor who has received little to no justice for her murder, as her death was by and large deemed to be unfortunate by officials. Mbembe is clear that "to a large extent, racism is the driver of the necropolitical principle insofar as it stands for organized destruction, for a sacrificial economy, the functioning of which requires, on the one hand, a generalized cheapening of the price of life and, on the other, a habituation to loss."[18] In addition to the prerogative of sovereignty to decide who gets to live and die, it is suggested here that we add to Mbembe's understanding of necropolitic's sovereignty the discretion on who gets incarcerated, *en masse*, and who gets to remain free. One need only to consider the thousands of black and brown people who were disproportionately imprisoned for drug usage and chemical dependency during the last quarter of the twentieth century, and the thousands of non-raced people who more recently are afflicted by opioid addiction and are now receiving *social compassion and assistance* via multibillion-dollar settlements from pharmaceutical companies that the courts have determined are culpable, in part, for the opioid epidemic. These are but modern-day examples of the manifestation of the racial imagination—a destructive imagination that is underwritten by social indifference, which in turn leads to degenerative spiritual decay.

16. These are excerpts from James Baldwin in a 1963 interview with Kenneth Clark in a Boston public television series; see Baldwin, "Conversation."
17. Mbembe, *Necropolitics*, 66.
18. Mbembe, *Necropolitics*, 38.

The mental and emotional inconsequentiality of black and brown bodies in the collective psychic space of the American republic represents the beginning of the process of dehumanizing *the other* and makes it easier to dispose of *the others' bodies*, or to passively witness the disposal of such bodies, without any experience of guilt, shame, shock, or outrage that should normally accompany sins against fellow human beings or crimes against humanity. While the notion that *time will magically heal all wounds* is an erroneous proposition for psychospiritual well-being, *the passage of time undoubtedly renders mental, emotional, and spiritual infirmities worse if left unattended to*. The writer of the Gospel of Matthew records a pastoral diagnosis Jesus makes of his contemporaries by using the category of unclean spirit to describe their collective spiritual condition:

> When the unclean spirit has gone out of a person, it passes through waterless places seeking rest, but finds none. Then it says, "I will return to my house from which I came." And when it comes, it finds the house empty, swept, and put in order. Then it goes and brings with it seven other spirits more evil than itself, and they enter and dwell there, and the last state of that person is worse than the first. *So also will it be with this evil generation.* (Matt 12:43–45 ESV; emphasis added)

Notwithstanding how the reader interprets the scriptural narratives on the demonic, what is undeniable is that the presence of an unclean spirit denotes some form of religious and spiritual ailment in an individual or community. It is suggested here that the unclean spirit leaving the person (as opposed to being cast out) speaks to apathy and indifference regarding spiritual degradation as opposed to the intentionality and self-work needed for spiritual health (i.e., intentionally casting out). The unclean spirit returning and finding the house empty, swept, and put in order denotes institutional religiosity that is only superficial and focuses on deceiving itself into believing it is well (despite the presence of clear evidence that it is not), as opposed to doing the hard and laborious self-work and repentance that is required for *actually becoming well*. The pastoral diagnosis Jesus puts forth is clear: not only is the last state of the individual or community worse than the first, but the prognosis can extend to an entire generation. Stated differently, the spiritual degradation is systematic. The same applies to the racial imagination. Appeasing it serves only to undermine the collective psychospiritual condition of the democracy.

With this in mind, it is ill advised to cast the insurrection events of January 6 as a mere aberration in the American democratic experiment. Prudence suggests that January 6, like any other historical act of racially motivated murderous mob violence inflicted on ethnic minorities in the United States (including Wilmington, NC, in 1898; Jim Crow-era lynch mobs; the multitude of race riots that swept the country in 1919; or the Tulsa white-on-black race massacre in 1921, to mention a few), should be understood as a *symptom of worse things to come if redemptive pastoral action is not undertaken to treat the unhealthy psychospiritual state of the collective self of the nation*. January 6 was not a blip. It is a painful wake-up call warning that we are moving dangerously in the wrong direction. Turning a blind eye to January 6 or trying to forget about it in the hopes that the collective sickness it represents will simply heal itself or go away is not a viable strategy—socially, politically, or morally. It will not work anymore than when individuals attempt to ignore mental and spiritual ailments; the condition only becomes worse. This history of using racially inspired mob violence or massacres in support of the racial imagination, or to maintain and restore a social order informed by white supremacy is in no way a spin-off of the American story; it is constitutional to the narrative. While it may be inaccessible to the immediate consciousness, the use of mob violence to terrorize ethnic minorities into subordination remains a dormant and unspoken, yet viable alternative in the psychic space of the democratic experiment. It is a spiritual sickness in the collective psychic space that requires a pastoral intervention. In his survey of black history, Lerone Bennett Jr. captures the growing use and prevalence of racial terror and mob violence at the top of the twentieth century. Because of its relevance, I quote him at length here:

> Negro Americans were being pushed to a point of no return. There were fifty-four lynchings in 1916 and thirty-eight in 1917. On July 2, 1917, white workers in East St. Louis, Illinois, turned on Negroes in one of the bloodiest race riots in American history. Estimates of the number of Negroes killed ranged from forty to two hundred. Nearly six thousand Negroes were driven from their home.
>
> Lynching increased. There were sixty-four in 1918 and eighty-three in 1919. More disturbing than the number was the increasing sadism of the mobs. The Mary Turner lynching of 1918 was undoubtedly one of the most barbaric acts ever committed in a civilized country. Though pregnant, the Negro woman was lynched in Valdosta, Georgia. She was hanged to a tree, doused with gasoline and motor oil and burned. As she dangled from the rope, a man stepped forward with a pocketknife and ripped open her abdomen in a crude cesarean operation . . . The next year, eleven Negroes were burned alive in six

> states. Then before the returning veterans [from World War I] could catch their breath, America erupted in the Red Summer of 1919. Twenty-six race riots marred the beauty of that summer. The biggest riots were in Washington, Chicago, Omaha, Knoxville, Longview, Texas, and Phillips Country, Arkansas. Six persons were killed and 150 were wounded in the Washington riots; fifteen whites and twenty-three Negroes were killed in the Chicago riots and 537 were injured. In Omaha, Nebraska, a white mob lynched and burned a Negro, hanged the mayor who tried to prevent the lynching and burned down the new county courthouse.[19]

Hubris alone will argue that the nation is no longer susceptible to enacting depravity and violence similar to what we witnessed in the twentieth century. The historical record clearly evidences that the only circumstance that follows appeasement, passivity, and indifference is further degeneration of the human spirit. From a psychological perspective, it is suggested here that the mob violence, *which is as American as apple pie*, is a manifestation of large-group regression in response to collective fear and anxiety. When a person or group is regressed, it suggests that they are using psychologically immature practices, such as aggression and denial, to manage their fear or anxiety. For our purposes here, America's long-standing affair with racially inspired mob violence (intended to subjugate ethnic minorities within a social caste system) reflects instances of large-group regression that is attempting to manage group anxiety associated with the perceived threat of having to relinquish the time-honored narrative of white supremacy. Another way of understanding this anxiety is the perceived threat of having to surrender the implicit assumption that the social construction of what it means to be white represents the global standard of what it means to be human. Altman describes the social construction of whiteness, which from a psychological perspective is to be understood as distinctly different from the ethnicity or culture of those who are of European descent. According to Altman then:

> Whiteness is thus an omnipotent fantasy, a fantasy of mastery and fullness. There is nothing inherently pathological about the impulse for mastery; indeed, much of what makes us human in a positive sense, many of the ways we have found to be safe and productive, depends on what has been called *effectance motivation* (White 1959). What makes the fantasy of whiteness a pathological defense is the way it is paired with blackness as its disavowed double. *The search for mastery becomes problematic*

---

19. Bennett, *Before the Mayflower*, 293–94.

> when it becomes so desperate that it must entail the construction of a subjected group of people and the disavowal of one's own helplessness—i.e., when the experience of helplessness is warded off, rather than integrated with the experience of mastery.[20]

When identity formation has been cultivated in racial ideology, and then further reinforced by Christian nationalism, then any threat to losing an identity crafted on the basis of a non-raced self (along with its long-standing perception of having a greater value in life or representing what it means to be normal in life) runs the risk of precipitating the deadly large-group regression we have historically witnessed in the form of deadly mobs and insurrections with the clear intent of restoring a social order inspired by the racial imagination and, more recently, Christian nationalism.

The role that identity development and formation have on the psycho-spiritual health of individuals and even entire groups or nations cannot be overstated. Identity formation represents a life-long process in which, when conducted in a healthy manner, the individual or group is in a dynamic process of constructing how they understand themselves to exist in life and in the world. Identity formation is not a destination, but a journey—a journey that is constantly influenced by history, culture, and context. Building on the work of Erik Erikson's notion of identity, Vamik Volkan argues that identity should be understood as:

> A person's subjective experience of him or herself and therefore should be distinguished from other, related concepts, such as "character" or "personality": these latter terms delineate the collected impressions that other people gather of an individual's emotional expressions, modes of speech, and habitual ways of thinking and behaving. Unlike character and personality, then, *identity designates the individual's [or group's] inner working model of him or herself and an individual's integration of his or her past, present, and future into a smooth continuum of remembered, felt, and expected existence.* An individual with a crystalized core identity therefore has a realistic body image, an inner sense of physical solidity, a subjective clarity about his or her gender, a well-internalized conscience, and, most importantly ... "an inner solidarity with one's group and its ideas." Thus, *an individual's core identity and large-group identity develop alongside one another.*[21]

---

20. Altman, "Whiteness," 55–56; first emphasis original, second emphasis added.
21. V. Volkan, *Blind Trust*, 32–33; emphasis added.

Volkan makes a distinction between ideological identity and identity underwritten by heritage and culture. In the former case, identity is appropriated after a certain political, social, or religious ideology or narrative that is more transactional in nature and designed to carry out the goals or objectives of a particular group. Ideological identity is akin to tribalism, is not necessary for survival, and can be altered. While ideological identity is value neutral and not inherently bad, it can prepare groups for deleterious behavior. Case in point: the ideology of "the lost cause" or *Birth of a Nation* is not constitutional to individual and group identity. These are secondary identities usually adopted during adulthood in furtherance of a destructive ideology that justifies harming other persons or groups. In another place Volkan suggests that destructive large-group identities "evolve during adulthood and lead to their members losing their moral attitudes—the superego-imposed restrictions which are linked to large-group identity that they acquired as children . . . the investment in their core large-group identities that had developed in childhood, drastically changes . . . [as] they become believers of ideas that were not available in their childhood environments."[22] *It is suggested here that such ideological identities can be changed with the appropriate communal and psychospiritual interventions.* Ideological identity does not have to be destructive or counterproductive to the uplifting of the human spirit. In the latter case, identity underwritten by heritage and culture—the inner design of how we understand and experience ourselves—is indispensable and represents the core of what makes us human. In my own religious experience in predominantly white institutions, whenever it has been suggested to me that black and brown heritage is irrelevant or not important to Christian identity, I understand such statements to be in line with the ongoing legacy of colonialism and the slavocracy—statements that are usually postulated against a backdrop of white invisibility.

In his project that examines how crisis and trauma can cause large groups, and even entire nations, to regress into destructive behaviors, Volkan goes on to observe that "like individuals, groups, from demonstrating crowds to religious cults to whole nations, can also regress—temporarily or for a long time, mildly or malignantly."[23] According to Volkan, regression is value neutral. That is to say, it is neither bad or good, as every human being can use regression to manage anxiety, fear, and stress. The obvious challenge is when regression yields destructive or deadly results over a prolonged period of time, or on a repeated basis that has become socially normalized. Volkan understands this as a "malignant" form of regression where

22. V. D. Volkan, "Large-Group Identity," 142–43.
23. V. Volkan, *Blind Trust*, 58.

"regression results in ruining the lives of many people, or killing people ... [whereas] a reparative leader, on the other hand, devotes him or herself to bringing the followers out of regression and promoting progression."[24] Similar to symptoms that individuals would manifest, Volkan outlines symptoms that large groups, and even nations, often manifest when operating in a regressed state. Those symptoms, to name a few, include individual members of the group losing their capacity to differentiate (i.e., self-identity is subsumed, and even lost, to the larger group identity); group members offering up blind or unquestioned loyalty to the group leader; intra-group psychological splitting where members who blindly follow the leader discern themselves to be *in good standing* and members who may demonstrate even the slightest sense of autonomy are perceived as *not in good standing*; inter-group or large-scale psychological splitting where group members perceive the events of world (and the people in the world) as either *all good* or *all bad*—thereby creating an *in-group all-good* category and an *out-group all-bad* category that is populated by *those other people*; and a system of social ethics where any action or decision that contributes to the development and maintenance of the regressed group's shared identity is automatically justified and rationalized as being the right decision or a moral action.

Otto Kernberg observes two types of regressed large groups: narcissistic and paranoid. The former is compelled in large part by a pervasive sense of psychological or emotional insecurity and the threat of losing a socially established understanding of individual and group identity. The latter is driven by a fear of being existentially overrun or consumed by *the mysterious other*. Consequently, the narcissistic large group is codependent on an individual or institution to soothe its insecurity. The paranoid large group is constantly in search of *another or the other* to either fight or wage war against as a way to soothe its internal anxiety. Because of its relevance to the discussion on regressed large groups, having been penned almost twenty years prior to this writing, I quote Kernberg at length:

> A narcissistic regression of the group ... stimulates the emergence of a narcissistic, self-congratulatory, self-assured leader who thrives on the admiration of others and assumes the role of an "all giving" parental authority, on whom everybody else can depend for sustenance and security. In the throes of its regression, the group's members become passive and dependent upon that leader, and assume that it is their right to be fed and taken care of. They begin to feel insecure and confused, unable to take an active stance toward their assigned task, instead competing

24. V. Volkan, *Blind Trust*, 59.

with each other in a greedy, envious way for the attention of the leader. This constellation of leader–follower behavior describes the "dependent basic assumption group."

> A group involved in a paranoid regression . . . becomes hyper-alert and tense, as if there were some danger against which it would have to establish an aggressive defense. The group selects a leader with a strong paranoid potential, a hypersensitive, suspicious, aggressive and dominant person, ready to experience and define some slight or danger against which he and the group following him need to protect themselves and fight back. The members of the group, in turn, tend to divide between an "in group," rallying around the group leader, and an "out group" who are suspect and need to be fought off. The mutual recriminations and fights between the in group and the out group give a frankly hostile and paranoid quality to the entire group, and may lead either to splitting into paranoid splinter groups, or the discovery of an external enemy against whom the entire group can consolidate around the leader. The fight then evolves between that paranoid group and the external world.[25]

The psychospiritual implications of Kernberg's observations are significant. Perhaps the most significant takeaway is that it is not a singular leader that precipitates the regression of a large group or even a nation. Instead, it is the regressed large group—over the long run—that attracts the leader who will cater to its psychological and spiritual deficits (i.e., "to suit their own desires, they will gather around them a great number of teachers to say what their itching ears want to hear [and] they will turn their ears away from the truth and turn aside to myths" [2 Tim 4:3–4 NIV]). Large-group regression of this type does not happen overnight. Instead, it is the product of decades and generations of actively and passively cooperating with the demands of the racial imagination until there is a cataclysmic social eruption that awakens us or *quickens those of us who have been dead in our trespasses and sins of silence and apathy.*

There are dire consequences to being indifferent about the events of January 6 and what it was socially symptomatic of in relation to the health of the democratic experiment. Some legal scholars have argued that Congress didn't have the legal authority to decertify the electoral votes of the states (and such an analysis is obviously beyond the scope of this book). Others have argued that the strength of the democracy was demonstrated in Congress returning to the Capitol to certify the election, and perhaps there is merit to this. It is also conceivable that it was more along the lines of dumb

---

25. Kernberg, "Sanctioned Social Violence," 684–85.

luck that the election was certified and that the democratic experiment was not turned on its head. To be indifferent towards the manifestations of the racial imagination is to play with fire, and we may not be able to put out the fire next time.

9

PENTECOSTAL WORSHIP

A Religious Revolution

I was convinced that worship at its best is a social experience with people of all levels of life coming together to realize their oneness and unity under God. Whenever the church, consciously or unconsciously, caters to one class it loses the spiritual force of the "whosoever will, let him come" doctrine, and is in danger of becoming little more than a social club with a thin veneer of religiosity.

—Martin Luther King Jr.

THIS BOOK RESISTS THE temptation to offer up a singular *fix-it* solution to the long-standing legacy of the slavocracy and the racial imagination. Such an approach would suggest that this centuries-old sickness is the result of cognition; that is, missing pieces of information or knowledge that, if secured, would crack the code and solve our problems. But for our purposes here, it is suggested that we cannot merely intellectualize our way out of the evil of the racial imagination and its systems of sin, evil, and domination. While there is always room for the individual or group to acquire more knowledge (in this case, knowledge and awareness about matters of race), the premise of this book forcefully argues that it is less about people not knowing what is right in terms of the legacy of racism and the slavocracy, and more about doing the necessary psychospiritual self-work to do what is right. Instead of suggesting strategies, what is offered up here are postures for how you can approach the work of challenging the racial imagination in your own context. As a nation, we have been here before. The example of the titans provides us guidance into how we can engage in the work of redeeming the soul of a nation.

FINDING YOUR COURAGE

Undermining the legacy of the slavocracy and the racial imagination, along with its psychosocial underpinnings of hatred (i.e., anti-love), animus, and resentment, which ultimately lead to structures of oppression, inequity, and injustice, is the work of righteousness. It is God's work. And when one dares to engage in God's work (which is to be distinguished from the busyness of church and ecclesial meandering), *courage is always required*. While the chapter on finding your courage profiled the voice of Martin Luther King, all of the titans—Fannie Lou Hamer, Benjamin Mays, and Ida B. Wells—labored to find their courage in order to do God's work. The telos of finding courage does not require one to be without fear, or to deny or repress fear. A healthy psychospirituality of courage involves acknowledging our fears, psychologically integrating into our interior world the emotion of fear as a vital and normative component of our humanity, acknowledging the real threats that precipitate the fears, and then *practicing forward movement in spite of the fear and the threats of danger*. In order to find your courage, you must practice courage.

Implicit in the discussion of courage is the willingness to endure resistance or suffering while engaging in the work of undermining the racial imagination. It is here that many individuals, groups, and institutions fail. Assuming they even want to engage with anti-racist or diversity work (and that is a big if), they are willing to do it in only the most *low-risk to status-quo* pain-free way that does not cost them anything. This approach is adopted because remaining accepted by the establishment community can be an intoxicating motivation for being passive and indifferent to the manifestations of the racial imagination. Remaining in the good graces of one's family or community of origin can be the driving factor in determining how matters of race are engaged with (or not). Pursuing righteousness is not a consideration, and instead is replaced by appeasement. Coming to terms with what may be lost or suffered, or the harm one may incur when doing the work of undermining the racial imagination is an inescapable cost-benefit analysis that must be undertaken by way of courage. Similarly to how the titans' biblical and theological understanding of *the cross they must bear* incorporated coming to terms with what they could possibly suffer on their journey, we must engage in the same self-work today. Like the titans, we must work to find our courage. Conversely, *establishment theology* tends to construct its God-talk in a way that (1) normalizes the racial status quo, (2) ensures comfort and convenience, and (3) justifies indifference and passivity in the face of racial hostility and injustice. The fact that the call of God might cost communal alienation, personal discomfort, painful change, or even personal harm or death is generally beyond the scope of establishment theology. Seminars and workshops on anti-racist strategies are meaningless without the individual and institutional courage that leads to contrition, metanoia, justice, and communities of equity and righteousness. Engaging in *the practice of finding our courage* is a necessary psychospiritual prerequisite to any manifestation of the beloved community.

YOUR LIFE-PROJECT: DOING YOUR WORK

Perhaps among the most potent threats to the racial imagination are people who labor in the pursuit of their life-project; that is to say, people engaged in doing their work. This is depicted in the life of Benjamin Elijah Mays. The alternative is to allow oneself to be typecast into a predetermined system of identities, roles, and performances dictated by racial ideology. The threat of being engulfed in a predetermined typecast, and the ensuing life of legalism whereby one adheres to the roles assigned to them in order to be deemed successful, can happen anywhere or at any point in life: in the family of origin, a vocational calling, a ministry calling, or in any organization or institution. Perhaps the most life-giving form of self-care and resistance in systems never designed to recognize and affirm black and brown life is to be actively involved in your life-project. Mays didn't conform to what society, and even his own family, thought a black man should be or how a black man should behave. Cultivated by the racial imagination, this is a trap that can be set even with the best of intentions. Mays understood this and taught it to the young men at Morehouse College. Mays constructed his identity and his life-project according to his own terms and conditions. Even in failure, to fail while in the process of doing your work is more conducive to psychospiritual well-being than succeeding while engaged in a life of legalism and conforming to what a social typecast dictates you should be doing. Living to be accepted is the condition precedent to spiritual death. Doing your work is the condition precedent to the beauty of becoming. This sort of self-care and self-work defies the racial imagination and leads to the beloved community. Perhaps Audrey Lorde understood it best when she expressed learning the difference between healthy growth and progress versus overextending herself in accordance with social expectations. It is a word of wisdom in self-care that serves us well today:

> Sometimes I feel like I am living on a different star from the one I am used to calling home. It has not been a steady progression. I had to examine, in my dreams as well as in my immune-function tests, the devastating effects of overextension. Overextending myself is not stretching myself. I had to accept how difficult it is to monitor the difference. Necessary for me as cutting down on sugar. Physically. Psychically. Caring for myself is not self-indulgence, it is self-preservation, and that is an act of political warfare.[1]

IDEALIZATION AND WORKING THROUGH EXISTENTIAL DISAPPOINTMENT

We all engage in idealization. It is a natural part of human development. The human project has a need to be associated with the hero (in a variety of forms), or exceptionalism and virtuosity, as a way of soothing debilitating emotions related to existential fears, hopelessness, feelings of insufficiency, despair, or annihilation anxiety. Idealization, in part, reflects the projection of our internal need to be affiliated with—even merge with—what we perceive to be greater than ourselves, or it can represent the externalization of our need for life itself to conform to our high values. Some idealizations are fair and realistic. More often than not, the vast majority of our idealizations are unfair and unrealistic. The challenge is when we become too codependent on our idealizations, as unhealthy idealizations can reflect our inability to engage with reality.

All idealizations are eventually undermined, or outright destroyed by the frailty and brokenness of people and institutions, the reality of loss and grief, or the vicissitudes of life. Ruptured idealizations precipitate the onset of existential disappointment, which left unattended or ignored, can eventually lead to disillusionment, and then nihilism. However, if existential disappointment is acknowledged and then worked through, the outcome can reflect psychospiritual growth as we discover our own capacity for genius, virtuosity, and high ideas. Humanizing the people, organizations, or institutions we have idealized can be an anxiety-provoking process but is a necessary component of healing and self-care. Such was the case for Ida B.

---

1. Lorde, *Burst of Light*, 130.

Wells in her life-long journey to combat the evil of lynching. The body of work that Wells generated over the course of her life (including her voluminous writings and scholarship) was second to none. It is suggested here that the genius of Ida B. Wells, in part, stemmed from her having worked through existential disappointment, as opposed to succumbing to the onset of disillusionment and nihilism. Potential idealizations for Ida B. Wells included (1) how she envisioned her fellow sisters and brothers of European descent would respond to speak and act against the terror of lynching (but in reality, failed to do much of anything), (2) how she envisioned being accepted and appreciated by her contemporaries in the black church and on several occasions was rejected because of their fear of speaking out against lynching or because she was a woman, and (3) Frederick Douglass, her mentor and perhaps the one person she had the greatest amount of respect for, fell short in publicly vouching for and affirming Wells at a perilous time in her life when she perhaps most needed such backing. Here, it is suggested that the writings of Wells reflect, in part, her working through such disappointment—disappointment precipitated by previously held idealizations. On the other side of the process of working through, Wells eviscerated her codependency on old idealizations, more fully discovered her own genius, and was able to live into the beauty of her own becoming. She offers up a compelling example of self-work for those engaged in the work of cultivating the beloved community.

THE LOOK OF LOVE

Fannie Lou Hamer compels each of us to ask within our own context and social location: *What does love look like?* As a practical theologian, I suggest that it is woefully inadequate to merely assert that we have love for our fellow human beings, and thus fulfil the divine mandate, while circumventing the burden of proof required for our professed love. As Hamer did in her own life and through her enormous body of work, love, in part, looks like our involvement in another's life for their benefit. For Hamer, it was not enough to disagree with injustice and systems of domination. She went beyond disagreement and got involved in the life and context of those suffering under the oppressive regime of the racial imagination. Hamer dared to cast her lot with the despised and disinheriterd of her community. And for this, it cost Hamer dearly. In our society that valorizes individualism, zero-sum competition, and even certain acts of incivility, the idea of love, let alone what love looks like, comes across as a utopian myth—perhaps even for the most religious-oriented or altruistic human being.

In my own experience (corporate world, church world, theological education), when manifestations of the racial imagination rear their ugly head, or any other form of bigotry (sexism, misogyny, etc.), it is usually not the case that others are unaware of the situation or that communities don't know the difference between right and wrong. Instead, more often than not, the community behaves as bystanders because they do not want to get involved on behalf of the person(s) suffering the abuse and mistreatment, or to challenge the perpetrators. The racial imagination thrives in this kind of environment, as people fear getting involved. In my experience, seasoned professionals, from senior executives in the corporate world or senior leaders in religious institutions, all the way down to those who hold junior roles in organizations, can all find an excuse not to get involved. This behavior is especially problematic for the church and theological education as well as other religious institutions, as Jesus's willingness to get involved with us—with humanity—is a strong indictment and rebuke of our unwillingness to get involved. Again, this is why for this project, I resisted the temptation of diversity or anti-racist strategies and instead focused on those personalities who came before us, those among the great cloud of witnesses, and highlighted their psychological and spiritual postures towards systems of domination and injustice. Fannie Lou Hamer was a formidable example for what love looks like. Diversity and anti-racist resources mean little if we do not address the human propensity to *not get involved*.

A RELIGIOUS REVOLUTION

In conclusion, it is suggested that a religious revolution in the form of Pentecostal worship is essential in undermining the racial imagination and redeeming the soul of the nation. When I invoke the term *Pentecostal*, I am referencing the pouring out of Spirit upon all the peoples of the earth that is attested to in the second chapter of Acts. The passage signals at once that the Divine is *most fully* represented in the multiplicity of human beings, and not simply one person or group. The Pentecost event turns the quest for human singularity and globalism that we witness at Babel in the eleventh chapter of Genesis on its head. Pentecost disrupts the colonial illusion of unanimity and consensus seeking with the multiplicity of languages (i.e., tongues), ethnicity, and culture, all of which attest to the works of God in the cosmos.

With this in mind, I understand Pentecostal worship as a radical recognition and affirmation of the image of God in every human being. The power of Pentecost makes us uncomfortable, reorients us (or introduces us) to what it feels like to be the stranger, destabilizes our need for power to control and dominate the other, and necessitates a divine interdependence on each other—without regard to heritage, creed, or color—if we are to more fully encounter God, and more fully understand what it means to be human. It is suggested here that Pentecostal worship holds revolutionary potential, as this paradigm disrupts the notion of a worship epicenter (usually situated somewhere in the West), an idea implicitly or explicitly offered up by the racial imagination, as it continues in its endeavor to tame the tongues of the earth through religious dogma, legalism, abuse of power, and illusions of doctrinal or religious purity. The psychosocial posture of a worship paradigm fashioned after the model of Babel and the trickery of the racial imagination reflects an arrogance whereby the community is eager for God and all the peoples of the earth to bear witness to the things they are doing, allegedly on behalf of God. Alternatively, the posture of Pentecostal worship is one of curiosity and earnest expectation to *bear witness to what God is doing* in the lives and spaces inhabited by all the peoples of the earth.

An example of Pentecostal worship is found in the tenth chapter of Acts with the encounter between Peter and the entire household of Cornelius. It is suggested here that the encounter between Peter and Cornelius was but an extension of the original Pentecost event in the second chapter of Acts, and represented the unfinished business of the Spirit, as Peter still did not comprehend the plan of God to identify with all people. Peter, like many of us, was fully convinced of his religious and doctrinal purity (i.e., *surely not, Lord . . . I have never eaten anything impure or unclean*). The highlight of this narrative is Peter's decision to baptize Cornelius and his household. But Peter did not arrive at this decision through intellection, or through a cognitive revision of his interpretation of the law. I suggest that Peter's revolutionary decision to allow gentiles to be baptized was the result of Pentecostal worship that involved (1) Peter being confronted with his own prejudices, (2) Peter being dislocated from a place of familiarity and where he had power, (3) Peter entering a space where he was the stranger and as such, (4) Peter being positioned in a place to bear witness to what God was doing in people whom Peter had considered up to that point as *those in the out-group*, or *the others*. Peter's embodied experience of the Divine at work in unfamiliar spaces (the outpouring of the Spirit on the house of Cornelius) expanded Peter's understanding of God (i.e., *God has shown me that I should not call anyone impure or unclean . . .* [and that] *I now realize how true it is that God does not show favoritism but accepts from every nation the one who fears him and does what is right*). It is difficult for the racial imagination to resist those whom God affirms and anoints in its presence. Witnessing the outpouring of the Spirit on all the peoples of the world begins the process of unraveling the racial imagination.

In the segregated South, Martin Luther King understood the revolutionary power of the *whosoever cometh logic* of Pentecostal worship. Whoever comes are co-creators of the space in Pentecostal worship. Pentecostal worship represents a divine liminal space of imagination and play where in the midst of a broken, cruel, and war-torn world, people can take time away from the realities of domination, oppression, animus, and hatred, and can dare to imagine a new Jerusalem and the beloved community. In another work where I describe the implications of imagination and play in worship, I suggest that "a person or a group is able to realize in transitional [or worship] space what he, she, or its members often are unable to accomplish in the exterior world . . . [and that] it is by playing [in the worship space] that personal emotional growth is achieved, that self-love, robust subjectivity, and agency are formed, that courage is cultivated, and thereby a constantly maturing engagement with the exterior world (i.e., reality) is achieved."[2] I suggest that when Peter and Cornelius came together, they co-created a Pentecostal worship space where they could imagine and play with the help of the Spirit. It precipitated a gentile religious revolution. Likewise, after being transformed, healed, and strengthened in Pentecostal worship, just like Ida B. Wells, Fannie Lou Hamer, Benjamin Elijah Mays, and Martin Luther King, we can return to doing the works of righteousness.

---

2. D. Gibson, "Black Religion, Mental Health," 254–55.

BIBLIOGRAPHY

1898 Wilmington Race Riot Commission. *1898 Wilmington Race Riot Report*. LeRae Umfleet, principal researcher. North Carolina Digital Collections, May 31, 2006. https://digital.ncdcr.gov/Documents/Detail/1898-wilmington-race-riot-report/2257408.
Addams, Jane. "Respect for the Law." *Independent* 53 (1901) 18–20.
Akhtar, Salman. *Good Stuff: Courage, Resilience, Gratitude, Generosity, Forgiveness, and Sacrifice*. Lanham, MD: Aronson, 2013.
Altman, Neil. *The Analyst in the Inner City: Race, Class, and Culture through a Psychoanalytic Lens*. 2nd ed. New York: Routledge, 2010.
———. "Whiteness." *Psychoanalytic Quarterly* 75 (2006) 45–72.
Anderson, James William. "Recent Psychoanalytic Theorists and Their Relevance to Psychobiography: Winnicott, Kernberg, and Kohut." *Annual of Psychoanalysis* (2003) 79–94.
Anti-Defamation League. *A Dark and Constant Rage: 25 Years of Right-Wing Terrorism In the United States*. New York: Anti-Defamation League, 2017.
Arendt, Hannah. *Eichmann in Jerusalem: A Report on the Banality of Evil*. New York: Penguin, 2006.
———. *Responsibility and Judgment*. 1964. Reprint, New York: Schocken, 2003.
Augustine. *The City of God*. Edited by Marcus Dods. Overland Park, KS: Digireads, 2017.
Baldwin, James. *Collected Essays*. Edited by Toni Morrison. Library of America 98. New York: Library of America, 1998.
———. "A Conversation with James Baldwin." Interview by Kenneth Clark. WGBH, June 24, 1963. http://americanarchive.org/catalog/cpb-aacip-15-9mo3xx2p.
Bass, S. Jonathan. *Blessed Are the Peacemakers: Martin Luther King Jr., Eight White Religious Leaders, and the "Letter from Birmingham Jail."* Baton Rouge: Louisiana State University Press, 2001.
Bell, Jeannine. "Pick the Lowest Hanging Fruit." *Journal of Criminal Law and Criminology* 112 (2022) 691–728.
Benjamin, Jessica. *The Bonds of Love: Psychoanalysis, Feminism, and the Problem of Domination*. New York: Pantheon, 1988.
Bennett, Lerone, Jr. *Before the Mayflower: A History of the Negro in America 1619–1962*. 1962. Reprint, Chicago: Martino Fine, 2016.
Blain, Keisha N. *Until I Am Free: Fannie Lou Hamer's Enduring Message to America*. Boston: Beacon, 2021.

Bloom, Paul. *Against Empathy: The Case for Rational Compassion.* New York: HarperCollins, 2016.
Brennan Center for Justice. *Democracy Can't Wait: Annual Report 2021.* New York: Brennan Center for Justice, 2021.
Brooks, Maegan Parker. *Fannie Lou Hamer: America's Freedom Fighting Woman.* Library of African American Biography. Lanham, MD: Rowman & Littlefield, 2020.
———. *A Voice That Could Stir an Army: Fannie Lou Hamer and the Rhetoric of the Black Freedom Movement.* Jackson: University Press of Mississippi, 2014.
Buschendorf, Christa, and Cornel West. *Cornel West on Black Prophetic Fire.* Boston: Beacon, 2014.
Butts, Hugh F. "Psychoanalysis, the Black Community and Mental Health." *Contemporary Psychoanalysis* 7 (1971) 147–52.
Cai, Weiyi, and Jugal K. Patel. "A Half-Century of School Shootings Like Columbine, Sandy Hook and Parkland." *New York Times*, May 11, 2019. https://www.nytimes.com/interactive/2019/05/11/us/school-shootings-united-states.html.
Cecelski, David S., and Timothy B. Tyson. *Democracy Betrayed: The Wilmington Race Riot of 1898 and Its Legacy.* Chapel Hill: University of North Carolina Press, 1998.
Cone, James H. *The Cross and the Lynching Tree.* Maryknoll, NY: Orbis, 2011.
Cooper-Lewter, Nicholas, and Henry H. Mitchell. *Soul Theology: The Heart of American Black Culture.* Nashville: Abingdon, 1991.
Crozier, Karen D. *Fannie Lou Hamer's Revolutionary Practical Theology: Racial and Environmental Justice Concerns.* Theology in Practice 9. Leiden: Brill, 2021.
Cytrynbaum, Solomon. "Implications of the Tavistock Model for Group Psychotherapy." Presentation at the America Group Psychotherapy Association Annual Meeting, San Diego, 1993.
Dalal, Farhad. *Race, Colour and the Processes of Racialization: New Perspectives from Group Analysis, Psychoanalysis and Sociology.* New York: Brunner-Routledge, 2002.
———. "Racism: Processes of Detachment, Dehumanization, and Hatred." *Psychoanalytic Quarterly* 75 (2006) 131–61.
Davidson, Leah. "Idealization and Reverence." *Journal of the American Academy of Psychoanalysis* 29 (2001) 127–36.
Denny, Sandy. "Who Knows Where the Time Goes?" Performed by Nina Simone. B-side of *Black Gold*. Recorded Oct. 26, 1969. RCA Victor LSP-4248, 1970, LP.
Dittes, James E. *Pastoral Counseling: The Basics.* Louisville: Westminister John Knox, 1999.
Doehring, Carrie. *The Practice of Pastoral Care: A Postmodern Approach.* Louisville: Westminister John Knox, 2015.
Douglass, Frederick. *The Lessons of the Hour.* Baltimore: Thomas & Evans, 1894. https://www.loc.gov/item/mss1187900483/.
———. *Life and Times of Frederick Douglass.* Hartford, CT: Park, 1881.
———. *My Bondage and My Freedom.* New York: Miller, Orton & Mulliga, 1855.
———. *Narrative of the Life of Frederick Douglass, an American Slave: Written by Himself.* Boston: Anti-Slavery Office, 1845.
———. *Oration by Frederick Douglass, Delivered on the Occasion of the Unveiling of the Freedmen's Monument in Memory of Abraham Lincoln, in Lincoln Park, Washington, D.C., April 14th, 1876. With an Appendix.* Washington, DC: Gibson Brothers, 1876. https://www.loc.gov/item/12006733/.

Du Bois, W. E. Burghardt. *The Souls of Black Folk: Essays and Sketches*. 2nd ed. Chicago: McClurg, 1903.

Dunbar-Ortiz, Roxanne. *An Indigenous Peoples' History of the United States*. Boston: Beacon, 2014.

Erikson, Erik H. *Identity and the Life Cycle*. New York: Norton, 1980.

Evans, James H., Jr. *We Have Been Believers: An African American Systematic Theology*. 2nd ed. Minneapolis: Fortress, 2012.

Fanon, Frantz. *Black Skin, White Masks*. Translated by Richard Philcox. New York: Grove, 2008.

Ford, Dennis. *Sins of Omission: A Primer on Moral Indifference*. Minneapolis: Fortress, 1990.

Ford, Julian D., and Christine A. Courtois. *Treating Complex Traumatic Stress Disorders in Adults*. 2nd ed. New York: Guilford, 2020.

Frankl, Viktor E. *Man's Search for Meaning*. Boston: Beacon, 1959.

Freire, Paulo. *Pedagogy of the Oppressed*. Translated by Myra Bergman Ramos. 50th anniv. ed. New York: Bloomsbury Academic, 2018.

Gates, Henry Louis, Jr. *The Black Church: This Is Our Story, This Is Our Song*. New York: Penguin, 2021.

———. *Stony the Road: Reconstruction, White Supremacy, and the Rise of Jim Crow*. New York: Penguin, 2019.

Gibson, Danjuma. "Black Religion, Mental Health, and the Threat of Hopelessness during the COVID-19 Pandemic." In *Racialized Health, COVID-19, and Religious Responses: Black Atlantic Contexts and Perspectives*, edited by R. Drew Smith et al., 252–56. New York: Routledge, 2022.

———. "Christian Triumphalism: The Antithesis to Trauma Recovery." *Calvin Theological Seminary Forum* 27 (Winter 2020) 8–11.

———. "Mentalizing the Classroom: Pedagogies toward Making the Other Matter in Social Activism and Public Theology." *Journal of Pastoral Theology* 27 (2017) 134–52.

———. "Trauma of the Heart: Augmenting the Family Paradigm to Stem the Spread of HIV/AIDS and to Facilitate Healing and Recovery in the Wake of HIV/AIDS." *Journal of Pastoral Theology* 25 (2015) 46–55.

Gibson, Danjuma G. *Frederick Douglass, a Psychobiography: Rethinking Subjectivity in the Western Experiment of Democracy*. Cham: Palgrave Macmillan, 2018.

———. "When Empathy is Not Enough: A Reflection on the Self-Experience of Black Boys in Public Spaces." *Pastoral Psychology* 67 (2018) 611–26.

Giddings, Paula J. *Ida: A Sword among Lions*. New York: HarperColllins, 2008.

Gladney, Margaret Rose, and Lisa Hodgens, eds. *A Lillian Smith Reader*. Athens: University of Georgia Press, 2016.

Glaude, Eddie S., Jr. *Begin Again: James Baldwin's America and Its Urgent Lessons for Our Own*. New York: Crown, 2020.

Goff, Phillip Atiba, et al. "The Essence of Innocence: Consequences of Dehumanizing Black Children." *Journal of Personality and Social Psychology* 106 (2014) 526–45.

Grinshteyn, Erin, and David Hemenway. "Violent Death Rates: The US Compared with Other High-Income OECD Countries, 2010." *American Journal of Medicine* (2016) 266–73.

Gump, Janice P. "Reality Matters: The Shadow of Trauma on African American Subjectivity." *Psychoanalytic Psychology* 27 (2010) 42–54.

Haley, John. "Race, Rhetoric, and Revolution." In *Democracy Betrayed: The Wilmington Race Riot of 1898 and Its Legacy*, edited by David S. Cecelski and Timothy B. Tyson, 207–24. Chapel Hill: University of North Carolina Press, 1998.

Hall, Deborah L., et al. "Why Don't We Practice What We Preach? A Meta-Analytic Review of Religious Racism." *Personality and Social Psychology Review* 14 (2010) 126–39.

Hamer, Fannie Lou. *The Speeches of Fannie Lou Hamer: To Tell It Like It Is*. Edited by Maegan Parker Brooks and Davis W. Houck. Jackson: University Press of Mississippi, 2011.

Harmon, Nolan, et al. "An Appeal for Law and Order and Common Sense." *Birmingham News*, Jan. 16, 1963.

———. "A Call for Unity." *Birmingham News*, Apr. 13, 1963.

Herman, Judith. *Trauma and Recovery: The Aftermath of Violence from Domestic Abuse to Political Terror*. New York: Basic Books, 1997.

Heschel, Susannah. *Moral Grandeur and Spiritual Audacity: Essays*. New York: Farrar, Straus & Giroux, 1996.

Holder, Eric H., Jr. *Our Unfinished March: The Violent Past and Imperiled Future of The Vote—A History, A Crisis, A Plan*. New York: One World, 2022.

hooks, bell. *All about Love*. New York: Morrow, 2000.

———. *Teaching to Transgress: Education as the Practice of Freedom*. New York: Routledge, 1994.

Horowitz, Pamela, and Jeanne Theoharis. *Julian Bond's Time to Teach: A History of the Southern Civil Rights Movement*. Boston: Beacon, 2021.

Izadi, Elahe. "Black Lives Matter and America's Long History of Resisting Civil Rights Protesters." *Washington Post*, Apr. 19, 2016. https://www.washingtonpost.com/news/the-fix/wp/2016/04/19/black-lives-matters-and-americas-long-history-of-resisting-civil-rights-protesters/.

James, William. *The Varieties of Religious Experience*. New York: Dover, 1902.

Janis, Irving L. *Crucial Decisions: Leadership in Policymaking and Crisis Management*. New York: Free Press, 1989.

———. *Groupthink: Psychological Studies of Policy Decisions and Fiascoes*. 2nd ed. Boston: Cengage Learning, 1982.

———. *Victims of Groupthink: A Psychological Study of Foreign-Policy Decisions and Fiascoes*. Boston: Houghton Mifflin, 1972.

Jelks, Randal Maurice. *Benjamin Elijah Mays: Schoolmaster of the Movement*. Chapel Hill: University of North Carolina Press, 2012.

Johnson, Sylvester A. *African American Religions, 1500–2000: Colonialism, Democracy, and Freedom*. New York: Cambridge University Press, 2015.

Jones, Mick. "I Want to Know What Love Is." Performed by Foreigner. B-side of *Agent Provacateur*. Recorded Dec. 1983. Atlantic A1-81999, 1984, LP.

Juergensmeyer, Mark. "Christian Violence in America." *Annals of the American Academy of Political and Social Science* 558 (1998) 88–100.

Kelsey, George D. *Racism and the Christian Understanding of Man*. New York: Scribner, 1965.

Kernberg, Otto F. "Sanctioned Social Violence: A Psychoanalytic View—Part 1." *International Journal of Psychoanalysis* 84 (2003) 683–98.

King, Martin Luther, Jr. *The Autobiography of Martin Luther King, Jr*. Edited by Clayborne Carson. New York: Grand Central, 1998.

———. *The Measure of a Man*. Minneapolis: Augsburg Fortress, 2001.
———. *Strength to Love*. 1963. Reprint, Philadelphia: Fortress, 1981.
———. *A Testament of Hope: The Essential Writings and Speeches of Martin Luther King Jr.* Edited by James Melvin Washington. New York: HarperCollins, 1986.
———. *Where Do We Go from Here: Chaos or Community?* Boston: Beacon, 1968.
Kohut, Heinz. *How Does Analysis Cure?* Chicago: University of Chicago Press, 1984.
———. *Self Psychology and the Humanities: Reflections on a New Psychoanalytic Approach*. New York: Norton, 1985.
Kohut, Heinz, and Ernest S. Wolf. "The Disorders of the Self and Their Treatment: An Outline." *International Journal of Psycho-Analysis* 59 (1978) 413–25.
Kohut, Thomas A. "Psychoanalysis as Psychohistory or Why Psychotherapists Cannot Afford to Ignore Culture." *Annual of Psychoanalysis* 31 (2003) 225–36.
Kunhardt, Peter, dir. *King In the Wilderness*. Pleasantville, NY: Kunhardt, 2018.
Larson, Kate Clifford. *Walk with Me: A Biography of Fannie Lou Hamer*. New York: Oxford University Press, 2021.
Leary, Kimberlyn. "Racial Enactments in Dynamic Treatment." *Psychoanalytic Dialogues* (2000) 639–53.
———. "Racial Insult and Repair." *Psychoanalytic Dialogues* 17 (2000) 539–49.
Lee, Chana Kai. *For Freedom's Sake: The Life of Fannie Lou Hamer*. Urbana: University of Illinois Press, 1999.
Lemann, Nicholas. *Redemption: The Last Battle of the Civil War*. New York: Farrar, Straus & Giroux, 2006.
Levin, Brian, et al. "U.S. Hate Crime Trends." *The Journal of Criminal Law and Criminology* 112 (2022) 749–800.
Lewis, John. "Together, You Can Redeem the Soul of Our Nation." *New York Times*, July 30, 2020. https://www.nytimes.com/2020/07/30/opinion/john-lewis-civil-rights-america.html.
Lorde, Audre. *A Burst of Light; And Other Essays*. Mineola: IXIA, 2017.
Lyle, Graham, and Terry Britten. "What's Love Got to Do with It." Performed by Tina Turner. A-side of *Private Dancer*. Capitol B–5354, 1984, LP.
Matthiesen, Noomi, and Jacob Klitmoller. "Encountering the Stranger: Hannah Arendt and the Shortcomings of Empathy as a Moral Compass." *Theory & Psychology* 9 (2019) 182–99.
Matuštík, Martin Beck. *Radical Evil and the Scarcity of Hope: Postsecular Meditations*. Bloomington: Indiana University Press, 2008.
Mays, Benjamin E. *Quotable Quotes of Benjamin E. Mays*. New York: Vantage, 1983.
Mbembe, Achille. *Necropolitics*. Durham: Duke University Press, 2019.
McClure, Barbara. "Pastoral Care." In *The Wiley-Blackwell Companion to Practical Theology*, edited by Bonnie J. Miller-McLemore, 269–78. West Sussex, UK: Wiley-Blackwell, 2012.
Means, J. Jeffrey. *Trauma & Evil: Healing the Wounded Soul*. Minneapolis: Fortress, 2000.
Miller-McLemore, Bonnie J., ed. *The Wiley-Blackwell Companion to Practical Theology*. Wiley-Blackwell Companions to Religion. West Sussex, UK: Wiley-Blackwell, 2012.
Mills, Kay. *This Little Light of Mine: The Life of Fannie Lou Hamer*. Lexington: University Press of Kentucky, 2007.

Morrison, Toni. "A Humanist View." *Mackenzian*, May 30, 1975. https://www.mackenzian.com/wp-content/uploads/2014/07/Transcript_PortlandState_TMorrison.pdf.

———. *Playing in the Dark: Whiteness and the Literary Imagination*. New York: Vintage, 1992.

———. "The Source of Self-Regard." In *The Source of Self-Regard: Selected Essays, Speeches, and Meditations*, 304–20. New York: Knopf, 2019.

Nelson, Deborah. "The Virtues of Heartlessness: Mary McCarthy, Hannah Arendt, and the Anesthetics of Empathy." *American Literary History* 18 (2006) 86–101.

Nelson, Stanley, dir. *Rise Up: The Movement that Changed America*. New York: Firelight, 2018.

Paris, Peter J. *The Spirituality of African Peoples: The Search for a Common Moral Discourse*. Minneapolis: Fortress, 1995.

Patterson, Orlando. *Slavery and Social Death: A Comparative Study*. Cambridge: Harvard University Press, 2018.

Payne, Charles M. *I've Got the Light of Freedom: The Organizing Tradition and the Mississippi Freedom Struggle*. Berkeley: University of California Press, 2007.

Perlitz, Daniel. "Beyond Kohut: From Empathy to Affection." *International Journal of Psychoanalytic Self Psychology* 11 (2016) 248–62.

Pitcavage, Mark. *Murder and Extremism in the United States in 2018*. New York: Anti-Defamation League, 2019.

Poland, Warren S. "Courage and Morals." *American Imago* 64 (2007) 253–59.

"Quotable Quotes." In *Jet* 66 (Apr. 16, 1984) 14.

Runyan, William McKinley. "Progress in Psychobiography." *Journal of Personality* 56 (1988) 295–326.

Said, Edward W. *Orientalism*. New York: Random House, 1978.

Santayana, George. *The Life of Reason: Introduction and Reason in Common Sense*. Cambridge: MIT Press, 2011.

Schachter, Judith S., and Hugh F. Butts. "Transference and Countertransference in Interracial Analyses." *Journal of the American Psychoanalytic Association* 16 (1968) 792–808.

Schaffer, Amy. "The Analyst's Idealization of the Patient: On Not Seeing the Dark Side." *Contemporary Psychoanalysis* 52 (2016) 602–21.

Scott King, Coretta. *My Life, My Love, My Legacy*. New York: Holt, 2017.

Smith, Lillian. "Are We Still Buying a New World with Old Confederate Bills?" *Georgia Review* 66 (2012) 480–87.

———. "The Right Way Is not a Moderate Way." *Phylon* [Clark Atlanta University] 17 (1956) 335–41.

Tart, Charles. *Waking Up: Overcoming the Obstacles to Human Potential*. Boston: Shambhala, 1987.

Thurman, Howard. *With Head and Heart: The Autobiography of Howard Thurman*. New York: Houghton Mifflin Harcourt, 1979.

Tillich, Paul. *The Courage to Be*. 2nd ed. New Haven: Yale University Press, 2000.

———. *Dynamics of Faith*. New York: HarperCollins, 1957.

"Tributes to Mays Mirror His Role as a Motivator." In *Jet* 66 (Apr. 16, 1984) 8–9, 12–13.

Turner, Marlene E., et al. "Threat, Cohesion, and Group Effectiveness: Testing a Social Identity Maintenance Perspective on Groupthink." *Journal of Personality and Social Psychology* 63 (1992) 781–96.

Umfleet, LaRae Sikes. *A Day of Blood: The 1898 Wilmington Race Riot*. Rev. ed. Asheville: North Carolina Office of Archives and History, 2020.

Volkan, Vamik. *Blind Trust: Large Groups and Their Leaders in Times of Crisis and Terror*. Charlottesville, VA: Pitchstone, 2004.

Volkan, Vamik D. "Large-Group Identity, Who Are We Now? Leader-Follower Relationships and Societal-Political Divisions." *American Journal of Psychoanalysis* 79 (2019) 139–55.

Weber, Max. *The Sociology of Religion*. Translated by Ephraim Fischoff. Beacon Series in the Sociology of Politics and Religion. Boston: Beacon, 1963.

Wells, Ida B. *Crusade for Justice: The Autobiography of Ida B. Wells*. 2nd ed. Edited by Alfreda M. Duster. Chicago: University of Chicago Press, 2020.

———. "Letter to Frederick Douglass." Apr. 6, 1894. https://www.loc.gov/resource/mss11879.10007/?sp=29&st=image.

———. "Letter to Frederick Douglass." May 6, 1894. https://www.loc.gov/resource/mss11879.10008/?sp=19&st=image&r=-0.382,-0.038,1.752,1.667,0.

———. "Lynching and the Excuse for It." *Independent* 3 (1901) 1133–36.

———. "Southern Horrors: Lynch Law in All Its Phases." In *The Light of Truth: Writings of an Anti-Lynching Crusader*, edited by Mia Bay and Henry Louis Gates Jr., 57–82. Penguin Classics. New York: Penguin, 1892.

———. *The Red Record: Tabulated Statistics and Alleged Causes of Lynching in the United States*. Chicago: Donohue & Henneberry, 1894. Kindle.

Wells-Barnett, Ida B. *Southern Horrors: Lynch Law in All Its Phases*. Pamphlet. New York: New York Age, 1892. https://digitalcollections.nypl.org/items/63ce23b0-4abc-0134-cda4-00505686a51c.

West, Cornel. *Black Prophetic Fire*. In dialogue with and edited by Christa Buschendorf. Boston: Beacon, 2014.

———. *The Radical King*. Boston: Beacon, 2015.

White, R. "Motivation Reconsidered: The Concept of Competence." *Psychoanalytic Review* 66 (1959) 297–331.

Wimberly, Edward P. *African American Pastoral Care*. Rev. ed. Nashville: Abingdon, 2008.

INDEX

abolitionists, 97–100, 181
acquisitive epistemology, 54
Addams, Jane, 112–14, 120
ADL (Anti-Defamation League), 162
affection, 171–72
affectionate understanding, 157–58
affective caste system, 25–27
affective exhaustion, 167
affective states, 25
African American religious tradition, sexism in, 135
African diaspora, 93–94
Akhtar, Salmon, 72
alter-ego connection, 80
Altman, Neil, 48–49, 194–95
AME conference, 134–35
American democratic experiment, 50–51, 60–61, 66, 97, 112, 141–42, 144, 159–60, 165, 174–75, 178–80, 182, 185, 187, 190–91, 192–93, 198–99
American landscape, 59–60
American progress, 3–4
animus, 23, 25, 29, 31, 114, 118, 122, 125, 142–43, 147, 158–59, 174, 201, 207
annihilation anxiety, 12, 44–46, 167, 184, 203
Anti-Defamation League (ADL), 162
anti-love, 158–65, 171, 174–75, 178, 179–80, 201. *See also* animus
anti-racism, 42–43, 60–61, 118, 120, 125, 143, 201–2, 205

anxiety/anxiety-provoking work, 8–11, 15, 19, 26, 45–46, 58, 79, 167, 184, 194, 203
apathy, 13–14, 17–18, 20, 22, 30, 46, 47–48, 123, 169, 177–78, 188, 191, 192, 198
"An Appeal for Law and Order and Common Sense," 35
appeasement, 5, 39, 89, 111, 121, 194, 201
Arbery, Ahmaud, 3, 161
Arendt, Hannah, 150–53, 170–71
"Are We a Race of Cowards," 117
Augustine, 158
Auld, Thomas, 27–28
authentic self, 111, 116
autobiography, 62–63, 71, 96–98, 116, 117–21

backlash, 2–4, 9–11, 14, 76, 182, 185, 187, 189
Baldwin, James, 95–96, 172–73, 178, 191
Barber, Rev. William J. II, 76
becoming, beauty of, 4, 5–10, 84–85, 87, 117, 202–3
behaviors, 11, 17, 65, 72, 196
Bell, Jeannine, 161–62
Beloved (Morrison), 119
beloved community, 8–9, 30–39, 48, 142–43, 158, 160, 175, 202, 203–4, 207
Benjamin, Jessica, 99
Bennett, Lerone, Jr., 193–94

Birmingham, Alabama, 6, 20–21, 35–39
Birth of a Nation (film), 183, 196
bi-vocational clergypersons, 94–95
black and brown people
    American progress, illusion of, 3–4
    black intellectual tradition, 98
    black religious tradition, 92–93, 94–96
    civil rights movement, , 1–4, 6, 35–39, 40, 51, 59–60, 66–69, 75–76, 159
    clergypersons, 94–96
    courage, 70–82
    dehumanization, 105–6
    diversity, 120
    existential frustration, 103–9
    Hamer's theology, 144–45
    idealizing historical personalities/figures, 63
    identity, 107–8
    intersubjective milieu, 5–6
    personhood, 87
    psychic space, 191–92
    psychospiritual condition, 190–92
    racial discourse, 51–52
    racial imagination, 24–25, 28–30
    racism, 1–4, 13, 18, 23–26, 29–30, 32, 33, 39–51, 79, 106–8, 122, 125, 142, 156–57
    voting rights, 183, 185–88, 190
black boys, 103–9, 146–49, 169, 171–73, 175
Black Lives Matter, 66
Black Power activists, 51
black women in African American religious tradition, 135
Bloom, Paul, 150
Bond, Julian, 38–39, 68–69, 75–76, 90
bondage, 7. *See also* becoming, beauty of
Bonhoeffer, Dietrich, 164
bystanders, 3, 9, 106, 118–19, 123, 126–27, 144, 145, 205

Cain and Abel, 30–31
Calvin, John, 45–47, 164

caregivers, 6–7, 59, 128, 142, 146–47, 148–50, 155–58, 167, 174
change, 41, 54, 64
check-the-box approach, 40, 156
Christian doctrine, 67
Christian ethics, 55, 72, 170
Christian faith, 32–37, 43–44, 52
Christian hope, 32–37, 52
Christian identity, 44–45, 55
Christian imagination, 62–63, 123
Christian nationalism, 67, 195
Christian praxis, 8, 36, 46, 55–56, 59, 63, 149, 183
Christian triumphalism, 123–25
Christian witness, 45
church, 10–11, 12–17, 43–46, 51, 61, 119–20, 123–25, 133, 153–54, 188, 205
civil rights movement, 1–4, 6, 35–39, 40, 51, 59–60, 66–69, 75–76, 159
The Clansman (Dixon), 183
Clark, Kenneth, 191
Clement, Rufus, 101
clergypersons, 94–96
coercive control, 79
cognitive dissonance, 17, 113, 152
collective soul, 24, 36, 39–40, 46–48, 53, 61, 112, 154, 159, 174, 178, 190
collective spiritual condition, 191–92
comfort and convenience, 15, 74, 78–79, 202
communal aspect of hope, 32–33
compassion, 157–58
Cone, James, 138
consensus trance, 164–65
Cooper-Lewter, Nicholas, 93
Cornell University's Roper Center for Public Opinion Research, 66
cosmic dimension of hope, 33
Countryman, Matthew, 51–52
courage, 8–10, 55, 70–82, 170–72, 201–2
Covey, Edward, 27
COVID-19 pandemic, 142, 161
Crozier, Karen, 145–46
cultural understanding of love, 165–69

Index

data consumption, 119–20
Davidson, Leah, 114–15
death of the heart, 191
defensive mechanisms, 17
dehumanization, 23, 105–6, 120, 190, 192
de-idealization, 114, 116, 129–38, 181–82
delinquency, 105
desegregation, 35–39, 41, 48
devaluation, 114, 116–17, 129–38, 148
developmental arrest, 62
Dexter Avenue Baptist Church, 70, 77, 101
Dexter Parsonage Museum, 70
disembodied theology, 14
disenfranchisement, 183, 185–88, 190
disillusionment, 186–87, 203–4
disprivileged class, 34–35
dissociation, 11, 152
Dittes, James, 149–50
diversity, 24, 119–20, 205
Dixon, Thomas, 183
do and practice equity, 53–54
Doehring, Carrie, 157–58
dominion theology, 164
Douglass, Frederick, 26–28, 91, 96–100, 117, 120–22, 130, 135–38, 179–88, 204
drug abuse, 48–49
"The Drum Major Instinct" (King), 81
Du Bois, W. E. B., 3–4
Dunbar-Ortiz, Roxanne, 67–68

education, 6–8, 142–43
efficacy of hope, 33
ego, 9, 16–17
Eichmann, Adolf, 152–53
eight ministers, 36–38
emotional bond, 116
emotional brutality, 100, 150, 156, 160, 165
emotional caste system, 25–26, 178–79
emotional contagion, 149
emotional experiences, 24–25
emotional needs, 25, 58–60, 73, 137, 149–50
empathic community, 128
empathic limitations, 148–51, 156
empathy, 20, 107, 147–54, 155–58, 172–73, 174–75
England, 136
enough is enough, 159
enslaved narratives, 120
Erikson, Erik, 167, 195
erotic transference, 157
eschatological hope, 52
eschatological plot, 90, 92–94, 107
establishment theology, 73, 184, 202
ethic of love, 142–43
ethnicity and homicide, 163
ethnic minorities, 40, 52, 65, 100, 119, 193–94
Eurocentric experience, 95, 145
Evans, James, 32–33, 37, 52
evil, 13–17, 32–33, 46–47, 55, 118, 122–29, 143–44, 158–65
exceptionalism, 13, 52, 118, 190, 203
existential disappointment or frustration, 10, 103–9, 115–17, 129–40, 203–4
existential exhaustion, 186
experienced as concept, 26
experiential pedagogy, 54

faith and racism, 42–46
false images, 116–17
false promises, 124, 150
Fanon, Frantz, 104–5
fear, 41–42, 44–46, 71–72, 194, 201
finding one's courage, 55, 70–82
"The Fire Next Time" (Baldwin), 172–73, 178
Floyd, George, 3, 161, 191
Ford, Dennis, 17–19
Foreigner (band), 168
forgetting, 64–65
Frankl, Viktor, 85, 102, 183–84
Franklin, John Hope, 183–84
Freedman's Monument, 180, 182
freedom, 2, 4, 7–8, 9, 32, 35–38
freedom fighters, 4, 56–57, 60
Freedom Riders, 66

Freire, Paulo, 6–7, 7n9
frustrated desire, 168. *See also* existential disappointment or frustration
fundamentalism, 73

Gallup surveys, 66
Garrison, William Lloyd, 99
Gates, Henry Louis, Jr., 179
Glaude, Eddie, 5
God, 10–11, 42–48, 63, 93–94, 123–24, 166, 169–71, 185, 201–2, 205–6
"God's Minute" (Mays), 85–92
Goff, Phillip, 105–6
Gospel of Matthew, 192
Green, Samuel, 86
Green, Sherman L., 101
grief work, 116
Grinshteyn, Erin, 162–63
group coping mechanism, 12–14
group-level splitting, 61
group psychology, 12–13, 112, 184–85
groupthink, 60
gun lobby, 67
gun violence, 162

Haley, John, 189–90
Hall, Deborah L., 156–57
Hamer, Fannie Lou, 1, 9–10, 141–75, 204–5
happiness, 13–20, 48
hate crimes, 161–62
hatred, 158–65, 201
Hayes, Rutherford B., 182
Haygood, Atticus G., 133
HBCUs (historically black colleges and universities), 89
healthy-mindedness, 16–17
Hemenway, David, 162–63
Herman, Judith, 79, 118–19, 126–29
Heschel, Abraham and Susannah, 90
high degree of empathy, 80–81
historically black colleges and universities (HBCUs), 89
historical personalities/figures, 1, 4, 58–69, 118, 184
historical record, 56, 65, 194

historical revisionism, 182
HIV/AIDS, 168–69
Holder, Eric, 187
Holocaust, 75–76
homicide, 162–63
hooks, bell, 5–8, 50, 173–74
hope in the Christian faith, 32–37, 52
human altruism, 131–33
human atrocities, 47, 119, 147, 178
human flourishing, 10–11, 32, 86, 89, 106, 116
human imagination, 26, 31, 45, 137
human spirit, 10, 88, 194, 196
human suffering and violence, 13, 73–74, 85, 123–26, 138–40, 142, 144–45, 148–50, 160–61
human-value caste system, 45

idealization(s)
   danger of distorting truth, 55–57
   and devaluation, 114–17
   existential disappointments, 115–17, 129–38, 203–4
   idealizing historical personalities/figures, 1–2, 4, 58–69, 118, 184
   maladaptive forms of, 11
   and reverence, 114–15
   undoing the harmful effects of, 38–39
identity, 3, 5–6, 25, 39, 44–45, 55, 60, 65, 84, 86–87, 107–8, 195–97
idolatry, 19, 42–48, 178, 185
impudence, 26–28
incarceration, 191
indifference, 12–22, 30, 46–47, 177–78, 181, 184–85, 188, 191–92, 194, 202
individual and collective self, 11–12, 26, 122, 180, 185, 188
individual and collective soul, 24, 36, 39–40, 48, 53, 87, 190
individual and collective splitting, 23, 113
individual and group, psychospiritual condition of, 178
individual and group, self-reflexive work, 164

Index

individual and group defensive mechanisms, 17
individual and group identity, 5–6, 44, 58–60, 65, 152, 156, 195–97
individual and group practice of denial and self-deception, 125
in-group, 184–85, 197
injustice, 3, 21, 56, 68–69, 71, 79, 82, 89, 107, 123, 164, 178, 184, 190, 201–2, 204–5
innocence, 9, 13, 27–28, 105–6, 118, 152, 183–84, 190
institutional racism, 25, 26, 29–30, 41
institutional redemption culture, 184–85
institutions, 13–20, 52, 53–55, 58–59, 163–64
insurrection of January 6, 2, 4, 10, 12–13, 19, 21, 40, 48, 60–61, 63, 69, 154, 159, 161, 165, 178, 188–90, 192–93, 198–99
intellectualism, 25, 28
interior questioning, 170
interior world, 23–26, 28, 31, 39, 79, 90–91, 99, 104, 117, 138
internalization, 29, 69, 121–22, 126
internalized racism, 5, 87–88, 103–9
intersubjective milieus, 5–6, 54
intracommunal dynamic, 99–100
intra-group psychological splitting, 197
ivory tower culture, 40, 49–50, 94–95, 118–19, 146
"I Want to Know What Love Is" (song), 168

Jaegerstaetter, Franz, 76–77, 80, 82
James, William, 13, 15–17, 20
Jean, Botham, 3
Jesus, 15, 31, 72–74, 192, 205
Jim Crow South, 6, 75–78, 87, 103, 144, 146–47, 163, 178, 180, 183
Johannine witness, 166
Jones, Rufus, 21–22
Juergensmeyer, Mark, 164

Kelsey, George, 42–45, 47

Kernberg, Otto, 197–98
King, Coretta Scott, 11, 70, 74, 78
King, Martin Luther Jr., 1–3, 9–10, 20–21, 35–39, 59, 70–82, 90, 97, 101–2, 154, 159–61, 169–70, 172, 174, 207
King, Martin Luther Sr., 101
kitchen event, 74–80, 90
KKK, 183
Klitmoller, Jacob, 150–51
Kohut, Heinz, 61–62, 75–77, 79–82, 115, 155, 157

large-group regression, 194–98
LBGTQ+ community, 161
Legacy Museum, 112
legalism, 91, 96–103, 107, 202
Lemann, Nicholas, 179
letter from a Birmingham jail, 20–21, 35–36, 38
Levin, Brian, 161
Lewis, John, 9, 56–57
Lexington, Mississippi, 144
liberal arts and culture, 166–67
liberalism, 164
life-project or doing your work, 10, 83–109, 202–3
limits of empathy, 148–51, 156
Lincoln, Abraham, 180–82
logotherapy, 85
Lorde, Audre, 202–3
lost cause narrative, 183, 196
Louis Harris & Associates, 66
love
    anxiety-provoking work, 8–11
    beyond empathy, 154
    cultural understanding of, 165–69
    ethic, performance of, 141–43, 146–47
    look of, 169–74, 204–5
    praxis of love and the welfare of the democracy, 174–75
    respect for the power of, 174–75
    self-experience of black boys in public spaces, 146–49
    spectrum of, 165–69
    and violence, 158–65

lynching
　anti-lynching work of Wells, 126, 130–38
　awareness of in Europe, 136
　bystanders, 126–27
　existential disappointments, 138–40
　Ida B. Wells, 111–14, 118–21, 204
　narcissistic injury, 136–37
　psychohistory, 185–86
　traumatological lens, 117–20, 122–29
Lyric Hall, 127–29

master and slave dynamic, 99–100
Matthiesen, Noomi, 150–51
maturity, 61, 64, 116, 123, 172
Matuštík, Martin Beck, 46
Matz, David C., 156–57
Mays, Benjamin Elijah, 1, 9–10, 83–109, 202
Mays, Hezekiah, 102–4
Mbembe, Achille, 191
McCarthy, Mary, 152
meaning-making process, 79, 93, 168
Means, Jeffrey, 164–65
Memphis, Tennessee, 127, 131–32
metanoia, 185, 202
Metropolitan AME Church, 120
mindfulness, 170
mindlessness, 120, 151–54
misogyny, 135
Mississippi Freedom Democratic Party, 144
Mitchell, Henry H., 93
mob violence, 130–31, 138–39, 185–86, 189–90, 193–95
moderation, 41, 48
Montgomery, Alabama, 70, 77–79, 101–2, 112–14
Moody, D. L., 121, 125, 133
moral action, 149–51, 153–54, 197
moral agency, 1, 9, 13–20, 28–29, 37, 39, 46, 63–64, 118–19, 150–52, 182
moral imagination, 3, 18
moral indifference, 17–18, 22
moral progress, 190

moral sloth, 19–20
moral universe, 97, 118
Morehouse College, 20, 85–89, 100–101, 107–8, 202
Morrison, Toni, 50–51, 108, 119
multi-vocational clergypersons, 94–96
musical arts, 166–67
mysterious other, 197
myth of black sexual deviance, 120–22, 126, 133

narcissistic injury, 26, 137
narcissistic regressed large groups, 197–98
nationalism, 4, 8, 12–13, 15, 40, 48, 67, 153, 185, 195
National Memorial for Peace and Justice, 113–14
Nazi Germany, 19, 75–82
necropolitics, 191
neighbors, 17, 31–33, 41, 72–74, 123
Nelson, Deborah, 151–52
New Oxford American Dictionary, 114
New York Age, 111
New York Voice, 121
Nichols, Tyre, 3
Niebuhr, Reinhold, 19, 164
nihilism, 203–4
nobility class, 34–35
noble courage, 72–75, 82, 117
non-raced people, 25, 29–30, 34, 42, 51, 99–100, 104, 106, 184, 191, 195
nonviolence, 37–39, 159–60
North Carolina, 188–90
Northern abolitionists, 97–100, 181
Nuremberg trials, 152–53

Obama presidency, 9, 162, 187
objectifying black sexuality, 130
one-off achievements, 52
open letters, 35–38
opioid epidemic, 191
organic epistemology, 53–54
organized religion, 92, 94–96
the other, 24–25, 42, 119–20, 122, 192
out-group, 185, 197, 206. *See also* the other

Index

Palm Sunday sermon, 154
parable of the good Samaritan, 15, 72–74, 123–24, 169–70
paranoid regressed large groups, 197–98
parents, 6–7, 59
Paris, Peter, 94, 96
Parks, Rosa, 59
pastoral ethics, 86, 149, 151, 165
pastoral imagination, 51
pastoral intervention, 26, 99
pastoral psychology, 125
pastoral theology, 10–11, 56, 154, 155–56
Patterson, Orlando, 31–32
Paul (apostle), 45–47
Payne, Daniel A., 134
Payne, Wallace, 88
pedagogy of racial justice, 53–55
Pentecostal worship, 120, 200–207
performance of the love ethic, 141–43, 146–47
Perlitz, Daniel, 157–58
permanent progress, 11, 52
perpetrators of evil, 118–20, 123–29, 144, 205
personal dimension of hope, 32–33
personal identity formation, 39, 107
personhood, 8, 80, 87, 95–96, 99, 117, 127–28, 129, 148, 173
Peter and Cornelius, 206–7
phobia-based courage, 72, 74
piety, 17, 91
Poland, Warren, 72
politicization of hope, 32, 35–37
polytheism, 43–44
posterity, 11, 63, 81, 91
post-traumatic stress disorder (PTSD), 124–28
practical theology, 10–11, 17–18, 143–45, 171
practices of love, 158–65, 171–72, 175
praxis of love, 142–44, 146–47, 154, 160–61, 165, 170–72, 174–75
pride, 42, 46
privatization of faith, 55–56
progress, 3, 8–9, 10, 11, 51–52
projection, 44, 122

proofs and support, 13
psychic space, 5–6, 13, 40, 55, 60, 65–66, 103, 122, 164, 166–67, 191–94
psychobiography, 10–11, 62–63, 65, 178
psychodynamics, 99, 184
psychohistory, 10–11, 26–27, 40, 65, 122, 178, 185
psychology
  group psychology, 12–13, 112, 184–85
  narcissistic injury, 26, 137
  psychohistory, 65
  psychological description of racism, 48–49
  psychological generativity, 81
  psychological splitting, 12, 23, 61, 113, 168, 180, 197–98
  psychological trauma, 117, 118, 124–27
  psychology of courage, 72
  psychology of mob violence, 194–95
  See also idealization(s)
psychosocial environment, 65, 126–27, 147, 182, 201, 206
psychospiritual assessment, 188–99
psychospiritual compensatory mechanisms, 184–85
psychospiritual condition, 60–61, 102, 122, 178, 185, 190–92, 195
psychospiritual death, 100, 106
psychospiritual energy, 116–17
psychospiritual ethic of love, 143
psychospiritual growth, 6–8, 116, 132, 203
psychospiritual implications of Kernberg's observations, 198–99
psychospiritual implications of slavocracy, 54
psychospiritual interventions, 11, 25, 29, 39, 40, 62, 88, 99, 196
psychospirituality, 29, 201–2
psychospiritual self-work, 6, 8, 9–10, 70–82, 116, 192, 200–201, 202, 204
psychospiritual sickness, 53, 103

PTSD (post-traumatic stress disorder), 124–28
public spaces, 146–49, 166

raced other, 44, 51
raced people, 29–30, 100, 104, 113
racial animosity, 8, 11, 12–13, 48, 66, 89
racial apartheid, 39–40, 41, 48, 183, 185, 189–90
racial caste system, 5, 72, 87–89, 94, 103, 112, 189
racial delusion, 121–22
racial discourse, 49–52
racial equity, 53–55
racial hatred, 10, 12–13, 63–64, 106, 111, 114, 142–43, 174. *See also* racial terror and violence
racial ideology, 12, 25, 29, 39–48, 49–52, 88–89, 195, 202
racial imagination
  and Addams, 112–14
  anxiety-provoking work, 9
  black voting rights, 187–88
  courage, 71
  eschatological plot, 94
  identity, 86–87, 108
  impact of, 51
  and indifference, 13, 178
  internalized racism, 87–88, 103, 106
  lost cause narrative, 183, 196
  myth of black sexual deviance, 120–22, 126, 133
  Northern abolitionists, 97–100
  objectifying black sexuality, 130
  pastoral theology, 11, 23–30
  pedagogy of racial justice, 53–55
  Pentecostal worship, 200–206
  praxis of love and the welfare of the democracy, 174–75
  psychic space, 122
  psychospiritual assessment, 188–99
  and racism, 39–49
  Redemption era, 178–79
  regressed idealization, 60
  romanticizing history, 183–84
  and silence, 89

truth-telling, 182
value gap, 5
racial integration, 7–8
racial justice, 2, 9–10, 39, 53–55
racially constructed other, 48–49
racially inspired mob violence, 193–95
racial oppression, 10, 26–28, 49–51, 54, 66, 69, 78–79, 84–85, 89, 100, 107, 111, 114, 159
racial reconciliation, 21, 30, 36–37, 53–55, 111
racial superiority, 31, 185
racial terror and violence, 39, 44–47, 55, 63, 76, 87, 106, 118–20, 125, 131, 138–40, 146–47, 178, 181–86, 189–90, 193–95. *See also* lynching
racing others, 30
racism, 1–4, 13, 18, 23–26, 29–30, 32, 33, 39–51, 79, 106–8, 122, 125, 142, 156–57
Racism and the Christian Understanding of Man (Kelsey), 42–45
Reconstruction era, 4, 52, 76, 178–83, 189
Redemption era, 4, 178–88
The Red Record (Wells), 130
regression, 194–98
  regressed idealization, 59–60
  regressed large groups, 197–98
religion
  religion and apathy, 169
  religion of happiness, 48
  religious icons, 79–80
  religious institutions, 163–64
  religious leaders, 15, 37–38, 40, 117, 123, 133
  religious moment, 90–91, 107
  religious other, 169
  religious racism, 156–57
remembering, 64–65
resistance, 10, 54, 66–67, 201–2
reverence, 114–15
revisionist history, 66–67, 178, 182–83
righteousness, 9, 201–2

"The Right Way Is Not a Moderate Way" (Smith), 41
romanticization of history, 1–2, 4, 8, 55–56, 58–69, 117–18, 159, 181–84
Roots (miniseries), 177

salvific virtue, 34, 44
Santayana, George, 64
Schaffer, Amy, 114–16
scholars of color, 50
Scholl, Hans and Sophie, 76–77, 80–82
Scripture, 67, 80, 123, 158
Second Amendment, 67
segregation, 35–39, 70, 89, 100
self-experience, 26
    of black boys in public spaces, 146–49
self-affirmation, 85, 172
self-aware subject, 99
self-care, 6–7, 84–85, 116, 202–3
self-courage, 8–9
self-harm, 78–79
self-reflexivity, 1, 97, 116, 164
self-work, 1, 5–8, 9, 116, 192, 200–202, 204
sense of humor, 76, 79–80
serenity, 80–81
Sermon on the Mount, 31
silence, 9–10, 12–22, 61, 89, 118–19, 121, 127, 151–52, 154, 177–78, 184, 188. *See also* apathy; backlash
Simone, Nina, 108
Sixteenth Street Baptist Church, 39
slavery, 31–32, 94, 99, 177–82
Slavery and Social Death (Patterson), 31–32
slavocracy, 9–10, 18, 23, 26–28, 39–40, 53, 54, 103, 121–22, 125, 130, 142, 178–79, 183, 185, 196, 200–201
sleep of everyday life, 164
sloth, 17–20
Smith, Lillian, 40–42, 48, 54
social action, 152, 170

social construction of whiteness, 194–95
social fundamentalism, 73
social isolation, 149
social oppression. *See* racial oppression
social violence, 190
sociology, field of, 130
sociopolitical messaging, Hamer's, 145–46
soul health, 9–10
soul theology, 93–94
Southern Democrats, 182
Southern Horrors (Wells), 132–33
spirituality in Africa, 94
subaltern, 151
subjugation, 5, 29–32, 65, 96, 98–99, 135
survival, 63, 76, 82, 87, 154, 196
syncretism, 43–44
systemic oppression, 1, 184, 190
systemic racism, 25, 26, 29–30, 45, 161

Tart, Charles, 164
Taylor, Breonna, 3, 161, 191
teachers, 6–7, 171–73
Theoharis, Jeanne, 68–69
theological education, 42–43, 50–51, 119–20, 145–46, 154, 166, 184, 205
theological reflection, 15, 37–38, 57, 184
Thurman, Howard, 21–22
Tillich, Paul, 45–47, 172
time, 85–87
transatlantic slave trade, 94
trauma of the heart, 168–69
trauma recovery, 79, 123, 126–29
traumatological lens, 117–20, 122–29, 139–40
travailing the existential threat of nonbeing, 77–79
tribalism, 11, 18–19, 73, 146, 196
tripartite engagement, 128–29
truth-telling, 180–83
Turner, Tina, 167–68

unclean spirit, 192
US Congress, 60

value gaps, 5–6
violence and love, 158–65
Vivian, C. T., 56
Volkan, Vamik, 195–97
voting rights, 90, 183, 185–88, 190

Washington, Booker T., 86
Washington, DC, 120, 180–81
Weber, Max, 33–35
Wells, Ida B., 1, 9–10, 110–40, 203–4
West, Cornell, 91
"What's Love Got to Do with It" (song), 167–68
white America, 143
Whitehead, Elizabeth, 86
white invisibility/whiteness, 29, 51, 194–96

white supremacy, 13, 25, 28, 31–32, 38, 40, 47–48, 51, 54, 56, 63, 75–76, 86, 96, 108, 111, 126–27, 140, 142–43, 159, 183, 188, 189–90, 193–94
"White Supremacy and the Founding of the NAACP" (Bond), 75–76
Willard, Frances, 120–21, 125, 133
will to act, 4, 9, 20, 55, 63, 150–51, 170
Wilmington, North Carolina insurrection, 188–90
Wimberly, Edward, 92
Winona, Mississippi, 143–44, 146–47
woke, 17–18, 153
Wolf, Ernest, 61–62
Wood, Wendy, 156–57

Young, Andrew, 5–6

www.ingramcontent.com/pod-product-compliance
Lightning Source LLC
Chambersburg PA
CBHW022014220426
43663CB00007B/1076